Rupert Shortt is a journalist and writer whose books include *Rowan's Rule: The Biography of the Archbishop*, *God's Advocates* and *Benedict XVI: Commander of the Faith*. He is Religion Editor of *The Times Literary Supplement*, contributes to the *Guardian* and *The Times*, and is a Visiting Fellow of Blackfriars Hall, University of Oxford.

By the same author:

Rowan Williams: an Introduction

God's Advocates: Christian Thinkers in Conversation (ed)

Benedict XVI: Commander of the Faith

Rowan's Rule: The Biography of the Archbishop

CHRISTIANOPHOBIA

A Faith Under Attack

RUPERT SHORTT

LONDON · SYDNEY · AUCKLAND · JOHANNESBURG

*Dedicated to all who suffer
for their beliefs*

1 3 5 7 9 10 8 6 4 2

This paperback edition published in 2013
First published in the UK in 2012 by Rider, an imprint of Ebury Publishing
A Random House Group Company

Copyright © Rupert Shortt 2012

Rupert Shortt has asserted his right to be identified as the author of this Work in
accordance with the Copyright, Designs and Patents Act 1988

The Random House Group Limited Reg. No. 954009

Addresses for companies within the Random House Group can be found at:
www.randomhouse.co.uk

A CIP catalogue record for this book is available from the British Library

The Random House Group Limited supports the Forest Stewardship
Council® (FSC®), the leading international forest-certification organisation.
Our books carrying the FSC label are printed on FSC®-certified paper.
FSC is the only forest-certification scheme supported by the leading
environmental organisations, including Greenpeace.
Our paper procurement policy can be found at:
www.randomhouse.co.uk/environment

Printed and bound by CPI Group (UK) Ltd, Croydon, CR0 4YY

ISBN 9781846042775

Copies are available at special rates for bulk orders. Contact the sales development
team on 020 7840 8487 for more information.

To buy books by your favourite authors and register for offers, visit:
www.randomhouse.co.uk

CONTENTS

CHRISTIANOPHOBIA

INTRODUCTION

In the video he made in early 2005 before committing suicide and mass murder, Mohammad Sidique Khan, ringleader of the 7 July London bombers, justified his action as revenge for the recent killing of Muslims by Western armies. Much has been said since about the moral vacuity of this statement, but far less made of its sheer incoherence. Looking beyond Iraq and Afghanistan, and on a time frame stretching back well before 11 September 2001, we can see innumerable Christian communities on the defensive against rampant forms of intolerance, both religious and secular. The problem has worsened dramatically since the turn of the millennium: about 200 million Christians are now under threat,[1] more than any other faith group. This ought to be a major foreign policy issue for governments across a vast belt of the world. That it is not tells us much about a rarely acknowledged hierarchy of victimhood.

Sidique Khan and his associates were allowed to practise their religion openly in Britain, yet there is scarcely a single country from Morocco to Pakistan in which Christians are fully free to worship without harassment. Muslims who convert to Christianity or other faiths in most of these societies risk harsh penalties. There is now a severe risk that the Churches will vanish from their biblical heartlands in the Middle East. The suffering is no less acute elsewhere. Before the partition of Sudan in 2011, for example, the regime in Khartoum was responsible for the deaths of 2 million Christian and other non-Muslim civilians over a thirty-year period. Before East Timor gained independence from Indonesia, 100,000 Catholic non-combatants were killed by agents of the Suharto government during the 1970s, 1980s and 1990s. As I write, the Grand Mufti of Saudi Arabia, Sheikh Abdul Aziz bin Amdullah, has officially declared that 'it is necessary to destroy all the churches' on the Arabian Peninsula,[2] and 50,000 Christians are thought to have been ousted from the city of Homs in Syria.

Christians in parts of Nigeria live in regular fear of violent attack; what is more, there is clear evidence that the attitudes underlying such aggression are fomented through official channels. One reason why Western audiences hear so little about religious oppression in the Muslim world is straightforward: young Christians in Europe and America do not become 'radicalised', and persecuted Christians tend not to respond with terrorist violence. Another explanation is linked to the blind spots that can affect bien-pensant opinion-formers. Parts of the media have been influenced by the logical error that equates criticism of Muslims with racism, and therefore as wrong by definition. This has further distracted attention away from the hounding of Christians, helping to cement the surprisingly widespread idea that Christianity is a 'Western' faith.

But this book is emphatically not based on polemics about a supposed clash of civilisations, still less on an uncritical attitude towards my fellow Christians. The Church's past record of violent intolerance – a record that persists in Russia, the Balkans, and other parts of the Eastern Orthodox world – is obviously shameful, too. And although the view that Muslims have been the perpetual victims of Christian aggression down the ages rests on a falsification of history, I reject the equal and opposite fantasy that holds Islam to be a uniquely violent religion. Misconceptions of this sort usually spring from a failure to distinguish between Islamic piety on the one hand, and Islamism as a religio-political ideology on the other.

My argument, rather, is shaped by two sorts of awareness. First, that much anti-Christian prejudice and violence – in China, India, Vietnam, North Korea, Burma, Sri Lanka, Cuba, or Israel, among other places – has nothing to do with militant Islam; and second, that a number of grievances felt by Muslims are reasonable. For example, I believe (in line with the clearly broadcast views of most church leaders around the world) that the invasion of Iraq in 2003 was a serious mistake, and I have a keen awareness of the West's role in promoting the sense of injustice felt by many Arabs in particular. More broadly, it seems equally clear to me that Christian mission in nineteenth-century Africa was often politicised, and geared to undermine the spread of Muslim influence; that Western (above all Anglo-French) adventurism in the Middle East during the twentieth century played into the hands of Arab nationalists and watered the seeds of Islamic revivalism; and that al-Qaeda drew strength from the West's indulgence of dictators in the region before the Arab Spring – and still now. These factors supply context to my case. They do not, however, invalidate it. (Statistical evidence on religious freedom around the world, collated by the Freedom House think tank, is set out in Appendix A.)

The oppression of Christians is especially worthy of note given the so-called return to religion over recent years. Whether you view this development with relief or unease, it has become increasingly obvious that Christianity and Islam are the two most formidable systems of belief in the world. Whatever the extent of secularisation in Western Europe – and even here the evidence is ambiguous, as various traditions experience revivals – almost all other societies on earth display high levels of religious belief and practice. Three-quarters of humanity professes a religious faith; that figure is projected to reach the 80 per cent mark by 2050.[3] The scale of the turnaround has been extraordinary. Thanks to the so-called third wave of democratisation during the 1970s, as well as smaller waves of freedom since then, millions were enabled to shape their public lives in new ways. In country after country, politically empowered groups began to challenge the secular constraints introduced by the first generation of modernising, post-independence leaders. Often, as in Communist societies, secular straitjackets had been imposed from on high; in other cases, such as Turkey, India, and Egypt, secularism retained legitimacy because the elites considered it essential to national integration and modernisation – and because of the sheer charisma of these countries' founding fathers. In Latin America, right-wing dictatorships, sometimes in cahoots with the Catholic Church, imposed restrictions limiting grass-roots religious influences, particularly liberation theology and Protestant 'sects'.

As politics liberalised in nations including India, Mexico, Nigeria, Turkey, and Indonesia in the late 1990s, religion's influence on political life increased steeply. Even in the United States, Evangelicals exercised a growing influence on the Republican Party during the 1980s and 1990s, partly because the presidential nomination process came to depend more on popular primaries and less on the decisions of party elders. Nowadays, where political systems reflect people's values, they usually also reflect people's strong religious beliefs. An inventory of faith-based political groups would include Vishva Hindu Parishad in India (which sowed the seeds of Hindu nationalism reaped by the BJP during the 1990s), the Muslim Brotherhood in Egypt and Jordan, Hamas in the Palestinian territories, Hezbollah in Lebanon, the Hahdlatul Ulama in

Indonesia, Pentecostals in Africa and Latin America, and in the Catholic world, an array of forces including European Christian Democrats, Opus Dei, and the newer religious movements. Faith communities are also developing remarkable transnational capabilities, appealing to foreign governments and international bodies deemed sympathetic to their cause.

Again, whatever one's opinion of the merits or coherence of religious belief, or the truth of one creed *vis-à-vis* others, the conclusion reached by two prominent American sociologists, Timothy Samuel Shah and Monica Duffy Toft, is hard to resist: 'The belief that outbreaks of politicized religion are temporary detours on the road to secularization was plausible in 1976, 1986, or even 1996. Today, the argument is untenable. As a framework for explaining and predicting the course of global politics, secularism is increasingly unsound. God is winning in global politics. And modernization, democratization and globalization have only made him stronger.'[4]

This should not surprise us. Atheism feeds off bad religion, especially fundamentalism, whose easily disposable dogmatic certainties now form one of atheism's main assets. On the other hand, it is much harder for atheism to replace the imaginative richness of a mature religious commitment, and the corresponding assurance that life is worth living responsibly, because it has an ultimate meaning. Yet faith is like fire, to cite a sobering analogy. It warms; but it can also burn. As the Jewish thinker Jonathan Sacks and others have pointed out,[5] people lived in self-contained spaces before the modern era – physically and therefore intellectually. It was possible to believe that 'our' truth was the only truth. That is naturally no longer possible in a globalised world. So while the twentieth century was marked by clashes of political ideology, there are strong grounds for thinking that interfaith relations, and the politics of identity that they betoken, will be one of the dominant challenges of the twenty-first.

In some ways, harmony between the religions remains a remote goal. Good religion promotes conflict resolution; bad religion fosters discord. As many commentators have pointed out, the destabilising effects of fanaticism can be seen far from Iraq and the ruins of the World Trade Center. Formerly secular challenges such as the confrontation between Israel and the Palestinians have taken on an overtly religious cast. Religion has played a role in recent and ongoing civil wars from Sri Lanka to Chechnya to Sudan. Along or near the tenth parallel of latitude north of the equator, between Nigeria and Indonesia and the Philippines, religious fervour and political unrest are reinforcing each other. This point should be granted even if one accepts religion's status as an immense – perhaps the pre-eminent – source of social capital in existence. On the positive side, faith-based conviction has mobilised millions of people to oppose authoritarian regimes, inaugurate democratic transitions, support human rights, and relieve human suffering. In the twentieth century, religious movements helped end colonial rule and ushered in democracy in Latin America, Eastern Europe, sub-Saharan Africa, and Asia.

Given the durability of faith, though, we can draw an equally certain lesson for today and tomorrow: that if religions – especially the six so-called global fellowships: Buddhism, Christianity, Hinduism, Islam, Judaism, and Sikhism – are not part of the solution, they will almost certainly be part of the problem. This much, perhaps, is common sense. (Another valid inference is that religious leaders function better as sources of influence at some distance from political leaders, not as wielders of direct power themselves.) To bring much-needed texture to the discussion, we should disentangle fair and tendentious accounts of the terrain, and be aware of how it gets hijacked by hotheads at either extreme of the divide between religion and secularism. It is above all unscientific to single out 'religion' (what religion? which manifestation of it?) for criticism, while ignoring both the colossal violence of twentieth-century anti-religious regimes, and the strife associated with other forms of social bonding, such as nation or ethnic group. In Northern Ireland, to cite an obvious example, religion is deeply interlaced with the legacies of British imperialism and Irish nationalism. In other parts of the world, religious affiliations often shade into ethnic differences, which in turn merge with claims to land, water, and oil. The tenth parallel is a case in point. Geography forms a major source of tension in several of the countries in this region, so faith differences can be exploited to intensify what are basically turf wars and other geopolitical conflicts. The subject also needs to be placed in the broader context of nineteenth-century and postcolonial nationalism. The imperial project of Russia from Peter the Great onwards – and especially Russia's conflict with the Ottoman Empire – brought waves of nationalism in south-east Europe and western Asia, often involving the redrawing of frontiers in ethnic or ethno-religious ways; population exchanges; and the subsequent persecution of minorities that were seen as being not truly Turkish or Bulgarian or Greek and so forth. Analogous processes later took place in the Indian subcontinent.

A powerful account of the population movements that unfolded continuously from the nineteenth century onwards is supplied by Tony Judt in *Postwar*,[6] his history of Europe since 1945. He charts how the consequences of events such as the Armenian genocide and the break-up of the Austro-Hungarian Empire were eventually held in check by the consolidation of the Soviet Union. The twilight of Soviet power then saw new homogenising pressures, including the impulse to ensure that people's political leaders belonged to the same group as themselves. Many factors came into play: economic, political, ethnic, linguistic, and religious: these combined with one another in what seemed to Judt and others a predominantly nationalist postcolonial framework. There are always local histories to make sense of particular contexts, of course, but the general processes round the world share broad common characteristics.

Determining the place of religion in conflict is therefore a matter of patient elucidation. Yes, faith can be put to corrupt use, largely because it is practised by fallible human beings. (The same applies in many other spheres of life.) But attacks on religion drawn from hit-and-run raids on history are callow and can be dangerous. The Churches are often on the receiving ends of such attacks, though as it happens, the classical critique of Christianity rested not on its violence, but on its *rejection* of armed conflict in the defence of a fragile social order. In what is plainly a perversion of Jesus's teaching, some Christians have ended up believing in saving conflagrations ushered in by war (just as, correspondingly, secular revolutionary bodies have had violent and non-violent wings). But by and large, as the sociologist David Martin has insisted, 'the Christian hope of a righteous kingdom "on earth, as it is in heaven", feeds into and is part of the hope of a secular transformation, and one has to understand that the good and the ill, like the religious and the secular, are mutually entangled.'[7] (This provides but one reason why President George W. Bush's division of the world into black and white wasn't authentically Christian.)

The complaint that church life outside Europe is somehow compromised, because Christianity often spread on the coat-tails of empire, forms a further instance of how a complex discussion can be short-circuited by ideology. These days, historians are more ready to acknowledge the substantial part played by indigenous people in Christian expansion. In Africa, Asia, and Latin America, many local Christians have long been critical agents in missionary work, given the small number of expatriate missionaries in relation to the size of these continents and their populations. The nurses, medical assistants, and compounders in mission hospitals, the teachers in the mission schools and colleges, the evangelists and 'Bible women' who go into villages and homes across vast areas of the world – these people are not only physical intermediaries with vastly varied local societies, but also 'translators', in a deeper sense, as they help interpret Christianity in local languages and cultures.

Anti-Christian feeling can regularly be premised more on envy than on fear. Indian Christians in Kerala, for example, are often more prosperous than their Hindu neighbours, and resented for the same reasons as prompted historic prejudice against Jews in Europe. In other parts of India, Christians are loathed by Hindu extremists for opposing the caste system. Sometimes Christians are disliked as well as admired for their enormously influential work in education. In Taiwan, only 3 or 4 per cent of the population is Christian (Nationalist Chinese persecuted the Churches as much as their Communist counterparts), but the Taiwanese educational system was largely founded by Canadian and Scottish Presbyterians. Taiwan itself is not noticeably hostile to Christians, but the climate is less benign in other countries where the Christian educational legacy is also strong. Sometimes, as in China, Christians are feared with reason, because they are heralds of a more open society. Nearly 9 per cent of China's population belongs to one denomination or another, and the journalists John Micklethwait and Adrian Wooldridge, authors of *God is Back* (2009),[8] are among many observers who forecast that a third of Chinese will be Christian within a few decades. That the Churches have faced large-scale persecution in China and elsewhere says much about their remarkable strength, as well as their vulnerability.

I hope it will be clear from the necessarily piecemeal material in this section that I do not assume the truth or falsity of any creed, merely that freedom of belief and association are unqualified goods. Nor am I seeking to offer either a comprehensive survey, or a grand narrative about an alleged global campaign against the Church. I am aware that 'Christianophobia', like 'Islamophobia', is an elastic term, perhaps implying a passive attitude, unlike the more active 'anti-Semitism'; and that prejudice should be distinguished from more overt forms of ill will manifested in state ideology or various sorts of behaviour. However, neither 'anti-Muslimism' nor 'anti-Christianism' has caught on, so Christianophobia seems to me a valid term.

Another point (clear from a glance at the Contents page) is that I have not set out to give a comprehensive account of my subject. There are no detailed discussions of the fast-changing situation in Sudan and South Sudan (though the two countries are covered briefly in chapter 13); of Malaysia and the Philippines, where a surge in Islamist militancy has caused widespread strife in recent years; of the Solomon Islands, where seven members of the Melanesian Brotherhood, an Anglican order, were martyred in 2003 while promoting peace talks with separatists; or of several other significant areas. My more modest aim has been to give the reader an overview of the landscape by turning the soil in twenty or so representative places.

The victims of Christianophobia can have more in common than the perpetrators. And among these shared characteristics is a reluctance – by turns admirable, understandable, and heart-breaking – to tell news of their respective Calvaries. Some brave souls, in obedience to the Sermon on the Mount and St Paul's appeal in Romans 12:12–14 ('Rejoice in your hope, be patient in tribulation . . . . Bless those who persecute you'), accept their suffering as a source of unity with Christ. But that does not mean that news of their plight should be suppressed. Nor, of course, does it exonerate the perpetrators.

This perspective calls for a brief sketch of shifting understandings of martyrdom held by Christians themselves. On the face of it, the subject is unpromising territory to anyone who does not share a cluster of faith-based assumptions. Before the crucifixion, Jesus himself represented his coming death in sacrificial terms. A distillation of the scholarly consensus about his mission is supplied by Andrew Chandler and Anthony Harvey in their study of Christian martyrdom in the twentieth century, *The Terrible Alternative*.[9] Jesus proclaimed the arrival of the Kingdom of God, 'with all that it entailed in terms of the remission of debt, the espousal of the poor and the marginalized, the casting out of evil spirits and the release of those resources of love, generosity and compassion which are so easily repressed by social convention and misguided religious scrupulosity.'[10] This mission led to Jesus's death, which he freely accepted, sensing that it would have redemptive power for the community of believers he inaugurated.

The opposition to Christianity voiced by the Jews and, later, the Romans led to protracted official persecution of Jesus's followers until the conversion of Constantine in the early fourth century. This seismic event caused anti-Christian sentiment to change shape for predictable reasons. Rome was the enemy to huge areas of Asia, including China, India, Persia, and Syria. As Constantine prepared to do battle with the Persians, Christians who had long been sheltered by Rome's enemies were now viewed as fifth columnists. Around AD 340, the Emperor Shapur II of Persia unleashed a campaign against Christians even bloodier than anything experienced during the previous three centuries. Those who refused to take part in Zoroastrian worship were killed; hundreds of bishops and priests were publicly executed. In total almost 200,000 Christians may have died.

But Shapur did not persecute Christians because he was offended by their beliefs. He acted from a sense that the Church was politically significant. One consequence of this was that the definition of martyrdom would in due course be tightened up, and the Vatican (to cite one of several examples) would declare that to qualify as a martyr, a candidate had to have been killed because of *odium fidei* – hatred of the faith as such. Sometimes, though, politics and theology cannot be disentangled. Chandler and Harvey are thus right to judge that we have come full circle in important respects: during the twentieth century, many Christian groups became progressively more identified with support for democracy and human rights – purportedly Enlightenment values which in fact originate in the Hebrew prophetic tradition and the teaching of Jesus. Models of martyrdom have thus been refreshed. The Jesuit liberation theologian Jon Sobrino has summed up the matter from his Central American context: 'The Church is being persecuted because it defends the life of the poor, denounces the unjust destruction of life and promotes the . . . practice of justice.'[11]

This is the light in which the discipleship of many recent Christian martyrs can be seen – there were more of them in the twentieth century than during the previous nineteen put together – figures as varied as Grand Duchess Elizabeth in post-Revolutionary Russia, Maximilian Kolbe in Nazi-occupied Poland, Lucian Tapiedi in Papua New Guinea, Esther John in Pakistan, Martin Luther King in the United States, Wang Zhiming in China, Oscar Romero in El Salvador, and the seven French Cistercian monks from Tibhirine in Algeria, whose lives were dramatised in the award-winning film *Of Gods and Men*. Since these people were in no doubt that values such as human dignity and equality are part of any account of Christian belief worthy of the name, it is not hard to see why they are sources of inspiration beyond as well as within their respective folds.

A final area of discussion seems relevant to this overview: the growing belief that Christians are persecuted in the West as well as elsewhere. The expression 'Christianophobia' has been used by some to designate what they see as a severe and mounting problem in Europe. I did not coin the term and claim no monopoly on its definition. But research for this book has taken me to Africa, the Middle East, and South Asia to meet people who have lost their loved ones, homes, livelihoods or career prospects because of their faith. Many have themselves been victims of unprovoked violence. This is persecution as I understand it.

The situation in Europe is largely another matter. There is no shortage of thoughtful people, liberal as well as conservative in outlook, who feel that employing the ideology of human rights to assault faith communities is very harmful. When a Christian airport worker is banned from wearing a cross, or a nurse sacked after a role-playing exercise in which he suggested praying for a patient, alarm bells ought to ring. Philosophically minded commentators have spotted a French-style, *dirigiste* impulse behind much recent equality legislation in Europe and elsewhere. Traditionally, the English model of liberalism defined the space in which governments may not intervene. English-style liberty set the limits of the state. French-style liberty, by contrast, has tended to be imposed by the State. Saluting its place in many contemporary democracies, Jonathan Sacks describes religion as 'part of the ecology of freedom because it supports families, communities, charities, voluntary associations, active citizenship and concern for the common good. It is a key contributor to civil society, which is what holds us together without the coercive power of law. Without it we will depend entirely on the State, and when that happens we risk what J.L. Talmon called a totalitarian democracy, which is what revolutionary France eventually became.'[12] It will be evident that Sacks prefers the traditional English way to the French. He has also voiced concern that UK legislation has started to display a worryingly 'French' tinge over the past decade. Broadly comparable sentiments to those of Sacks have been repeated by churchmen including Pope Benedict XVI and George Carey, the former Archbishop of Canterbury. One does not need to endorse all their views in areas such as sexual ethics to grant that their broader concerns deserve a serious hearing.

Elsewhere in the West today, Christians are mocked or caricatured as soft targets by an irreverent media often much warier about turning its fire on other faith groups, and by an academic establishment sometimes incongruously deferential to political fashion. Anti-Christian blasphemy is common, but public figures who spurn secular multicultural orthodoxies may expect trouble. Campaign groups such as the Christian Legal Council tell us that Christian beliefs are now under threat, because Christian guesthouse-owners and would-be foster parents who disapprove of homosexuality have themselves incurred the disapproval of the state. Some complaints about these (very varied) developments are fair; others overlook the benefits of a free press and a robust public conversation; others again are in my view marks of special pleading. Whatever their status, though, none of the opinions, insults, or laws judged offensive by many Western Christians amounts to persecution as chronicled in the pages ahead.

1
EGYPT

'I came to England in 1979', Dr Ibrahim Habib told me, 'after all the Christian students in my year at medical school were marked down.'

We got to know each other after I visited the Coptic church in West London, where Ibrahim worships regularly, even though he lives and works in the Midlands. Originally from Minya, near Asyut in Upper Egypt, where about a third of the population is Christian, he is a stolid, soft-spoken figure with an eager smile. But his professional success and blithe manner were belied by the melancholy tale he told me:

> Christians were either passed or failed; not a single one was placed in the 'Good', 'Very Good', or 'Excellent' categories. This meant that none of us Christians would achieve a high-flying career. The modern phase of anti-Christian violence in Egypt really began in 1972, with the establishment of the Gama Islamiya, a militant group. They started attacking Christian students on the university campus at Asyut, barging into our rooms and tearing down pictures of the Virgin Mary and other religious materials. A fight ensued. I and other Christians were expelled from university accommodation, but the Muslims who caused trouble were allowed to remain.
>
> The upsurge in militancy can be blamed to a great extent on President Sadat. After the assassination attempt on Nasser in 1954, many fundamentalists were rounded up and sent to prison.

Sadat, faced with heavy challenges from the Left, indulged the Islamists and let many in from Saudi Arabia. He also called Egypt a Muslim country, even though 15 to 20 per cent of the population were then Christian. That figure has now fallen to 12 per cent, because of all the emigration.

In the lead-up to my own graduation from Asyut in 1976, several Christian students were thrown from the balconies of buildings and injured. Others were killed. A local priest in Asyut, Fr Gabriel Abd al-Motgaly, was murdered. I felt that my decision to leave Egypt was vindicated, because a major flare-up took place in 1981. A piece of land belonging to a Christian in the al-Zawia al-Hamra suburb of Cairo was seized by Muslims who wanted to build a mosque. At least eighty people were killed in the violence, some people were burnt alive in their homes, and the police just looked on, according to eyewitness accounts.

There were many similar attacks on Christians in Upper Egypt as well, and no prosecutions, apart from in one case. A monk was murdered in front of the gates of his monastery at al-Moharaq. Two men were arrested, and eventually received prison sentence of three years.

The situation deteriorated steadily during the 1980s and 1990s. Hundreds of Christians died in many attacks during this period. A few Christians I knew were given good jobs for propaganda purposes, and because they were very loyal to the Mubarak regime. But my own prospects would have faded if I'd stayed.

The future of Egypt is pivotal to interfaith harmony in the Middle East, because about 10 million people are Christians of one stripe or another. Most of these are Copts – part of the Oriental Orthodox family that includes the Syrian, Armenian, and Ethiopian traditions. The country was a more tolerant place a hundred years ago than today. Muslims of both sexes were widely involved in culture and education. But from the 1970s onwards, Egypt began to be influenced by the Salafist Wahhabi ideology deriving from Saudi Arabia. Alaa al-Aswany, the journalist and author of the bestselling novel *The Yacoubian Building*, has ascribed the rise of Salafism in Egypt to a chain of causes. With the quadrupling of oil prices in 1973, Salafists suddenly acquired the finance to export their ideas around the world. Millions of Egyptians sought employment in the Gulf States, where they came under the influence of extremists. In time, Wahhabi sympathisers infiltrated Egypt's security forces as well: unlike the Muslim Brotherhood, the country's largest organisation, Wahhabis did not menace the state directly. They are nevertheless widely seen as heralds of theocracy. As well as opposing music, theatre, and general education, or insisting that women wear the burqa – jettisoned by earlier generations many decades ago – the Wahhabis deny that Christians can be full citizens. Rather, they see the Copts as *dhimmis* (protected non-Muslims) occupying a subordinate role. As al-Aswany puts it,

In Wahhabis' eyes, Copts are . . . infidels and polytheists prone to hating Islam and conspiring against it . . . Anyone who follows the portrayal of Copts on dozens of satellite channels and Salafist websites is bound to be saddened. These forums, followed by millions of Egyptians daily, openly declare their hatred of Copts . . . Often they call on Muslims to boycott them. There are countless examples, but I will cite here what I read on the well-known Salafist website 'Guardians of the Faith', which devoted a whole article to the subject, 'Why Muslims Are Superior to Copts'. 'Being a Muslim girl whose role models are the wives of the Prophet, who were required to wear the hijab, is better than being a Christian girl, whose role models are whores,' it says.

3

'Being a Muslim who fights to defend his honor and his faith is better than being a Christian who steals, rapes, and kills children . . . Being a Muslim whose role models are Muhammad and his companions is better than being a Christian whose role models are Paul the Liar [sic] and the whoremongering prophets.' As this enmity towards Copts spreads, is it not natural, even inevitable, that it should end in attacks on them?[1]

The effects of these Salafist pronouncements are not confined to cyberspace. Among the starkest recent examples of Islamist aggression against Christians were the murders of nine worshippers as they emerged from St George's Church in Nag Hammadi, 80 kilometres from Luxor, in January 2010; and the bombing of the Two Saints' Church in Alexandria on New Year's Eve of the same year. Twenty-one people attending Mass were killed, and seventy wounded, in this attack, which was allegedly prompted by a false rumour that senior clerics were holding two female converts to Islam against their will.[2]

It goes without saying that a large number of Egyptian Muslims, and Arabs more generally, bear no ill will whatever towards their Christian fellow citizens. Many pious Muslims, including a significant fraction of the Muslim Brotherhood, are committed to peace and consensus as Egypt moves fitfully in a more democratic direction. For their part, overseas observers are now familiar with images of Muslims protecting Christians as they celebrated the Eucharist in Tahrir Square at the dawn of the Arab Spring, just as Christians stood guard for Muslims while they performed their own devotions during the same period. But the fresh start promised by the overthrow of Hosni Mubarak in February 2011 was soon tarnished by a resurgence of the attacks on churches that had become common beforehand.[3]

A recent story highlighted by the American human rights campaigner Nina Shea helps to bring the tragedy of the Copts into clearer focus. In July 2008, Thomas, Catholic Coptic Bishop of El-Qussia in Upper Egypt, gave a lecture in Washington, DC, called 'The Experience of the Middle East's Largest Catholic Community during a Time of Rising Islamization'. Bishop Thomas ended his address with a lament over the decline of an ancient community: 'We are worried about the large number of [emigrants] that are leaving Egypt, like all the Middle East; we are worried that the Christians are leaving this area.'[4]

Forthright but uninflammatory, the bishop's words prompted a vitriolic response in Egypt's government-controlled mosques and media. Thomas was denounced in hundreds of newspaper articles, many of which called for his arrest and prosecution. He was accused, among other things, of supporting a Zionist plot and of working as a Western agent. During Friday prayers shortly afterwards, the sheikh at the al-Rahma mosque in El-Qussia commended a violent response to the lecture: '[I say to] you the traitors, there are men among the Muslims who will spill your blood . . . [M]y helpers will sever the legs of all those who assist the traitor [Bishop Thomas].'[5]

Oblivious of the irony, the sheikh thus confirmed the truth of Thomas's initial comments. The conclusion drawn by Nina Shea from this episode is that Egyptians have been witnessing 'a reinvigorated effort by some of the country's more radical Islamists to establish Egypt's identity as a thoroughly Islamicized . . . state'. More moderate elements in the Muslim Brotherhood have expressed a commitment to pluralism and democracy. But Salafists remain largely implacable. In February 2011, Ayman al-Zawahiri – soon to become leader of al-Qaeda after the killing of Osama bin Laden – described Copts as 'one of

Egypt's main problems'. He also referred to Pope Shenouda III, the Coptic spiritual leader from 1971 to 2012, who was renowned for his open-handed attitude towards Muslims, as a 'Zionist traitor'.

*

Given the volatility in this most important of Arab nations, the wider context is more than usually important. Egypt already had a venerable Christian history before the birth of Muhammad: 'Copt' derives from the Arabic *Qibt*, an abbreviation of *Aigyptios*, the Greek word for Egypt; the Coptic patriarch – also called pope – is held by tradition to be the successor of St Mark the Evangelist; and St Antony of Egypt (*c.250–c.350*) is the father of Christian monasticism. From the fourth to the early seventh centuries, Egypt was part of the Eastern Roman Empire and a centre of debate, regularly escalating into controversy, over core Christian doctrines. Jesus's followers were hardly models of toleration at this time: the sobering truth for Christians is that the Coptic Church welcomed the prospect of Muslim rule in the seventh century because it offered relief from Byzantine control.

After the Islamic conquest, Egypt became a province of an empire whose capital was at first Damascus, then Baghdad. The territory was ruled by semi-autonomous governors. Christian–Muslim relations were at first peaceful: the Copts absorbed Islamic culture in general, and even showed a willingness to sideline their ancient language in favour of Arabic. But they were not the equals of their Muslim neighbours. Under the Umayyad and Abbasid caliphs between the seventh and ninth centuries, Christians were obliged to pay a poll tax, known as the *gizya*, demanded of all free, non-Muslim men, and a property tax called the *kharâg*. Muslims only paid alms (the *zakât*). This led many Copts to convert to Islam. The Christian population fell for other reasons besides. Following Muhammad's command, a Christian who wanted to marry a Muslim had to convert to Islam, and the children of a mixed marriage were considered Muslim.

It is now thought on the basis of financial records that up to half of the Christian population became Muslim in under half a century, and that by the year AD 800 only a fifth of the population remained Christian. Others estimate that Muslims did not become a majority until the end of the tenth century. Muslim dominance led to greater interfaith tensions in time, even though some members of the Coptic elite held important government posts. Christians objected to the Caliph Yazid's destruction of Christian icons in 722; uprisings against Muslim rule took place across the Nile Delta later in the eighth century.

A more concerted revolt in 829 led to a bloody crackdown on Christians, when thousands were sold into slavery in Baghdad. Thereafter, the position of Copts became a good deal more testing. Laws were introduced forcing Christians to wear distinctive clothing, and (as elsewhere in Muslim domains) stopping them from riding horses or taking part in church processions. Persecution of Christians fell and rose in intensity at different times after this, but the long-term template was set – especially as Copts were suspected of Western sympathies during the Crusades, despite their generally loyal attitude towards Saladin, founder of the Ayyubid dynasty and Sultan from 1169 to 1193.

The status of Copts deteriorated under the Mamluks, who ruled for 300 years from the mid-thirteenth to the early sixteenth centuries, although the Church still experienced artistic and theological flowerings from time to time. Day-to-day life for many Copts became harder still after the Mamluks were succeeded by the Ottomans as Egypt's masters, although, as Febe Armanios has confirmed in her recent study,[6] rich and powerful lay Copts – the so-called *archons* – continued to flourish in senior administrative postions. Scholars accompanying Napoleon's expeditionary force in 1798 nevertheless estimated that only around 160,000 Christians remained in Egypt, though some experts today judge this estimate to have been too conservative.[7]

The Napoleonic conquest proved a fillip to the Copts (who at least shared the faith of the invaders), and a natural source of resentment to Muslims. Abd al-Rahman al-Jabarti (1753–1825), author of the celebrated *History of Egypt*, thought that religious minorities were flourishing rather too much after 1798. The period, he protested, brought forth 'the elevation of the lowliest Copts, Syrian and Greek Orthodox Christians, and Jews. They rode horses and adorned themselves with swords because of their service to the French; they strutted around haughtily, openly expressed obscenities, and derided the Muslims.'[8]

Egypt was returned to notional Ottoman rule, with the Mamluks as administrators, after Napoleon's defeat at the hands of Britain and its allies. But in 1811, an officer in the Ottoman army, Muhammad Ali, supplanted the Mamluks and became ruler of Egypt, assuming the title of Khedive (viceroy). In interfaith terms, the reigns of Muhammad Ali and his successors were broadly positive. Copts were promoted to senior levels of the civil service, not least as a means of promoting ties with the Christian powers of Europe. In the mid-1850s, for example, the Khedive Muhammad Saïd allowed Copts to join the army, and abolished the *gizya*: important steps towards the establishment of full citizenship for Christians. Muhammad Saïd's successors, the Khedives Ismail and Tewfiq, also helped to grant legal equality to Copts – a move codified in 1913 and confirmed in the

1922 constitution. (Since then, there have always been Coptic members of Egypt's legislative assembly.) The country even had a Coptic prime minister, Boutros Ghali, who was murdered by a Muslim extremist in 1910.

As Alastair Hamilton, a leading scholar of Coptic history, has observed,[9] the greater profile of Copts led to rising educational standards and ecclesiastical reform. Egypt's greatest nineteenth-century churchman was Pope Cyril IV, who served from 1854 to 1861. He set up the first Coptic schools based on the European model, which helped members of his flock to take a full part in Egyptian public life. But his successors – who were selected from monastic ranks, like most bishops in the Eastern Churches – were far less disposed towards cross-cultural dialogue. This led to a long-term rift, still evident today, between educated laypeople and conservative prelates.

Change benefited Catholic Copts (namely those reconciled with the see of Rome), as well as their Orthodox counterparts. Western missionary groups, both Protestant and Catholic, spread across Egypt during the nineteenth century. The Jesuits founded the Collège de la Sainte Famille in Cairo in 1879, and as Hamilton argues, with the founding of the American University in Cairo in 1908, 'the Presbyterians set up what was to remain one of the best centres of advanced education in the entire . . . Middle East.'[10]

The British imposed a protectorate on Egypt at the outbreak of the First World War, then installed King Fuad three years later. In response, a broad alliance of Muslim and Christian activists established the Wafd Party. By the 1930s, however, the national mood had polarised under the impact of Islamic revivalism. Organisations – notably the Muslim Brotherhood – were set up to promote a tight link between national identity and their own brand of religion. The reign of King Farouk from

1936 until Gamal Abdel Nasser's coup in 1952 saw prolonged general instability and defeat at the hands of the newly formed Israeli state in 1948. Nasser's vision was secularist. The Muslim Brotherhood and other faith-based associations were banned. Many tracts of church-owned land were confiscated in 1955. But although a significant proportion of wealthier families of both main faiths emigrated, the period also saw a monastic renaissance nourished by Pope Cyril VI, in office from 1959 to 1971.

Despite the spread of Islamism, the position of Copts improved in some respects under Sadat. Egypt was placed on a path of economic liberalisation known as *infitâh*; and the Coptic Foreign Minister, Boutros Boutros-Ghali (later Secretary General of the United Nations), proved vital to the success of the Camp David peace talks, which brought peace between Egypt and Israel. Islamist paranoia was partly stoked by the visibility of Christians. When a period of inter-religious violence began during the summer of 1981, both Copts and their Muslim assailants faced collective punishment. Pope Shenouda was temporarily deposed. Sadat himself was assassinated by Muslim fundamentalist militants on 6 October of that year.

*

The reasons for the steady decline of Christian populations in Egypt and across the Middle East are partly socioeconomic. Christians are overwhelmingly monogamous and tend to have fewer children than Muslims. Marriages between Muslim men and Christian women are much easier to contract than unions between Muslim women and Christian men, and it is very hard for mixed couples to bring up their children outside the Islamic faith. But forced emigration forms the greatest single reason for shrinking Christian populations. This can arise from local factors, such as real or imagined apostasy, but Islamist demagogues frequently use events thousands of miles away as a means of scapegoating their Christian neighbours. Examples of this include the Danish cartoon controversy of 2005, in which images of the Prophet Muhammad clothed as a suicide bomber triggered violent demonstrations around the world and the burning of churches in Iraq; and a comparable response the following year after Benedict XVI's Regensburg lecture. On a visit to the university in southern Bavaria where he had once taught, the Pope quoted a fourteenth-century Byzantine emperor's opinion about the link between Islam and violence. Benedict merely intended to stress the complementarity of faith and reason, but the address induced apoplexy among Muslim demonstrators in parts of Africa and Asia. Dozens lost their lives. Other forms of conflict nearer to home – notably the battle between Israel and Hezbollah in 2006 – also offered a pretext for attacking Christians, even though the antagonists were Muslims and Jews. Palestinian Christians, viewed with suspicion both by the Israelis and by their more militant compatriots, who see them as fifth-columnists, have faced growing hardship ever since.

The exit strategy of Arab Christians has been traced in an essay by Habib Malik, a Coptic observer.[11] Many will at first flee to another country in the region – Iraqis to Syria, for example, or Lebanese to Cyprus – before finding a long-term home in the Americas or Europe or Australia. Chicago's Assyrian community is in consequence large enough to have its own patriarch. Armenians and Copts have gravitated towards California; and there are hundreds of thousands of Lebanese Christians in São Paulo, Montreal, Sydney, and Paris.

Pessimists may judge the exodus of Christians to be inevitable – even, perhaps, desirable. But Malik and others see a robust church presence in the Middle East as vital for the region's cultural and political health. As he suggests, 'influential Arab Christians such as . . . Albert Hourani, Constantine Zurayk, Michel Aflaq . . . and Hanan Ashwari, along with many other . . . scholars, monks and legal experts, have mediated the transmission of Western ideas, including individual rights and freedoms, to the Middle East while simultaneously explaining the Middle East to Westerners . . . The Arab world would be far more insular had their work not been done.'[12] Questions on topics such as religious freedom, the status of women, and blasphemy are more likely to be engaged with constructively if the non-Muslim components of these societies can flourish alongside their neighbours.

Less sanguine observers stress the scale of the challenge. The Muslim Brotherhood's underground status under Mubarak provided fertile ground for the formation of radical splinter groups such as Al-Tafkir wa al-Hijra, Al-Gama'a al-Islamiya, and Al-Jihad al-Islami. The members of these offshoots were responsible for a stream of violent attacks on Christians, moderate Muslims, and tourists during the 1980s and 1990s. These events in turn served as triggers for periodic crackdowns on the militants in which many thousands were imprisoned without trial. The Mubarak regime also employed a creative interpretation of Egypt's penal code to persecute 'unorthodox' – usually Shia – Muslims.

In recent decades Christians have been under assault not only from Islamists but also from police and security officials who have refused to protect them or go after those responsible for attacks on churches or congregations. Coptic deputies (appointed, not elected) made up under 1 per cent of Egypt's parliament under Mubarak, and Copts have faced systematic obstacles to promotion in the army, the police, and the legal system. At the end of the Mubarak period, there were two Coptic ministers (one a nephew of Boutros Boutros-Ghali) and one Coptic provincial governor. But there were no Coptic judges, university vice-chancellors, generals, or senior police officers. Ottoman-era legislation had severely curtailed the ability of Copts to rebuild or even renovate their churches. A description of significant incidents in recent years might flag up a report in the *Al-Midan* newspaper on 13 October 2005, which alleged that a play performed in St George's Church, Alexandria, had 'insulted Islam'. The work (part of a summer programme for young Copts) was really about strategies for resisting forced conversion to Islam, but word spread among local Muslims that the production was discourteous towards Muhammad. A crowd of more than 5,000 surrounded the church: four people were killed and about ninety injured in the ensuing violence. Seven other churches in Alexandria, and one in Cairo, were attacked. Pope Shenouda received multiple death threats.

Over the New Year period in 2000, twenty-one Christians and one Muslim were killed in the village of El-Kosheh, in Sohag Governorate, Upper Egypt. The conflict sprang from an argument between two traders, a Muslim and a Christian, on New Year's Eve. Shops were damaged or destroyed as the violence escalated; the Muslim who died was hit by a stray bullet. No one suggested that the killer was a Christian, but the death of the Muslim shopkeeper was followed by a large escalation in the violence. As the mayhem unfolded, the police were reported as watching without intervening, and in some cases of actively taking part in anti-Christian attacks.[13]

Other examples flesh out the broader story. On 7 November 2003, an unidentified group attacked Christian homes and property in Gerza, a village near the northern city of al-Ayyat; five Copts were injured. On 14 and 21 October 2005, a large crowd of Muslims attacked St George's Church in Alexandria, an assault causing three deaths.[14] A seventy-eight-year-old Copt, Nishi Atta Girgis, was killed, and five other Christians injured, when three churches in Alexandria were attacked on 14 April 2006. In May of the following year, the imam of the mosque in the village of Bemha, south-west of Cairo, instructed his flock to defend Islam in response to a rumour that a new church was to be built nearby. About seventy Christian-owned homes were set on fire in consequence, shops were looted, and dozens of Copts were injured.[15] This fracas came hard on the heels of violence against Christian-owned property across Upper Egypt, after the spreading of rumours about a love affair between a Muslim woman and Christian man.[16]

As has often been pointed out, many Egyptian Muslims think that Copts are implicated in what they see as a Christian assault on the Muslim world, because of George W. Bush's use of the term 'crusade' after 9/11. Others maintain that Bush's ill-chosen words and mistaken policies have provided a convenient excuse for aggression against minority groups which patently have no connection with Western governments. But however the motivation for violence is measured, the early twenty-first century has seen a steady rise in the strife endured by Christians. Coptic women have been kidnapped and forced to become Muslims,[17] while converts from Islam to Christianity have been arrested and sometimes tortured. One convert died in police custody in November 2003.[18]

For decades, Egyptian citizens have needed identity cards for internal travel, education, employment, and other administrative reasons. These stipulate a person's religion, but only the so-called divine faiths – Judaism and Christianity, as well as Islam – are permissible options. Converting from Christianity to Islam is straightforward. But converts to Christianity have rarely been allowed to change their identity cards. This brings us back to apostasy – as vexed a problem for Egypt as for Pakistan. On 2 August 2007, Muhammad Ahmed Hegazy, a twenty-five-year-old Christian from a Muslim background, took an unprecedented step. He filed a lawsuit against Habib al-Adly, Minister of the Interior. After his conversion in 2002,[19] Mr Hegazy had been tortured in custody, but still launched an unsuccessful bid to change his religious affiliation on his identity documents. His case was thrown out in January of the following year. Judge Muhammad al-Husseini's ruling, based on Article 2 of the Egyptian constitution, stated that since Islam represents God's final revelation, to be a Muslim is by definition to 'practise freedom of religion', and that therefore leaving the Islamic faith was not possible.

Given the link between religion and social identity in the Middle East, it is unsurprising that conversion can look like an act of betrayal to many. Converts can bring shame on their communities; this then feeds a corresponding urge for restitution. A Muslim who becomes a Christian or Baha'i, for example, may be shunned, physically harmed, or even killed. The Qur'an does not set out specific punishments for apostasy in this life. The notion that converts to other religions should be killed fed into all the main branches of sharia law via later collections of teaching, especially the Hadith. It is partly for this reason that Muslim attitudes should not be considered immutable – either by Islamists on the one hand, or hostile critics of Islam on the other. A growing number of jurists in the West insist on the priority of the Qur'an over the Hadith in this and other areas, and no less a figure than Egypt's Grand Mufti, Ali Gomaa, has urged that apostasy lies beyond the scope of human judgement. Many other senior Muslims are far less circumspect, though. When the Grand Mufti stated on 'Muslims Speak Out', a *Washington Post/Newsweek* online forum, that Muslims were free to change their religion, he was rapidly contradicted by Dar al-Iftaa, Egypt's most authoritative theological council. In fact, the council declared, 'Islam forbids Muslims from renouncing their faith . . . if a Muslim did so [he or she] would be committing a mortal sin.' It added that apostasy was 'a sort of crime' that 'requires punishment'.[20]

The acute sensitivity of this issue was established in an important test case, heard in 1996, involving Nasr Hamed Zayd, formerly Professor of Arabic Literature at Cairo University, who renounced his Muslim identity and was deemed an apostate, even though he did not embrace another religious creed. Egypt's Court of Cassation ruled that the 'apostasy of a Muslim is not an independent matter that the Islamic law and its state can pardon and overlook as one of the rights of the individual . . . because exiting from Islam is a revolt against it . . . Nobody is entitled to call for whatever contradicts public order or morale, nor use the freedom of opinion to harm its foundation.'[21] The court has never defined the 'proper' punishment for an apostate. Mr Zayd and his wife fled from Egypt to Holland after the ruling.

From a Christian perspective, there is naturally a double standard in the rule that allows a Muslim man, but not a Muslim woman, to marry across the faith divide. The rule can also affect female converts whose new allegiance is not officially recognised: a woman who has become a Christian, and wishes in consequence to marry a Christian husband, will have great difficulty in fulfilling her aim. Some Christians with Muslim backgrounds will therefore forge their documents – both in order to marry, and to register their children as Christians. If the deception is uncovered, those involved may have to flee abroad to avoid harsh reprisals.

In 2007, monitors from Christian Solidarity Worldwide examined two such cases: one of an Egyptian Christian from a Muslim background who was seeking asylum, and another of a young Egyptian couple who fled to Jordan and sought refugee status from the UN Refugee Agency, UNHCR. A Coptic priest, Fr Matteos Wahba, was sentenced to five years' imprisonment in October 2008. His 'crime' was to have granted a marriage certificate to a Christian woman from a Muslim background and a Coptic man, based on documents provided by the couple showing them both to be Christians. Fr Wahba was accused of helping in the forgery of documents, even though the couple had stated publicly that he did not know the documents were not genuine. The couple then went into hiding.[22]

The State Security Intelligence Service (SSIS) was especially feared by converts under the Mubarak regime. In one notorious instance, three young men who had converted from Islam to Christianity were arrested in September and October of 1990 and detained for ten months. They were tortured throughout this period by methods that included electric shocks to the genitals, beatings, cigarette burns, sexual humiliation, and isolation in cells too small to enable detainees to lie down. They were eventually set free only after recanting their Christian beliefs, and an international campaign on their behalf. The men remain in Egypt but have faced long-term intimidation from the authorities in the years since their release.[23]

Evidence garnered by the human rights organisation Freedom House confirms this trend. To cite a representative case, twenty-two converts to Christianity and several of their supporters were arrested in 2003. One, Isam Abdul Fathr, died in custody;

others were tortured.[24] Just after New Year in 2005, Gaseer Muhammad Mahmoud, a Christian convert, was arrested by the police and his toenails were pulled out. He was transferred to the El-Khanka mental hospital near Cairo a few days later, on 10 January, where he was 'kept in solitary confinement, put in a water-filled room, beaten, whipped, and told that he would be incarcerated until he renounced his faith'.[25] He was released in June 2005 after a tide of international pressure.

Rumours that Copts are planning to extend church premises can be as inflammatory as suggestions of interfaith romance. On 25 October 2007, for example, Coptic villagers at Gabal-el Teir, in the al-Minya region south of Cairo, were attacked after local Muslims heard of plans to expand the local diocesan headquarters. The walls of the compound, which had already been rebuilt a number of times after earlier incursions, were attacked afresh. A church member rushed to report the attack at the local police station, only to be detained himself. The police took two hours to attend the scene of the attack, by which time most of the wall had been destroyed. Even then, though, they did not intervene directly, but allowed the violence to continue. Local Christian-owned farms were set on fire, irrigation pumps were stolen, two trucks were attacked, and eighteen people ended up in hospital. Later, twenty-two Copts and nineteen Muslims were arrested and questioned by the prosecutor. A 'reconciliation' process was launched: its result was that permission to build a wall was granted, but only as long as it was three metres inside the compound's boundaries. No compensation was offered to the victims.[26]

To be fair, the authorities can sometimes show less partiality. When attacks were launched in Esna, near Luxor, on twenty-six Christian-owned businesses and on the Church of the Holy Virgin on 16 December 2007, leaders of the local Coptic community at first refused to sign a reconciliation agreement. In what proved to be an unprecedented solution, however, an accord was reached when the governor's office granted compensation totalling 1,295,000 Egyptian pounds (approximately £129,000) to those whose property had been damaged.[27] But another anti-Christian attack in rural Egypt shortly afterwards was more typical. A dozen men set upon worshippers in the village of Qasr Hur with clubs as they were leaving church after a Palm Sunday ceremony. Even though five Copts were injured, and no one was charged in connection with the assault, a reconciliation process was foisted on the community. At roughly the same time, a group of Muslims in the village of Ezbet Adam attacked a Christian household in which the birth of a baby was being celebrated. The assailants were apparently angered about the close ties between the Christians and their Muslim neighbours, who had visited them to offer drinks and food.

About sixty armed men attacked the Abu-Fana monastery in Minya on 31 May 2008, after workers had begun building a wall around the monastery. Some of the attackers started destroying the wall; others attacked a chapel. Two monks and two workers were shot and injured during the ensuing clashes. A local Muslim, Khalil Muhammad, was killed. The attackers abducted three monks on their way out. After refusing to spit on a cross, deny their faith, and accept Islam, the monks were beaten, whipped, and had thorns stuck into the soles of their feet, before being released early the next morning.[28] Two of the monastery's contractors, Rifaat and Ibrahim Fawzy, were held for thirteen months in relation to Khalil's murder, despite the presentation of evidence that exonerated them, and court decisions ordering their release.

No one was charged with the attack or the kidnap and torture of the monks. The terms of a reconciliation meeting after an earlier attack on the monastery in 2006, including a fine of 500,000 Egyptian pounds (£50,000) in the event of a future attack, were ignored in the aftermath of the May 2008 attacks. In July 2009, there was an official reconciliation agreement, which resulted in changes to the testimony given by the monks and villagers. Both parties publicly acknowledged that they did not know who their attackers and the murderer of Khalil Muhammad were. After this agreement, the Fawzy brothers were finally released by the SSIS.

Among the most graphic recent examples of harsh religious discrimination in Egypt has been the cull of pigs ordered in April 2009. Officially presented as a precaution to eliminate any risk that the H1N1 (swine flu) virus might spread from pigs to humans, the move was disastrous for many thousands of Christians, as well as scientifically flawed. The main facts of the case are reasonably familiar outside Egypt. Alarm – whether genuine or contrived – over the pandemic led the Mubarak government to order a cull of the country's 300,000-strong pig population, a move gratifying to many Muslims because of Islamic dietary laws. This proved a serious blow to the country's pig-farmers, most of whom were Christians. A less-discussed aspect of the affair involved the harm inflicted on the *Zabbaleen* – outcasts of Egyptian society who have long survived by refuse collection. They, too, are predominantly Christian.

The *Zabbaleen* ('garbage people' in Egyptian Arabic) were able to recycle up to four-fifths of the rubbish they collected. Pigs played a crucial part in this process, consuming up to 50 per cent of organic waste, which in Cairo amounted to 5,000 tons per day. By selling on non-recyclable material, the *Zabbaleen* were able to boost the small income they received from rubbish-collection, and to perform a valuable service for the broader community in the process. When the cull was announced, pig-owners were told that they would receive 50 EGP per pig – that is, 10 per cent of their market value. After protests, 250 EGP was offered for every sow culled. The action not only decimated the livelihoods of farmers and butchers: levels of organic waste soared in Egypt's cities as well. The *Zabbaleen* were offered employment by private refuse-collecting firms for 400 EGP per month, a quarter of their normal wage, while Cairo's pig-farmers were told that they could have a new breeding site in future at an unsuitable desert location 70 kilometres from the city.

There has still not been a single case of transmission of the H1N1 virus from pigs to humans. Before the health scare arose, the Egyptian government had already tried unsuccessfully on several occasions to force pig-farmers to move to out-of-the-way spots. Human rights observers were thus almost certainly right to conclude that the swine flu pandemic provided Mubarak's government with a convenient pretext for eradicating pig-farming.

*

We now have a vantage point from which to ponder the Arab Spring. Two main narratives have governed interpretation of this seismic period. Optimists maintain that governments across the spectrum are acknowledging a need to be more responsive to the demands of their people. Cheerier commentators can point to Tunisia, where there is a democratic government, the first since the 1950s, and women occupy a quarter of the parliamentary seats. In Morocco, for the first time in the country's history, the prime minister has not been chosen by the monarch. Elsewhere, Jordan, Yemen, and Bahrain are on journeys towards reform.

The less sanguine can naturally base their case on the Syrian bloodbath of 2011–2012, and buttress it by pointing out that theocratic rebels hardly mark an improvement on secular forms of hardline rule. (We have already noted the estimate that 50,000 Christians were expelled from their homes in the Syrian city of Homs in late 2011 and early 2012.)

Egypt's case lends credence to both sides, Tahrir Square in Cairo having become a symbol of pro-democracy activism before Hosni Mubarak's downfall, and of military violence after it. Copts have therefore been living on a knife-edge. Shortly before the president's resignation on 12 February 2011, more than twenty worshippers were murdered, and at least seventy others injured, when a car bomb exploded outside St Mark's Coptic Church in Alexandria. On 20 March, vigilantes in the province of Qena entered the village where Ayman Anwar Mitri, a school administrator, lived and cut off his right ear. Mr Mitri's alleged crime was to have let a flat to a woman his attackers claimed was a prostitute. They told him that 'Nazarenes' (that is, Christians) like himself were no longer protected by Mubarak's hated secret police, and would henceforth be liable to face Islamic justice. The perpetrators of this and similar attacks were Salafists. Their antics are a sign of how Christians (even those who don't face active persecution) are seen across large parts of the world: as somehow not fully part of their respective nations, despite long traditions of peaceful coexistence with the majority communities.

Members of a large crowd crying '*Allahu Akbar*' set fire to St Mina and St George's Church in Sole, a village 30 kilometres from Cairo on 4 March. They were spurred by a romance between a local Christian man and a Muslim woman, and the refusal of the woman's father to restore the family's 'honour' by killing her. Within a few days, a group of Copts had decided to draw national attention to the attack by protesting outside the headquarters of state television in Cairo. But on 8 March they were confronted by a much larger group of Muslims carrying guns, clubs and Molotov cocktails. The Coptic demonstrators responded with sticks and stones. Though called in to keep the peace, soldiers fired live ammunition: thirteen people were killed and more than a hundred wounded. The violence spread around the eastern area of the capital where many *Zabbaleen* live. Throughout the night mobs marched through the area, setting fire to vehicles and Christian-owned homes and business premises.

Some Muslim protesters claimed that the guards at St Mina and St George's had opened fire on them, but army searches of Copt-owned property failed to uncover either weaponry or the alleged convert.[29]

The following day, Coptic demonstrators marched to the headquarters of state television on the banks of the Nile, demanding that Egypt's Supreme Military Council clamp down on the 'criminals' behind the wave of anti-Christian violence. Muslim counter-demonstrators attempted to thwart the action at first, but they were turned away. Several thousand Copts then helped erect tents matching recent scenes in Tahrir Square, which is only a few minutes' walk away – but this time the scene was festooned with large wooden crosses, banners, and images of Christ and Pope Shenouda.

In mid-May, I visited the demonstration, known as the Maspero sit-in, with a group of journalists from *Watani*, the leading Coptic newspaper. The atmosphere was at once light-headed and deeply serious. Though hardly free of anxiety, these Christians had the poise of those who sense that there will be no going back. Their chief refrains had not changed. They wanted Salafist zealots brought to justice, and national unity against destabilising forces. 'We just want the army to do its job and follow the law,' commented Fadi Philipe, a member of the Maspero Youth Union, which organised the protest. 'We are peaceful people but we are not cowards. If the army won't defend us, then we'll defend ourselves.'

Youseef Abdullah, a lawyer gathering signatures for a petition demanding international intervention to end 'crimes against humanity', was clear that recent violence formed part of a pattern. 'These [assaults] are not spontaneous, as some describe them,' he declared. They were 'planned, serial attacks on . . . Copts', which had been going on with greater or lesser intensity for centuries. Fr Matthias Nasr Mancrious, a priest with a renowned ministry to the urban poor, emphasised that interfaith relations were often good. 'Muslims are not against Christians: it is only the Salafists who embrace violence. But the nation and all its elements must apologise for allowing this, not just in words but in deeds.'

The broad contours of debate have not altered greatly since then. In the first round of parliamentary elections, held in November 2011, Islamists from both the Muslim Brotherhood's Freedom and Justice Party, and al-Nour, the Salafist party, did very well, polling over 60 per cent of the vote between them. It remains to be seen how far the two groupings will cooperate over the longer term, but their success owed much to good organisation (not a forte of more liberal groups) and the social-support structures that Islamists have long fostered around the country.

Shortly before Christmas, Wagih Yacoub, a Coptic activist, told the campaign group International Christian Concern that 'Salafists are one of the largest threats to Christians in Egypt. The Muslim Brotherhood is also very dangerous, but the difference is the Salafists don't negotiate.'[30] Fr Gameel, a Coptic priest in Cairo, commented to the *al-Ahram* newspaper that the election results so far showed that Egypt had 'replaced the Mubarak dictatorship with a new dictatorship, but this time it is religious'.[31]

Writing with more equanimity about the situation in the newspaper *al-Hayat*, another commentator, Elias Harfoush, declared that 'One of the most important achievements of the Arab Spring is that it restored the right to free choice to the regular citizens. This right is not violated by the fact that the Islamic movements have accessed power. Indeed, these are the societies and this is their choice.'[32]

Liberals are naturally despondent. Most of those I interviewed in Cairo foresee great strife ahead. Their view is summed up by Wael Gamal, a distinguished economist and managing editor of another Egyptian newspaper, *al-Shorouk*, who believes that the country's institutions are too weak to cope with the groundswell of pro-reform opinion. 'I have no doubt we will see another confrontation, another uprising, very soon,' he said in early 2012.[33]

Mohamed Morsi's election as President several months later lent support to both sides of the argument. Egyptians now have their first-ever elected leader. That is a hopeful sign in principle, notwithstanding the country's gargantuan social and economic problems. So was the President's dismissal in August of the Defence Minister, Field Marshal Hussein Tantawi, and other senior military figures associated with the Mubarak era. But major questions clearly remain. Will the Muslim Brotherhood serve the interests of all communities, as it has promised, or will it seek to impose a theocratic model of government? Pragmatists have stressed that Turkey's ruling party provides the Brotherhood with its preferred way ahead, but this, as we shall see in Chapter 5, is hardly a source of reassurance to

Christians. Turkey jails more journalists than either China or Iran. In any case, will the army – and agents of the so-called deep state – really be prepared to give up power? One point cannot be gainsaid. Copts (whether in Cairo or Kensington or further afield) remain deeply concerned about the future of their battered Church.

2
IRAQ

Few Christian populations on earth have suffered as acutely as Iraq's in recent years. The onslaught against an ancient and peaceful body of believers has prompted responsible pastors to wonder about the very survival of their communities, who mainly belong either to the Chaldean Catholic Church, the Assyrian Church of the East, or the Oriental Orthodox Churches.[1] In 1990, there were between 1.2 and 1.4 million Christians in the country. By the time of the second Gulf War in 2003, this figure had fallen by about half a million.[2] Today, fewer than 200,000 remain.

Though it is commonly assumed that Saddam Hussein's Baath regime afforded protection to Christians, the idea requires heavy qualification. The truth is that Christians suffered displacement and discrimination, if not outright persecution, throughout the later decades of the twentieth century. There were almost 250 Christian villages in northern Iraq at the end of the Second World War, for example; even by the end of the 1960s, dozens of them had been destroyed. The year 2003 nevertheless marked a watershed. Chaos followed the American-led invasion in the spring of that year; with chaos came an explosion of sectarian strife. Iraqi Christians became more vulnerable than ever: as one of them later put it, 'Extremist Sunnis and Shiites are at war over everything else, but united by a common denominator, the persecution of Christians.'[3] For some, the more targeted nature of the attacks was encapsulated by the beheading in 2006 of a kidnapped Syrian Orthodox priest, Fr Boulos Iskander, even after a ransom had been paid. Between 2006 and 2010, seventeen Iraqi priests and two Iraqi bishops were kidnapped in Baghdad and in the northern cities of Mosul and Kirkuk. All were assaulted or tortured by their captors. Most were released, but one bishop, four priests, and three subdeacons (junior clerics) were killed. In most cases, those responsible declared that they wanted all Christians to be expelled from the country.

Speaking about this turn of events during a visit to Ireland in 2011, the Chaldean Catholic Archbishop of Erbil in Iraqi Kurdistan, Bashar Warda, emphasised the price paid by laypeople – shopkeepers, mothers and children, the elderly – as well as by church leaders. He said that common expressions of sectarian belligerence included direct threats in letters with bullets enclosed; text messages mentioning potential targets by name; direct, person-to-person threats on the street; threatening language from policemen and army personnel; burglary and extortion; threatening graffiti, including quotations from the Qur'an on the walls of Christian homes; and the periodic appearance of armed men outside Christian households.

The systematic desecration of Christian places of worship began with an assault on a church in Mosul in 2004. On 1 August of that year, a bomb was detonated at St Peter and St Paul's Church in the Christian town of Al Dora. Five other churches around the country were bombed on the same day; twelve people were killed, and many injured.[4] By early 2011, at least sixty-six other churches had been bombed or invaded: forty-one in Baghdad, nineteen in Mosul, five in Kirkuk, and one in the city of Ramadi, about 70 miles west of the capital. Two convents, a monastery, and a church-run orphanage had also been bombed.[5]

Later in the address already mentioned, Archbishop Warda told two stories that crystallised the trauma facing his fellow believers. One was about a Mr Dahan, the father of a teacher at a church-run kindergarten. He was the first of at least eight Iraqi Christians to be killed in Mosul before the elections of 2010. The abduction that ended with his death was the second time he had been kidnapped. Two years before, he had been seized, beaten, and stuffed into the back of a car until his relatives had paid a ransom of $5,000. The family did not move after this, because Mr Dahan himself refused to leave. As a family member put it, 'Our father said, "If all of us Christians leave, who is going to stay in the land of the prophets and pray in our churches?" He added, "We were all born in Mosul and we will die in Mosul."' The second story involved a priest, Fr Mazen, from the town of Qaraqosh (also called Bakhdida) in the north, who was kidnapped four days after his ordination. He was released; but a year later, armed men entered his home and killed his father and two brothers in front of his mother and sister-in-law. Despite this tragedy, Fr Mazen has continued to serve the displaced families in his congregation with unflagging faith.

'There are thousands of examples of such senseless injury and killing,' the archbishop added. 'The grief and sorrow in our congregations is palpable, where not one person has been unaffected by tragedy since 2003. Moreover, each family has suffered decades of losses from the Saddam regime, the sanctions prior to the occupation, the devastation of the Gulf War as well as the Iran–Iraq war. Iraqis are a people who have experienced immense suffering but who are also strong, resilient, and prepared to claim their right to existence.'[6]

In some ways the lack of attention paid to Iraqi Christians is understandable, given the far greater bloodletting between the

Shia and Sunni communities, and the immense suffering of the population as a whole. More than 100,000 civilians are thought to have died violent deaths since 2003; but even this figure is eclipsed by the effects of UN sanctions during the 1990s, which claimed the lives of over 500,000 children.[7] A sense of the particular horrors being endured by Christians probably began to filter into Western public consciousness after 31 October 2010. This was the date of an attack by ten al-Qaeda militants on the Syrian Catholic Cathedral in Baghdad, when over fifty people were murdered and many more maimed.

Though the cathedral, Our Lady of Deliverance (Sayidat al-Najat), is near the heavily protected Green Zone, this did not stop a posse belonging to the 'Islamic State of Iraq' group from approaching the building shortly after the start of worship at 5.30 p.m. First, the terrorists detonated a car bomb outside the semi-fortified cathedral gates. One of the priests present, thirty-two-year-old Fr Thaier Saad Abdal, thought that the noise was caused by random shooting. He pressed a button beside the altar to turn on some soothing sacred music. Watching him from near the front of the aisle was his mother, Um Raed, and several other members of their family. Speaking later to the journalists Hala Jaber and Christine Toomey of the *Sunday Times*, Um Raed recalled what happened next: 'I turned and saw gunmen with suicide belts strapped around their waists scrambling in through a hole they'd blown in the church doors. They were screaming "Allahu Akbar! Allahu Akbar!"' She saw another priest, twenty-seven-year-old Fr Wasim Sabieh, close to the cathedral entrance pleading with the terrorists to stop. 'They shot him through the mouth, then again in the chest, shouting "We've killed an infidel!",' explained Um Raed, who, turning back in horror to face her own son, saw him fall on the steps of the altar, gasping, 'God, to thee I commend my soul.' 'I saw his blood spill across the floor,' she continued. 'I fell to my knees and started rubbing my hand through his blood. They shot me too. They shot my hand in my son's blood.'

As terrified worshippers threw themselves between the pews, Um Raed saw her eldest son, Raed, push his wife and baby daughter in the direction of the sacristy beside the altar, where other worshippers were scrambling for shelter, before reaching out to embrace his brother. Then they shot him. 'Both my sons fell by the altar,' Um Raed explained to Jaber. 'I lay between them. They shot me again in my leg.' Desperate to protect his mother, Raed hissed at her, 'Mama, don't move, be still.'

'I lay between my sons,' recalled Um Raed. 'I lay there thinking Raed was keeping quiet too, so they wouldn't know he was alive. I kept my hand in my son's blood; I caressed it as I lay there listening to the gunmen shout out "We've killed an infidel! We've killed another one! We have hostages!" as they shot more people. When their ammunition ran out, they started throwing grenades.'

Samer and Emil, two brothers who would become refugees in France, were sitting three rows from the altar when the gunmen arrived. Emil was shot and collapsed between the pews. Samer, thinking his brother dead, threw himself to the floor and crawled to the sacristy where he and others quickly barricaded themselves in with a bookcase pushed against the door. 'Every beat of my heart in that place felt like a year. Every scream we heard outside took part of my life away,' he said.

Above the din Samer heard a woman pleading for the door to the sacristy to be opened so that she could hide too. He recognised the voice as that of his friend Raghda. She had gone to the cathedral that day with her husband for a blessing after learning that she was expecting their first child. Others in the sacristy argued that the door should not be opened. But Samer pulled the bookcase away just enough to draw his friend inside. 'Raghda was sobbing, telling us they had killed her husband,' said Samer, who then threw a book at the one light in the room, plunging the group into semi-darkness. 'Outside,' Jaber wrote, 'terrorists were picking off worshippers one by one. Husbands were slaughtered in front of wives. Babies were killed in front of parents. One mother who whimpered that she did not know how to stop her infant crying was told by one of the gunmen, "I'll show you how!" He took aim at the child's head and fired, then shot the baby's mother, father and grandfather.'

Unable to get through the sacristy door, the terrorists began throwing flares and sound grenades through a ventilation shaft into the sealed room. One man beside Samer, Muhammad Munir, was severely injured. He had only been back in Baghdad for a month, after five years of studying engineering in Russia. Shrapnel blew off his left arm below the elbow and the toes of his sister, Manal, beside him. 'She fell on top of those sitting on the floor, spilling her blood. I thought both would bleed to death,' Samer said. When he noticed Raghda's breathing was growing heavier, Samer implored her to talk to him. 'Then I felt something warm on my leg. It was Raghda's blood. She was bleeding to death. She died in my arms, her unborn child too . . . her only crime being that she prayed to her god.'

Meanwhile, Um Raed lay between her sons for the next five hours, hardly daring to breathe, until after 10 p.m. Only then did the Iraqi security forces arrive at the cathedral to confront the terrorists. By dawn on the following day – coincidentally All Saints' Day, on which the persecution of the early Christians has long been commemorated – forty-four worshippers, two priests, and seven personnel from the security forces lay dead. About sixty people had been wounded.

Like many of their fellow believers, Um Raed and her family had moved from their home (in their case Mosul) to Baghdad. After the first Gulf War, Christians began moving in numbers from Iraq to Syria, Jordan, Europe, and the United States. The situation deteriorated severely after 2003, as Um Raed's daughter, Najlaa, recalls: 'Immediately after the fall of Saddam, nothing much changed. We continued to dress normally. We would go to clubs. Until 2008, life was more or less normal. Then we started hearing of entire families killed because they were Christians. All Christians became more afraid. But despite this, we left things in the hands of God.' Hala Jaber and Christine Toomey later published a powerful account[8] of the atrocity based on the witness of survivors, many of whom became refugees in France.

Within two weeks of the cathedral attack, nearly a hundred surviving members of the congregation sought refuge in the city of Sulaimaniya, in eastern Kurdistan. Many others had fled elsewhere. Twelve people were arrested in connection with the crime, but the churchpeople were largely sceptical about whether the real culprits had been found, suspecting that the detentions were mainly intended to reassure the Americans.[9] Very soon after this, on 5 December 2010, an elderly Christian couple, Hikmat and Samira Sammak, were stabbed to death at home in the Baladiyat neighbourhood of Baghdad. They had already moved away – to Ainkawa-Erbil, in the north – and had simply returned to finalise the sale of their property.[10]

Najlaa's impressions are borne out by a few more statistics. In January 2005, the Syrian Catholic Archbishop of Mosul, Basile Georges Casmoussa, was kidnapped and subsequently released after international pressure. As noted above, Fr Boulos Iskander was snatched in 2006 and beheaded several months later. In January 2008, over a year after Fr Boulos's abduction, nine Chaldean and Assyrian churches in Mosul, Kirkuk, and Baghdad were bombed. A few weeks later, a very senior Chaldean Catholic leader, Archbishop Paulos Faraj Rahho, was kidnapped and killed, and his body was deposited in a shallow grave.[11]

*

History casts a revealing sidelight on the current affairs explored in this chapter. The hounding of local Christians seems to me all the more heartrending given that the roots of their communities are almost as old as the New Testament itself. Westerners are often shamefully ignorant when it comes to the Middle East's patchwork of faiths: as I have suggested, many even assume that Christianity is an import to the region, 'rather than an export from it', as Rowan Williams has said. The Archbishop of Canterbury expanded on this insight during a parliamentary debate about the persecution of Christians in 2011.[12] He reminded his audience that for two millennia, the Christian presence in the region had been an integral part of successive civilisations: 'a dominant presence in the Byzantine era, a culturally very active partner in the early Muslim centuries, a patient and long-suffering element, like the historic Jewish communities of the Maghreb and the Middle East, in the complex mosaic of ethnic jurisdictions within the Ottoman Empire and, more recently, a political catalyst and nursery of radical thinking in the dawn of Arab nationalism.' To be ignorant of this was

> to risk misunderstanding a whole world of political and religious
> interaction and interdependence and to yield to the damaging
> myth that, on the far side of the Mediterranean or the Bosphorus,
> there is a homogeneous Arab and Muslim world, a parallel

universe. . . . The Middle East is not a homogeneous region, and the presence of Christians there is a deep-rooted reality. We are not talking about a foreign body, but about people who would see their history and their destiny alike bound up with the countries where they live, and bound up in local conversations with a dominant Muslim culture, which they are likely to see in terms very different from those that might be used by Western observers.[13]

Dr Williams later told me how some London schools had illuminated his point by their inept treatment of refugee children from the Middle East. Arab pupils had been pulled out of assembly by overzealous staff who assumed that they were all Muslims, when many were in fact Orthodox Christians.

We could supplement this cluster of insights by noting that beyond the Christianity of Byzantium, beyond the Euphrates and into Persia, Central Asia, China, and India, thousands of congregations, under the oversight of scores of bishops, arose during the first millennium. The faith spread early into modern-day Iraq from south-east Turkey and established itself during the second century in the city of Seleucia-Ctesiphon, on the banks of the Tigris near what would become Baghdad. Here, as Anthony O'Mahony, a highly respected expert on Middle Eastern Christianity, has noted, the Church of the East became the most successful missionary launchpad in the world – all without ever becoming a state religion.[14]

Why is this seam of Christianity so unfamiliar to Western eyes? A full explanation would entail a long chapter in itself, because it centres on the fallout of complex church disputes about the relationship between Christ's human and divine identities that came to a head during the fifth century. The Assyrian Church of the East became separated from the rest of the Christian world after the Council of Ephesus in 431, and was thereafter known by the inaccurate label 'Nestorian', at least until the modern era. The Oriental Orthodox Churches went their own way after the even more momentous Council of Chalcedon, held near Constantinople in 451.[15]

Doctrinal differences were naturally magnified by geopolitical factors, among them that a large proportion of Assyrian Christians lived outside the Eastern Roman Empire. Much later, the frisson of discovering another Christian culture at once familiar, alien, and exotic was encapsulated by an early twentieth-century traveller such as Adrian Fortescue. 'The stranger who passes the Turkish–Persian frontier near Lake Urmi, the stranger who goes to delve among the ruins of Ninevah, will perhaps wonder to find in these parts buildings which are plainly Christian churches,' he wrote. This was the 'last tragic remnant of a Church whose history is as glorious as any in Christendom'.[16]

Fortescue notes that what he variously calls the Nestorian or 'Persian' Church evolved in part by defining itself against the Roman Empire. For example, clerical celibacy was abolished, even for bishops. Commenting on the Catholikos (senior bishop) Babai II, in office from 497 to 502, Fortescue quipped that 'this man marks almost the lowest degradation of the Persian Church. He could even read, and he had a wife.'[17]

These are the words of a confident Catholic untroubled by the ecumenical niceties of a later era. Fortescue loses few opportunities to put down those he judges to be heretics or schismatics. But he has the grace to acknowledge the Assyrians' extraordinary missionary endeavours. These led not just eastwards, as we have seen, but also to westward expansion, especially after the rise of Islam, because caliphs in regions such as Egypt and Syro-Palestine were indifferent to doctrinal squabbles between Christians and allied attempts to outlaw 'Nestorianism'. But it was the Assyrians' missionary ventures into Asia, including countless places where the gospel had never yet been preached, which most impressed Fortescue. He salutes them as follows:

> Those forgotten Nestorian missionaries, they were not Catholics but they were Christians. Braving long journeys, braving heathen tyrants and horrible danger, they brought the name of Christ north to Lake Baikal [in Siberia], south to Ceylon, and east right into the heart of China. They must have baptized thousands, and they taught the wild men of Tartary [namely the Great Steppe, stretching from the Caspian Sea to the Pacific Ocean] to worship one God, to serve Christ . . . to love his mother . . . Let that be remembered to their honour.[18]

The point is summed up in a different way by Philip Jenkins in his 2008 book *The Lost History of Christianity*.[19] In terms of 'the number and splendor of its churches and monasteries', he writes, 'its vast scholarship and dazzling spirituality, Iraq was through the late Middle Ages at least as much a cultural and spiritual heartland of Christianity as [were] France or Germany, or indeed Ireland.'[20] Jenkins's subtitle tells its own story: *The Thousand-year Golden Age of the Church in the Middle East, Africa, and Asia – and How it Died*. The author deals with longer-term civilisational currents, but judges the impact of the death of Genghis Khan in 1259 to have been decisive. His Christian deputy, Kit Bugha, was defeated by a Mamluk army from Egypt in 1260. This tide of Mongol conquest – and an allied tradition of religious tolerance – was now over. Churches and church-run institutions were razed in Mesopotamia and Egypt by radical adherents of Ibn Taimiyyah (1263–1328), sometimes seen as a spiritual ancestor of today's Wahhabis. The Christian population then plummeted.

But the decline cannot be ascribed to outside forces alone. The Assyrian Church of the East developed major weaknesses, and was in due course supplanted by the Chaldean Catholic Church, which began as an offshoot from it. By the twentieth century, about 70 per cent of Iraqi Christians were Chaldeans. Their origin lay in a split within Assyrian ranks over the practice of hereditary patriarchal succession (the mantle of leadership passed from uncle to nephew), which arose during the fifteenth century. A very young and totally inexperienced candidate became Patriarch in 1552. Alarmed by this turn of events, several Assyrian bishops sought union with Rome, taking their people with them. An abbot, Yuhannan Sulaka, was proclaimed Patriarch Simon VIII 'of the Chaldeans' by Pope Julius III in St Peter's Basilica in 1553. Soon after returning home, the patriarch was tortured and executed by the Ottoman ruler of Amadya. This set the tone for several centuries of conflict between pro- and anti-Catholic parties in territories that had been subsumed into the Ottoman domains. The wound was staunched in 1830, when Pope Pius VIII confirmed Metropolitan (or Archbishop) Yuhannan Hormizd as leader of the Chaldean Catholics, and styled him Patriarch of Babylon.

The Chaldean Catholics endured heavy losses during the First World War, when between 70,000 and 100,000 of them were killed, the fallout of battles between the Russian and Ottoman Empires. The survivors came to refer to 1915 as 'the year of the sword'. In later decades of the twentieth century, their lives were upset by more familiar forms of turbulence: revolutions in 1958, 1963, and 1968, the last of which was spearheaded by Saddam Hussein; the Kurdish revolt of the 1960s; and the Iran–Iraq War of the 1980s. The number of

Christians in northern Iraq fell from 1 million in 1961 to around 150,000 in 1995.

The Assyrian Church's evolution during the twentieth century had much in common with that of the Chaldean Catholic Church, especially as its heartland also lay around the unstable border between Kurdistan and Iraq. A large number of Assyrians were displaced from the Hakkari region of the newly formed Turkish republic, and assembled in northern parts of Iraq with their fellow Christians. They then formed so-called Iraqi Levies, becoming one of the most loyal and effective sections of the British army, hoping thereby to secure their eventual independence. But an Assyrian state never materialised – a mark, critics say, of colonial treachery. When the British Mandate ended in 1933, 3,000 Assyrians were slaughtered in a bloodbath. Christians began to emigrate as a result. Those who remained had to cope with recurring instability, including the assassination of Patriarch Mar Eshai Shimun III in 1975. His successor, Mar Dinkha IV, moved his Church's headquarters to Chicago the following year. But there was encouraging ecumenical news to soften the gloom. Pope John Paul and Patriarch Mar Dinkha signed a historic joint declaration in 1994 that paved the way for intercommunion between the two Churches. In consequence, Assyrians and Chaldean Catholics have drawn closer.

The second half of the twentieth century brought a more general growth of Iraqi diasporas – in the Antipodes, as well as in traditional refuges such as Lebanon, Syria, Turkey, and Jordan. As suggested, then, the regime of Saddam Hussein was not especially propitious for Christians. Despite its secular credentials, the Baath Party recognised Islam, but not Christianity, as a core element in Arab culture, and Islam was the de facto state religion. Although congregations were allowed to build or repair their churches and worship more or less freely, Christian involvement in public life was highly restricted. As O'Mahony notes,[21] the 250-member National Assembly of 1984 included just four members (a proportionate representation would have been at least twice that figure); and no Christian held a senior public post, with the exception of the long-serving Foreign Minister, Tariq Aziz. This was probably no bad thing. It meant Christians could keep their heads down. Yet this did not stop many of them – especially those with an eye to the consequences of Islamic revivalism in Iran and elsewhere in the region – from thinking of Saddam as the lesser of disagreeable alternatives. One anonymous bishop commented prophetically that Christians would have nothing positive to gain from either the implosion of the regime, or from an Islamic revolution.[22]

This point is well taken. The emergence of eighty new political parties – five of them Christian – since the downfall of Saddam is hardly compensation for all the mayhem and carnage. The picture is not even encouraging in theory, as a glance at the new constitution of 2005 proves. Time and again, this document enshrines competing principles. One strand in the text is based on individual rights and notional equality; the other on a traditional Islamic pattern where people's status varies according to their gender or faith allegiance. Article 2 stipulates both that no law may go against 'the principles of democracy', and that 'no law contradicting the provisions of Islam may be established'. Article 39 does not lay down a clear right to settle family law disputes through recourse to civil rather than religious courts. Article 89 declares that the Supreme Court should include 'experts in Islamic jurisprudence', with no counterbalancing requirement that they be trained in civil law as well. Tellingly, this matches the models already operating in Afghanistan, Iran, and Saudi Arabia.[23]

A revealing snapshot of a fast-worsening situation came in 2007, when the Chaldean Church decided to hold its synod in Iraq as a mark of solidarity with the population. (The previous such event had been held in Rome two years earlier.) On 31 May, the day before the gathering was due to start, a terrorist gang shot dead Fr Ragheed Ganni in front of the Holy Spirit Church in Mosul, where he was parish priest. The deacons accompanying him were also murdered.[24] Fr Ganni had survived several earlier attempts on his life, but would have known that he was very likely to be martyred. When his colleagues convened hours later at the al-Qosh monastery near the city, the agenda included debate on the drastic shrinkage of the Chaldean population – which had fallen by 50 per cent because of emigration – and the enormous rates of internal displacement within Iraq. By 2007, 2 million people had moved to the north of the country in search of peace.

Life in Baghdad had become even harder. Fatwas banning the wearing of the cross had been issued; churches were under threat for displaying the cross. On 4 June 2007, a declaration put out by the Mahdi Army, a group led by the extremist cleric Moqtada al-Sadha, purported to impose the wearing of the veil on Christian women.[25] And on the following day, Shia militants took over the Chaldean convent of the Angel Raphael in Baghdad's Doura quarter.

The other Christian family in what is known as the Syriac tradition consists of the Syrian Orthodox on the one hand, and another group in communion with Rome, the Syrian Catholics. There were between 30,000 and 60,000 of the former, and about 60,000 of the latter in Iraq in 2004,[26] many of whom were from families that had emigrated southwards towards cities such as Baghdad and Basra. At this period, there were also between 20,000 and 25,000 Armenian Orthodox in cities including Baghdad, Mosul, Kirkuk, Basra, and Zakho. Western-rite (Roman) Catholics are mainly foreigners, and the same is largely true of the small Anglican and Protestant communities. St George's Anglican parish in Baghdad is overseen by Canon Andrew White, president of the Foundation for Relief and Reconciliation in the Middle East, who has ministered with exceptional courage in the city since 2005, despite having multiple sclerosis. Evangelical and Pentecostal missionaries, mainly from the United States, have become an additional item on the country's religious landscape since 2003.

In the northern Kurdish areas, where until recently some 30 per cent of the Christian population was living, the local authorities have discriminated strongly against two other minorities, the Mandeans (a Gnostic group) and Ezidis (whose teachings derive from Zoroastrianism), as well as Christians, and have excluded Mandean villages from US-funded water and sewage works, electrical provision, and other essential services. Many families have been forced to leave their ancestral homes for safer areas of the country. After their departure, their properties were taken over by Kurds, or, in many cases, confiscated by the local authorities.

The plight of minorities is not improving at the time of writing. Attacks on Christians continued steadily in 2010 and on into 2011, the year of full American withdrawal from Iraq. Archbishop Warda has described the shock of his people after an Orthodox Christian, Arakan Yacob, was shot dead in Mosul on 31 May 2011. In an interview with Aid to the Church in Need,[27] the archbishop said that the murder had prompted many members of his flock to express a wish to emigrate. But emigration was becoming even more difficult, owing to the growing political crisis in Syria. 'The latest murder adds to the pessimistic view that there is no future,' he said. 'No matter how you try to convince people things are getting better, they say, "Look at what is happening." Even the situation in Turkey is not that good.' But he refused to be downcast. 'A message of hope is always there – life should go on – that's the message.'[28]

On 2 August 2011 – early in Ramadan – terrorists struck in Kirkuk at the Syrian Catholic Church of the Holy Family. A bomb was detonated beside the building at 5.30 a.m., injuring up to twenty-three people, including a twenty-day-old baby. The blast was severe enough to wound people in their beds nearby with broken glass. An electricity generator was sent flying, which blew a hole in the side of the church. Fr Imad Yelda, one of the parish priests, was also slightly hurt. In fact, the Christian population had a near escape. The militants also planted a bomb at the Presbyterian Evangelical Church in the city centre, but it failed to go off. Speaking afterwards,[29] the Archbishop of Kirkuk, Louis Sako, explained that the attack had occurred during a summer conference at the cathedral on the subject of Christian witness. He had asked the participants whether they were prepared to continue: virtually all had said yes. He added that local Sunni and Shia leaders had joined him in condemning the violence.

Kirkuk, with a population of almost a million, stands near the heart of an ethno-political struggle between Arab, Turkmen, and Kurdish groups. Kurds want the city to be absorbed within Kurdistan; Arabs and Turks wish to remain under the control of Iraq's central government. The violence against Christians probably reflected this instability. Yet there is irony in this as well. As the archbishop pointed out, Christians, besides being peace-loving and not very numerous, almost wholly lack political power.

It would be a false picture of Iraqi Christians which did not record their heroism. We have been reminded that they are very far from resigning themselves to a slow demise, not least because falls in the Christian population in some parts of the country have caused numbers to swell elsewhere. For example, the diocese of Erbil in Kurdistan has grown by 30 per cent in recent years, so that housing and school places are in short supply. Housing costs have risen steeply: rent levels have leapt by 200–300 per cent to take advantage of rising demand. In his address to Irish churchpeople, Archbishop Warda said that Christian schools in his diocese were having to run two shifts a day to cope with demand, while class sizes had risen substantially. Thanks to charitable donations from outside Iraq, new churches were springing up. Damaged buildings were being restored.

A new Catholic primary school had recently been built to ease the burden of public education in the area. Church leaders were overseeing the construction of low-cost housing for displaced families as a long-term investment against rising land values. Diocesan leaders were also seeking to develop church investments to stimulate jobs. 'Lastly,' the archbishop said,

> we want the presence of the Church to be apparent [through] a vibrant . . . parish life symbolized by church buildings and obvious public spaces. We do not want to hide our faith or identity out of fear for our lives. We want to be seen and remembered by all Iraqis; those who threaten us, but [especially] those willing to stand in solidarity with us . . . This is not a time to hide our faith or our identity . . . In Iraq, forty years of war and oppression have strengthened our endurance and our resolve to stand strong and to claim our legal and historical right as a Church and as a people . . . We have not come this far to give up.[30]

3

IRAN

When spokesmen for Iran's theocratic government shake their fists at Christians, the complaint of choice is that the Churches form a fifth column for Western influence. In October 2010 (to cite one of innumerable examples), the country's Supreme Leader, Ayatollah Ali Khamenei, declared that 'the goal of the enemies of Islam is weakening religion in Iranian society, and towards that end they engage in spreading immorality and nihilism, false mysticism, Baha'ism and the expansion of home churches.'[1] The verbal aggression makes that of a figure such as George W. Bush look mild by comparison, but this is not to suggest that it is wholly irrational. If Iranian Christians and other religious minorities are ever granted the right to worship without hindrance, the country's cultural climate will have liberalised significantly.

Western perceptions of the mullahs as overbearing bigots are familiar. But the widely held Iranian sense of the Americans and British as being oil-hungry bullies cannot be swept aside as the 'wrong' sort of generalisation. Iranians have long memories, fed by a toxic mélange of grievances. Older heads also remember the British and American meddling that resulted in the overthrow of Muhammad Mosaddegh's democratically elected government in 1953. They recall that they were treated like a colony (even though never a part of the British Empire) when the UK took control of Iran's treasury, armed forces, and transport system in

1919. Before this, towards the end of the nineteenth century, a British company had won a 'concession' to run Persian industry, a deal that Lord Curzon, the Viceroy of India, called 'the most complete and extraordinary surrender of the entire industrial resources of a kingdom into foreign hands'. When asked by a journalist in 1980 about comparable examples of American high-handedness – in this case the restoration of the Shah by the United States in 1953 – President Jimmy Carter replied, 'That's ancient history.'[2] The comment was ill-judged.

But Khameni's accusation reflects very high levels of paranoia all the same. Just 2 per cent of the 75 million people in Iran are non-Muslims. Only the Baha'i faith (considered heretical by many Muslims) is formally banned. Baha'is are deemed to be 'unprotected infidels', and may be murdered with impunity. Their places of worship have been destroyed, and they are denied access to a university education. Sufis have fared better, but not well. The constitution awards notional freedom of worship to Christians, Jews, and Zoroastrians, who have reserved seats in the Majlis or parliament, but conditions are very different in practice. Inequalities based on what one human rights organisation has termed 'religious apartheid'[3] are widespread. Neither the government nor any state-owned company employs non-Muslims. Muslim-owned businesses are officially banned from hiring non-Muslims, and members of religious minorities may not prepare food for Muslims.

The problem extends well beyond discrimination alone. For more than thirty years, members of Iran's religious and ethnic minorities have faced imprisonment, execution, and murder, as well as legal inequality. When Muhammad Khatami became President in 1997, freedom of speech and other rights were extended. Hopes of a more liberal future appeared to be confirmed by parliamentary elections. But these results prompted a backlash from religious conservatives, followed by electoral victory for hardliners in 2004, when many reformists were banned from standing. Mahmoud Ahmadinejad claimed the presidency a year later after another rigged poll – 1,006 out of 1,014 candidates were rejected by Iran's ruling Council of Guardians – and was re-elected in 2009 with a similar disregard for fair play. The clerical establishment retains its grip through a terror network – torture, arbitrary detention, disappearance, summary trial, and frequent use of the death penalty. The past few years have seen a renewed crackdown on non-Muslims, especially Baha'is and converts to Christianity.

Almost 300 Christians were officially arrested and detained during the twelve months after June 2010, but Christian Solidarity Worldwide judges that 'the full figure is almost certainly much higher'.[4] While the majority were released after short periods of imprisonment, several dozen spent between a month and a year in jail. Torture is used to achieve false confessions and extract information on fellow Christians and religious activities. CSW adds that exorbitant bail demands,

> some in excess of $30,000, secure the release of individuals, along with illegal documents that religious detainees are forced to sign. Such documents demand an end to participation in Christian activities, the renunciation of faith and compliance with further questioning when summoned. Laptops and mobile phones are often confiscated during raids on private Christian homes, and are used to obtain information on the activities and identities of other Christians.[5]

Among much else, the acrid rhetoric pouring out of the regime reflects its longstanding ideological confusion. On 7 January 1994, Iran's then President, Akbar Hashemi Rafsanjani, preached one of many sermons claiming that there was no validity in non-Muslim faiths. Moreover, he continued, the Islamic world confronted the same challenges as those that Muhammad had faced during his own ministry. Therefore Iran and the entire Muslim world must adopt 'the Prophet . . . and jihad as the model'.[6] Just as the first small Muslim community in Arabia succeeded in conquering the Christian world of the period, Rafsanjani avowed, so would the contemporary Muslim world, once more under attack by the forces of Christianity, ultimately triumph over its oppressors.[7]

Variations on this theme are regularly broadcast through official channels. In October 2010, Ayatollah Khamenei announced at the holy city of Qom that Christianity was being deliberately spread by Iran's enemies as a means to weaken Islam within Iranian society. A few weeks later, the Governor of Tehran, Morteza Tamadon, threatened further arrests of church members and declared that Evangelical Christians had inserted themselves into Islam 'like a parasite', with the backing of the West. Ayatollah Hadi Jahangosha said in August 2011 that 'the West is trying to divert our youth by publishing and advertising false Gnostic books . . . our enemies have noticed that Satanism and false Gnosticism are not popular in Iran and because of that they are taking a religious approach to expand Christianity.'[8] He identified house churches (newer, free-range congregations without an institutional structure) as a deviant sect by stating that 'the "real Christians" do not believe in this distorted Christianity-Protestantism'.[9]

Although Christians did not enjoy an easy life under the Shah, Muhammad Reza Pahlavi, conditions for them deteriorated almost as soon as he was overthrown in 1979. Hassan Dehqani-Tafti was Anglican Bishop in Iran from 1961 to 1990 – the first Iranian to become a bishop outside the Armenian and Assyrian

Churches since the seventh century. An attempt was made on his life in 1979 and although he fervently wished to stay on among his people, he was persuaded that this was now impossible. He continued to serve his diocese from exile in Britain.

Born in 1920 of Muslim parents in a village near the city of Yazd, Dehqani-Tafti attended a Christian school in Isfahan, converting to Christianity as a student at Tehran University. He served in the Iranian army at the end of the Second World War, before moving to England for ordination training. As a parish priest in the 1950s he gained renown, and set up two schools during his time as bishop. He greatly expanded the Church's ministry to blind people, as well as promoting interfaith dialogue around the Middle East. Having deplored the extent of corruption under the Shah's regime, at first he welcomed Ayatollah Ruhollah Khomeini's promise of a more just society. The bishop even wrote to the new leader with a pledge of support. Then the climate changed abruptly. Church-run hospitals and schools were confiscated. The Dehqani-Tafti household was looted. One night, at the end of 1979, two gunmen climbed over the walls of the bishop's house in Isfahan before opening fire on Dehqani-Tafti and his wife, Margaret, in their bed. Remarkably, the first four shots narrowly missed, and the fifth passed through the hand of Mrs Dehqani-Tafti as she threw herself across her husband's body to shield him.

Jean Waddell, the bishop's secretary, was shot and badly wounded the following May, but she, too, survived. The Dehqani-Taftis' son Bahram (at that time doing a stint as an English teacher at Tehran University as part of his national service) was less fortunate. He was fatally shot a few days later when his car was ambushed.[10]

Another much-publicised tragedy involved the murder of Haik Hovsepian-Mehr, leader of an Evangelical grouping, the

Assemblies of God. He prompted fury among hardliners by supporting the case of Mehdi Dibaj, a Christian convert, who had been imprisoned for apostasy and sentenced to death on four occasions during his decade-long incarceration. An international campaign spearheaded by Hovsepian-Mehr – known as Bishop Haik to his flock – ended with Mr Dibaj's release in Tehran on 16 January 1994. But Bishop Haik himself disappeared three days later. Officials announced shortly afterwards that he had been murdered. His family were never allowed to see his remains. On 24 June of that year, Dibaj also disappeared. His body was found in a Tehran park on 5 July, shortly after the discovery of the corpse of Bishop Haik's successor, Tateos Mikaelian.[11]

Sunni Muslims have also suffered severely at the hands of their Shia co-religionists. Sunnis make up 8 per cent of Iran's population, and 1 million of them reside in Tehran; yet they are not allowed a single mosque in the city. *Religious Freedom in the World* nevertheless reports that '[Shia] zealots who have practised widespread discrimination against Sunni communities have not been rebuked, nor has anti-Sunni violence been punished.'[12] The authorities destroyed a Sufi place of prayer at Qom, in north-west Iran, in February 2006, and dozens of worshippers reportedly sustained heavy injuries.

No overview of religious freedom in Iran should omit the treatment of the country's Jewish community. Jewish families are not allowed to travel abroad together; no Jew may visit Israel; Jewish schools are banned. Ahmadinejad is a Holocaust-denier. His statements on the subject have been described by prominent clerics as 'the heartfelt words of all Muslims in the world'.[13] Despite the travel restrictions, the Jewish population has fallen by about a half since 1979.

Nevertheless, Hadi Ghaemi, executive director of the International Campaign for Human Rights in Iran, sees the rise of a 'very targeted persecution and prosecution of Christians' at present,[14] attributing this to the rise of house churches, which are attracting converts disenchanted by the hardline Shia milieu in which they were raised.

As I have emphasised, Christians can sometimes score own goals. On occasion, the anger of the authorities has been stoked by sensationalist claims from some house churches about mass conversions from Islam. In the Iranian government's eyes, 'apostasy' on such a scale is highly threatening, even though the complaint masks a double standard. According to a report published in November 2010, for example, the number of Assyrian Christians had fallen from 100,000 in the mid-1970s to about 15,000, even though Iran's population had almost doubled during this period.[15] The core point is simply that people should be free to practise the faith of their choice.

Christian groups such as the Assemblies of God, which refuse on grounds of conscience to pledge not to evangelise among Muslims, are liable to face especially tight curbs. Copies of the Bible in Farsi are difficult to get hold of, while permission is not given to construct new churches, even though existing structures can sometimes be repaired. Evangelical churches continue to be closely monitored and are obliged to report to Irshad, the Ministry of Information and National Guidance, before admitting new members to their congregations.

*

Anti-Christian sentiment is also fed by tacit awareness of the country's pre-Islamic roots. The church presence in Persia dates from the second century. Within roughly a hundred years of this, about twenty dioceses had been established within the territory; and soon afterwards missionaries were being sent as far afield as

China and South East Asia. The Churches would in due course develop a complex ecology, which partly explains their frequent failure to present a united front against governments and other religious groups. The main indigenous Christian communities are the Armenians, the Chaldean Catholics, and the Assyrians.

The absence of strong cooperation between these Churches can be put down to cultural factors, as much as the theological differences sketched in the previous chapter. The Assyrians, for example, are mountain people, even though their patriarch lives in exile in Chicago. The Chaldeans reside mainly on the plains – either in Mesopotamia or Shahpour, a region in Iranian Azerbaijan, and their hierarchy is based in Iraq. The Armenian community is important relative to other parts of the Armenian diaspora, but its numbers have dropped from around 170,000 to approximately 100,000 since 1979.

The immensely deep roots of all these groups are worth tracing in outline. We have already noted in the Introduction that fourth-century Persian Christians faced a torrent of persecution under the Sassanid dynasty (the last pre-Islamic dynasty to rule Persian territory, which lasted from 224 to 651), most notably after war erupted with the Romans in 337. Peace was restored under the Emperor Yazdjard, who issued an edict of toleration for Christians in his domains in 410. It was not always adhered to – converts from Zoroastrianism, the ancient faith of Persia, to Christianity could still face severe penalties, for example – but the Assyrian Church of the East nevertheless became a *Millat* or officially recognised religious minority, with major implications for the evolution of what would become the Muslim world. The Church had its own senior bishop, the Catholikos, appointed with the reigning Shah's approval; it could make its own laws, and control its own buildings and institutions. Similar rights were extended to other Christian groups in Persia over the succeeding centuries. As Bishop Michael Nazir-Ali has pointed out in a valuable essay on Persian Christianity,[16] the *Millat* system represented the codification of an arrangement that had existed in de facto form during the Jewish Exile in the sixth century BC (Ezra 7: 11–26).

After the Islamic conquest of Persia in the mid-seventh century, the practice was integrated into the *Dhimma* system for non-Muslims. At its best, this way of managing minorities fostered unity and self-sufficiency among the groups concerned. But it also encouraged political submissiveness. As Nazir-Ali observes, 'It has enabled the survival of non-Muslim communities in the Islamic world, but the price has been very great, not only in terms of reductions in numbers, but in being easily identifiable and, therefore, vulnerable to persecution, exile and abuse.'[17]

Much depended on relations between individual bishops and Muslim leaders. Under the Abbasid dynasty, for example, a friendship arose between Patriarch Timothy I (728–823) and the Caliph al-Mahdi, even though the two men engaged in a vigorous debate on the truth claims of their respective traditions. Interfaith courtesies aside, however, the Assyrian Church's missionary activities were increasingly restricted. This propelled the community's eastward expansion – at least until the rise to dominance of the Turkic and Mongol peoples. Under Shah Abbas I (1588–1629), the Georgian and Armenian populations were forcibly moved to different parts of Persia. Many Georgians converted to Islam, while others accepted martyrdom. In 1604, Abbas razed the city of Julfa, a Christian centre on the Aras near today's Iranian border. Armenians moved to Isfahan, the Safavid capital of Persia, in large numbers, from where their descendants spread across the globe in the face of further persecution – to Aleppo, Venice, Amsterdam, and London; to Tibet, China, and the Philippines; and even, in the early eighteenth century, to the New World via the Pacific. In many cases, Armenians who stayed on in Persia remained in touch with their kinsmen abroad. They thus played a notable part in opening Persia up to the rest of the world during the nineteenth century and later.

As elsewhere, the Christian presence has long been impaired by inter-church divisions as well. The healing of the breach between Catholicism and the Chaldean Church served to sideline the Assyrians for a time, though as we have seen, contemporary ecumenical advances mean that it, too, may be formally reconciled with Rome over the coming decades. Not that Christians were incapable of cooperation before the modern era. When Protestant missionaries reached Persia (as it was then still known) in the early nineteenth century, many sought to revive the country's ancient Churches, even when some indigenous Christians were tempted to embrace Western forms of the faith. Nazir-Ali notes that the Church Missionary Society, which began its work in Iran in 1869, sought to promote the growth of a genuinely Persian Church, and announced that it would not proselytise among the members of the ancient Oriental Churches. 'When the Episcopal (Anglican) Church came to be established in Iran, receiving its first bishop in 1912, the membership was drawn largely from Zoroastrian, Jewish, or Muslim converts rather than from the ancient Christian communities.'[18]

It is this impulse – laudable from a Christian point of view, but problematic for many Muslims – that forms a major element in Iran's interfaith problems today. If non-indigenous Christian groups were not committed to mission, then the authorities would be less severe. But there are at least 10,000 converts to Anglicanism, or to Evangelical fellowships such as the Assemblies of God. Tension is such that influential voices in the regime have supported the reintroduction of traditional punishments for apostasy, namely the death sentence for a man and life imprisonment for a woman. Whether or not this happens,[19] the experience of converts to Christianity since 2005 has prompted rising alarm among NGOs and other observers. At the very least, officials apply intense pressure on 'apostates' to recant. Extra-judicial violence against Christian converts is also widespread. Between June and August 2009, at least thirty ex-Muslim converts to Christianity were arrested and detained across the country, mostly during church gatherings. The human rights group Middle East Concern reported that in one incident on 31 August, some twenty-five members of a house church in Amameh, near Tehran, were arrested. Although most of the worshippers were subsequently released, seven members were kept in the Evin prison. They were eventually released in September after surrendering the title deeds of their homes as bail. Official charges have not been levelled against them.

In the same year, two Christian women from a Muslim background, Maryam Rostampour, twenty-seven, and thirty-year-old Marzieh Amirizadeh, were detained in the same prison without facing a formal indictment. Security officers arrested them on 5 March, after their apartment was searched and their Bibles confiscated, along with other items. Neither woman had committed a crime under Iranian law. On 9 August, they were taken to court and ordered by the judge to recant their Christian faith, and threatened with further imprisonment and apostasy charges. After their refusal to recant, they were sent back to prison. Subsequently released, they have now left the country.[20]

During 2008, reports continued of the detention of Christians from Muslim backgrounds and leaders of underground house churches in Shiraz, in the south-east; Mazandaran province, in the north; and Tehran. In all of these cases, those arrested were kept incommunicado and in solitary confinement for days or weeks without charge or legal representation. They were interrogated regularly, verbally abused, threatened with apostasy and treason charges, and released only after signing documents pledging no further involvement in Christian activities. They were also made to turn over deeds to their properties, with no guarantee that the investigations against them would be dropped.[21]

In September 2008, a prosecutor at the Public and Revolutionary Court in Shiraz requested the death penalty for two men, Mahmoud Muhammad Matin-Azad and Arash Ahmad-Ali Basirat, by evoking the judge's constitutional obligations to refer to sharia law, and by citing Ayatollah Khomeini's book *Tahrir-ul-Vasile*, which prescribes the death penalty for apostasy. Mr Matin-Azad and Mr Basirat were later released after international pressure. Also in 2008, the passports of at least forty Christian converts were confiscated at airports on their return from attending church meetings abroad. They were all required to present themselves in front of judges, who told them that they should return to Islam if they wanted to regain their travel documents without facing criminal charges. A significant number reportedly yielded under duress.[22] Christian Solidarity Worldwide monitors were able to interview one of these Christians. He was summoned to court five times during the year. At each hearing, he was asked for the reasons behind his conversion and put under pressure to renounce his faith. He repeatedly refused to do so. Not only is he no longer allowed to travel abroad, but he was also sacked from his job, because his colleagues refused to work alongside an apostate. This reaction arose from the belief that non-Muslims, particularly apostates, are *najess* (meaning 'impure'), and thus that any physical contact with them or even with products used by them can potentially defile a Muslim. Ayatollah Khomeini himself declared that 'non-Muslims of any religion or creed are *najess*'. He held that although a handshake with a non-Muslim was not *najess*, contact with the bodily liquids of a non-Muslim was. Thus, washing the clothes of non-Muslims and Muslims together, eating food, consuming products or using utensils touched by non-Muslims are seen as potential sources of defilement.

Although physical intimidation and torture during detention is rarely reported, on 25 June 2008, Compass Direct News noted that a couple, who are Christians from a Muslim background, were detained for four days, during which they were subjected to physical harm.[23] Two women, Tina Rad and Makan Arya, were arrested for holding a Bible study at their house, and Ms Arya was charged with participating in 'activities against national security'. During their detention, they were threatened with the death penalty and told that the police would place Ms Arya's four-year-old daughter in care if they did not stop attending the church. Before being released on bail, they were forced to sign documents promising not to take part in church-related activities.

The scale of the problem is further illustrated by a clutch of recent cases – most importantly, that of Pastor Youcef Nadarkhani, a house-church leader. He was arrested in October 2009 in his home city of Rasht, 150 miles north-west of Tehran, and charged with apostasy after questioning the Muslim monopoly on the religious education of children in Iran. This monopoly contravenes the country's constitution, which allows parents to raise their offspring in their own faith, and violates international statutes such as the Convention on the Rights of the Child. He was found guilty in September 2010 and sentenced to death after refusing to reconvert to Islam. Pastor Nadarkhani denied ever having been a Muslim, but the prosecution argued successfully that his embrace of Christianity was illicit, owing to his 'Islamic ancestry'.[24]

The accused, who has two young sons, was then given three further chances to renounce his beliefs over the following twelve months, but refused to do so. Despite public pleas on his behalf from the US State Department, the British Foreign Secretary William Hague, and Western church leaders, the pastor's life remained in the balance in mid-2012. At the end of 2011, human rights monitors received unconfirmed reports suggesting that the case had been passed from the Supreme Leader to the head of Iran's judiciary, and that Mr Nadarkhani's possible execution was being postponed by a year to allow time to persuade him to recant.

Much of his time in prison has been spent in solitary confinement. Another pastor in a similar position is Behrouz Sadegh-Khanjani, a second-generation Christian from Tehran, who has been held in a high-security prison since June 2010. He faces charges of apostasy, blasphemy, and 'contact with the enemy'. Other members of his congregation (a part of the Pentecostal Church of Iran), including Mehdi Furutan, Muhammad Beliad, Parviz Khalaj, and Nazly Beliad, were also arrested. Each of these men has suffered acutely for his faith. Mr Furutan, for example, was picked up by undercover police officers, who told him that if they wished, they could beat him so hard as to draw blood from any part of his body. The prisoner stood his ground, explaining how he had struggled with substance abuse as a teenager, before eventually finding faith in Christ at university. This angered his captors, one of whom said: 'I asked you to tell about your crime, not evangelise us.' After months in captivity in Shiraz prison and then at Adelabad security prison, where torture is common, Furutan was released unexpectedly, but remained in considerable danger. His parents had given the deeds of their house to the authorities as bail. He and his fiancée decided that their best option was to enter Turkey as refugees. This involved escaping through the mountains, because Furutan's documents had been confiscated.[25]

The following stories from 2009 confirm a pattern of human rights abuse.[26] In that year, an Islamic Court in Shiraz sentenced three Christian converts – Seyed Allaedin Hussein, Homayoon Shokouhi and Seyed Amir Hussein Bob-Annari – to an eight-month suspended sentence and five years on probation. They were accused of 'cooperating with anti-government movements' – a reference to Christian TV stations – and told not to contact one another or take part in public worship. The judge threatened to enforce the sentence and have them tried for apostasy if these instructions were not obeyed.

Shortly afterwards, a sixty-two-year-old Muslim pensioner, Abdul Zahra Vashahi, was arrested in the Western city of Bandar Mahshar in an attempt to curb the activities of his Christian son, John Reza Vashahi, who has been living in Britain for a decade. John Vashahi founded the Iranian Minorities human rights group the previous year, and writes a blog: 'Jesus for Arabs'. His father was released after a six-day interrogation.[27] In July, police raided a meeting of Christian converts from Islam in Fasham north of Tehran. All twenty-four participants were arrested; devotional objects and other materials were seized. Seventeen of the detainees were released the following morning. Two days earlier, another eight Christians from the same group were arrested in Rasht, on the Caspian coast. Local Christians ascribed the move to rising tension over President Ahmadinejad's re-election the previous month: the suspects were accused of collusion with 'foreign powers'. At the same time, several satellite channels, including the Christian broadcaster

SAT-7, found their signals into Iran had been blocked by the government.

Religious festivals can also see extra restrictions on house churches. On Christmas Day 2010, more than seventy members of house churches were arrested and around fifty detained.[28] The contempt for house-church members shown by the government had been reflected a year earlier, when the Governor of Tehran declared that 'Just like the Taliban . . . who have inserted themselves into Islam like a parasite, [Evangelical Christians] have crafted a movement with Britain's backing in the name of Christianity.'[29]

Numerous complaints have been voiced by officials connected to the regime. In August 2011, a consignment of 6,500 Bibles was confiscated as it was being taken from Zanjan to Abhar, two cities in the north of the country. Soon afterwards, Dr Majid Abhari, an adviser to the Majlis, complained that Christian missionaries were attempting to deceive people, especially the young, with an expensive propaganda campaign. He also repeated a view, common among some Muslims, that other faith groups were dedicated to undermining Islam.

*

Iran's grim human rights record should not lead us to take a dim view of Shia Islam as such. We are unlikely to understand the position of Christians at the grass roots without some grasp of the power struggle unfolding at the top of Iran's highly spasmodic regime. Theology is crucial to such an understanding, because Ahmadinejad's power grab springs from a malign twist on Shia thought.

The President's mentor is Ayatollah Mesbah Yazdi. Both men are disciples of Muhammad Baqer al-Majlesi (1627–99), a highly influential Savafid theologian. Al-Majlesi is particularly associated with a downgrading of the importance of reason in religious discourse, and a parallel insistence on the need for unquestioning obedience to the clergy. Behind this stands a fundamental tenet of Shi'ism (often judged by other Muslims to encourage superstition): that there are a dozen semi-divine imams, beginning with Ali, the Prophet Muhammad's son-in-law, who bridge the gap between the supernatural and created realms, and that the twelfth figure in this line – the so-called Hidden Imam – will reappear on earth as the Mahdi to sweep away injustice shortly before the Day of Judgement.

Contemporary scholars such as Ali Rahnema, author of *Superstition as Ideology in Iranian Politics: From Majlesi to Ahmadinejad*, have done much to trace Ahmadinejad's use and abuse of this tradition.[30] In essence, the President is the self-appointed representative of the Hidden Imam, and claims to be preparing the way for his reappearance. Ahmadinejad thus casts any criticism of himself as de facto criticism of God's messenger. More specifically, the President has lavished large amounts of cash on the Jamkaran mosque near the city of Qom, Ayatollah Mesbah Yazdi's headquarters. Here, the ayatollah tells pilgrims to entrust their well-being to the Hidden Imam, forgetting current hardships in the process.

More liberal figures, including the former President Khatami, are aghast, seeing Ahmadinejad's pretensions as bordering on blasphemy. But as Rahnema observes, even many conservatives, including the anti-reformist Ayatollah Mahdavi Kani, are shocked, arguing that Ayatollah Khomeini himself would not have voiced claims so inflated. It is the beliefs underlying these claims that prompted Ahmadinejad to falsify the results of Iran's election in 2009.

With this bridge between religion and politics in mind, we can get a better view of Iran's stance in foreign affairs. Even if the regime's problems are self-inflicted, it is nevertheless clear that the world appears a menacing place from Tehran. Pakistan and India have nuclear bombs, there are American troops stationed in Afghanistan and the Gulf, and Iran is surrounded by mainly Sunni societies. The West supported Saddam Hussein during the Iran–Iraq War, even after the Iraqi dictator had used weapons of mass destruction on his own people.

Iran's wish for nuclear weapons is easier to understand against this background, even though the process has led to international ostracism, severe economic sanctions, and the killing of Iranian scientists, perhaps by Israeli agents. The wider ramifications of this are beyond the scope of our discussion. A few developments are worth noting. One is that the regime is weak, for all its bluster. The most notable aspect of the attacks on Israeli diplomatic targets in New Delhi, Tbilisi, and Bangkok in February 2012 is not that they occurred, but that they failed so miserably. As the journalist Martin Fletcher and other regional specialists have suggested,[31] they were in the same league as Iran's odd conspiracy to use Mexican drug-dealers to assassinate the Saudi Ambassador to Washington in 2011, and unlike its lethal bombing of the Israeli Embassy in Buenos Aires in 1992. Furthermore, the position of Iran would be weakened still further by a change of regime in Syria, its principal client state.

Internally, the government's unsteadiness is reflected in all sorts of ways, from the simmering tensions between Ahmadinejad and Khamenei over corruption and cronyism, to the causes célèbres that are much more familiar to Western audiences, including the treatment of dissidents, Western hostages, and individuals such as Sakineh Mohammadi Ashtiani, who was sentenced to death by stoning for alleged adultery, and has now been on death row for many years. The government is terrified by the prospect of a velvet revolution; it would thus probably welcome the propaganda value flowing from an American or Israeli bid to bomb Iran's nuclear facilities. Authorities such as the author Amir Taheri[32] believe that Iran's posturing on the international stage is precisely designed to trigger the Western attack that would play into Khamenei's hands.[33] Whether such a strike takes place or not, the link between a febrile political situation and our core theme is readily apparent. While the collective tragedy endured by Iran since 1979 continues to be played out, the prospects for Christians and other minority groups remain desolate.

4
PAKISTAN

The recent atrocities against Christians in Pakistan will sear
the imaginations of countless people of all faiths throughout
the world. As the Minister of Law in the Punjab has already
said, such actions are not the work of true Muslims: they are
an abuse of real faith and an injury to its reputation as well
as an outrage against common humanity, and deserve forthright
condemnation.

Christians in Pakistan are a small and vulnerable minority,
generally with little political or economic power. They are
disproportionately affected by the draconian laws against
blasphemy, which in recent years have frequently been abused
in order to settle local and personal grievances. They need to
be assured of their dignity and liberty as citizens of a just and
peaceful society. Their good, their security, is part of the good of
the whole Pakistani nation. Those of us who love Pakistan and
its people, whatever their faith, feel that the whole country is
injured and diminished by the violence that has occurred.[1]

These words were written in August 2009 by Rowan Williams
after a deeply shocking turn of events at Gojra, a town in the
Pakistani region of Punjab. Eight Christians, including a child,
had been burned alive in their homes as mobs went on the
rampage after reports spread that a copy of the Qur'an had been
desecrated in the nearby village of Korian on 30 July of that
year. A false rumour suggested that at a Christian wedding, the

guests had not thrown paper money into the air, as is customary, but pieces of the Qur'an cut into the size of banknotes. Talib Masih, one of the hosts, was ordered to explain himself in front of a sham village council or panchayat, established in haste with the involvement of men from outside the area. About forty Christian households were set on fire. Pessimistic about whether the culprits would face justice, the victims' families drew attention to their plight by laying the coffins of their loved ones on the tracks at the town's railway station.

The majority of the perpetrators of this violence remain at large, so the victims live in fear of further attacks. After facing threats and aggression from those released on bail, the main targets and witnesses of the violence have been forced to go into hiding or leave Pakistan.

Seventeen months later, another forceful statement from the normally mild archbishop reflected a change for the worse: 'In the story of some countries there comes a period when political and factional murder becomes almost routine – Russia at the beginning of the 20th century, Germany and its neighbours in the early 1930s.' Pakistan had just taken 'a further step down this catastrophic road', Dr Williams added.[2] Two points deserve emphasis here. First, that the archbishop was referring to the chaos of the pre-Hitler period in Germany, not comparing Pakistan's government with the Nazis; and second, that although some may have looked askance at the words of a church leader perceived to represent the former colonial overlord, his words would almost certainly be endorsed by a large number of educated Pakistani Muslims. Dr David Gosling, an Anglican priest who served as Principal of Edwardes College in Peshawar for nearly five years from 2006, and who faced death threats for promoting coeducation, underlines the high standing of Christian colleges and schools generally. 'The former ruler, General Pervez Musharraf, was educated at Forman College in Lahore,' he told me. 'Twelve of the seventeen most senior figures surrounding him studied at Christian institutions.'

The cause of the archbishop's second intervention was the murder of Shahbaz Bhatti, Pakistan's Minister for Minorities and a Catholic, who was fatally shot by militants in Islamabad on 2 March 2011. His 'offence' was to oppose the country's anti-blasphemy laws, introduced by the dictator General Zia ul-Haq during his Islamicisation programme in the 1980s. Mr Bhatti's killing came nine weeks after that of Salmaan Taseer, the Muslim Governor of Punjab, who had also enraged extremists by speaking out in defence of religious minorities.

For all its chronic problems, Pakistan does not lack a civil-society movement. A small group of campaigners had been seeking a repeal of the blasphemy legislation. After the violence in and around Gojra in 2009, the drive became more vocal. Observers say that the prospects for a change in the law seemed relatively propitious: Shahbaz Bhatti was in the Cabinet, and Salmaan Taseer also favoured reform – as did prominent Muslim Members of the National Assembly such as Sherry Rehman, Jamila Gilani, and Bushra Gohar.

Besides standing up for Gojra's Christians, Shahbaz Bhatti had backed Aasia Bibi (also known as Aasia Noreen), a Christian sent to prison for alleged blasphemy in 2009. She had been working in the fields near her home in the Sheikhupura district of Punjab before being asked to fetch some drinking water for her fellow labourers. When she brought the water, however, they refused to consume it, arguing that it must be 'unclean' because Aasia Bibi was not a Muslim. During an argument following this incident, she was attacked by a crowd of her neighbours who accused her of insulting the Prophet. A police investigation was launched. Initially, the government responded with an investigation of Aasia Bibi's case and the setting up of a body to review the blasphemy laws, both headed by Shahbaz Bhatti. He proposed the creation of penalties for false accusations of blasphemy, a requirement that judges investigate cases before they were registered, and judicial monitoring of the police. These suggestions were deplored by an array of conservative Islamist parties: thirty of them formed a coalition in early 2010 to oppose any changes to the law. In November 2010, Mrs Bibi, who has five children, was sentenced to death by a court at Sheikhupura. Reformers were galvanised by the announcement of the death sentence. Both Mr Taseer and Mr Bhatti visited her in prison.

Salmaan Taseer's support for Mrs Bibi was the trigger for his murder on 4 January 2011 by one of his bodyguards. During the weeks that followed, demonstrations against any watering down of the blasphemy law were staged by ultra-conservative faith-based parties. The government yielded to this pressure, promising to maintain the status quo. Reformers were left vulnerable; Mr Bhatti received several further death threats. One day on his way to work, his car was sprayed with bullets. The gunmen who assassinated him deposited literature declaring that they represented the Tehrik-i-Taliban Pakistan (TTP) and citing Mr Bhatti's attitude to blasphemy legislation as the cause of their actions. Some observers have taken this apparent admission of responsibility at face value. The official explanation is that the culprits were Indian agents seeking to foment sectarian strife.

Shortly after Mr Bhatti's death, it emerged that he had made a video to be publicised if he were killed. In it he declared: 'I am living for my community and for suffering people and I will die to defend their rights. I prefer to die for my principles and for the justice of my community rather than to compromise. I want to share that I believe in Jesus Christ, who has given his own life for us. I know . . . the meaning of the Cross and I follow him on the Cross.' At memorial events held a year after his death, it was noted that no one had been brought to justice for the crime.[3] Aasia Bibi remains on death row.

The fire-breathers have not had it all their own way. On the contrary, it was Shahbaz Bhatti's achievements that raised their hackles. Gains made for minorities since the end of 2008 include the declaration of a 'National Minorities Day' to be celebrated on 11 August each year, the date of Muhammad Ali Jinnah's landmark speech to the Constituent Assembly of 1947; the creation of a 5 per cent quota for minority applicants in federal government jobs, and the eventual extension of this principle to the provincial level; the recognition of non-Muslim religious holidays, including Christmas Day; a 50-per-cent increase in the state development fund for minorities; the establishment of district-level 'interfaith harmony' committees; and the introduction of four reserved minority seats in the Senate.

The Pakistani government has also made many positive statements in favour of minority rights. On Christmas Day 2009, for example, President Zardari reavowed the commitment of the ruling Pakistan People's Party to

continu[e] to fight along with our Christian brothers and sisters for the rights of all Minorities and deprived people in the country. Together we will struggle for establishing a liberal and pluralistic society in Pakistan in which every citizen is allowed to participate freely in the social, political and economic development of Pakistan irrespective of his cast, creed and colour. Let me also reiterate on this occasion our pledge that the PPP [Pakistan People's Party] will continue to uphold the right of the Christians, indeed of all minorities, to be treated as equal citizens of the state and allowed to partake in its development on an equal footing.[4]

So worthy sentiment is not scarce. The difficulty, as we have seen, lies in translating the ideals into action.

*

It is common knowledge that Pakistan's birth in 1947 occurred amid the bloodshed of Partition. Since Partition, Pakistanis have had an abiding suspicion of their eastern neighbour, India. This dislike is revealed over and again by authors such as Farzana Shaikh[5] and Anatol Lieven.[6] Lieven quotes a very senior soldier's view that an officer in the Pakistani army 'has no doubt in his mind that the adversary is India, and that the whole *raison d'être* of the army is to defend against India. His image of Indians is of an anti-Pakistan, anti-Muslim, treacherous people. So he feels he must always be ready to fight against India.'

This stance lay behind the quest for allies such as the United States and China to help neutralise India's influence, and, later on, Pakistan's acquisition of nuclear bombs. It also prompted bids to assist Islamist separatists in Indian-held Kashmir. The Soviet takeover of Afghanistan in 1979 led to a rise of Indian influence in Kabul, and thus fed Pakistani fears of encirclement. These worries were greatly stoked during the aftermath of 9/11, partly by dint of the Bush administration's growing friendship with India, and partly because of American attempts, seen as arm-twisting, to encourage Pakistani action against al-Qaeda. This in turn stimulated a tide of anti-American feeling and hostility to rulers deemed to be American pawns, especially General Pervez Musharraf and his successor, Asif Ali Zardari.

Writing before the death of Osama Bin Laden, Lieven concluded that 'while radical Islamism is very limited', hostility towards the United States is 'overwhelming'.

One reason for this is that a party such as Jamaat Islami, the largest Islamist grouping, represents a highly austere brand of the faith that is uncongenial to the majority. Pakistani Muslims are broadly split between the Deobandi and Barelvi traditions – a contrast that in some ways resembles the Protestant–Catholic divide. Deobandis are puritans, deeply committed to undefiled living as they understand it, and to a literalist reading of sacred texts. They are ferociously hostile to *ijtihad* – the idea that the Qur'an, and other texts such as the Hadith (which records supplementary traditions about Muhammad's life and teaching), can be reinterpreted in the light of fresh circumstances. Most Pakistanis are Barelvis, whose devotions include pilgrimages, the veneration of saints, and other practices reckoned by Deobandis to constitute a threat to pure monotheism. What is more, most possess a rural, clan-based mindset, which leaves them unwilling to give up the bonds of kinship.

Nor is the religious radicals' message all that attractive to the urban poor, with their love of popular culture, Bollywood films, and fondness for hashish and alcohol. As Lieven puts it:

> The Jamaat has enjoyed its greatest success among the educated classes, and has made gaining influence in the universities and the media a key part of its strategy – a sort of Islamist version of the reform-Marxism 'long march through the institutions'. However, this also reflects the party's failure to appeal to the masses in general or to transcend the 5 per cent or so of the electorate which has been its average for the past sixty years.[7]

Jamaat faces both ways over violence, condemning Taliban militancy on the one hand, while also consorting with other violent extremists and arguing that US bombing along the border with Afghanistan warrants retaliation. And the unpopularity of the United States, as well as of India, gives Islamists a crucial fillip. Unable to rally more people under their religious banner, they have nevertheless been able to mobilise large numbers of their countrymen in support of their nationalist agenda since 9/11. (It is also clear that Pakistani militants, like terrorists the world over, do not require a broad basis of support in order to inflict mayhem.)

This in outline is the background against which Pakistani Christians are living. Another factor, signalled by Lieven's subtitle, is the severity of life in Pakistan – a reality confirmed for me as I talked to Kashmiri villagers while travelling from Islamabad to the Chinese border in a student group in 1988. Thanks to the international language of cricket, we kindled warm relations with local men, especially, during a week around the town of Gilgit and the region of Hunza, an area that would now be off-limits to almost all Western visitors. The local women in Hunza also talked to us at length – something which scarcely happened in cities such as Karachi, Lahore, and Rawalpindi.

Our novelty value was enhanced by a near disaster. The bus in which we were travelling suffered a double puncture at four o'clock in the morning. This caused the driver to lose control for several moments near a hairpin bend on the side of a mountain. The atmosphere was already tense: a man with a radio tuned to the BBC World Service had earlier announced that General Zia's plane had exploded, killing everyone on board. For hours we had scarcely passed another vehicle in this exceptionally remote area; now everyone was obliged to sit by the roadside till a rescue party arrived after daybreak.

The delay in our journey seemed to bring out the best in our hosts. Several days later, it was clear that they were rooting for us when we were urged to set off for Peshawar, a long journey south, before dawn to avoid the climax of 'Mourning of Muharram' ceremonies, in which Shia Muslims lash themselves with chains to commemorate the martyrdom of Hussain ibn Ali, grandson of the Prophet Muhammad.

As elsewhere in Pakistan, the hardship of life along the Karakoram Highway – where immense valleys and ravines are shadowed by glaciers and cone-shaped peaks – is much more than physical. You need family or tribal links to protect you, so that your people will stick with you and make sacrifices for you whatever happens. Members of your tribe will get you out of trouble – avenge you if necessary. Where the rule of law is patchy, legal cases and police work advance through the cutting of deals with senior tribesmen and other community leaders. Justice may sometimes be served by such processes. Often, though, it leads to a culture of rampant impunity. Christian Solidarity Worldwide defines impunity as

a problem which thrives when shrouded in fear and secrecy – police officials susceptible to bribes (or indeed, intimidation), victims in too weak a position to consider complaining about their problems (even when many others share them), rumours spread throughout communities and leading to false accusations and distorted versions of events and, ultimately, the false perception that one can commit certain crimes against certain communities without fear of punishment by the state. The present scale of vigilantism and extra-judicial killings in Pakistan underlines that neither prevention nor follow-up are adequate.[8]

In a setting where personal contacts matter so much, Sunni Islam – the faith of around 76 per cent of Pakistan's 180 million-strong population – supplies a critically important anchor to the majority. The benefits include access to charitable resources and links to the pre-colonial past. The flipside of this, as so often, is hostility to the outsider. Shias and Ahmadi Muslims (members of another sect of Islam who hold that the promised messiah appeared in the nineteenth century), as well as Christians, have been viewed with growing suspicion as the legacy of Zia's Islamicisation has developed.

A sharply etched illustration of this is given by Michael Nazir-Ali, who was born in Pakistan and paid a large price for opposing Zia. Dr Nazir-Ali and members of his flock cooperated with more liberal groups, mainly Muslim, in resisting educational and other restrictions placed on women, for example. 'We also felt', he said, 'that we could not go along with the *sharia hudud* punishments that [Zia] was introducing, because they not only mutilated the body but also humiliated people, like public flogging.'[9]

The bishop extended his ministry among the very poor during the 1980s, particularly those involved with bonded labour in brick kilns. The owners were happy for Nazir-Ali to take services in these communities, but opposed him when he started talking about a possible way out – 'if not for the grown-ups, perhaps for their children'. He faced harassment from Islamists which he describes as 'bearable', but changed his mind when threats began to be directed at his children. Nazir-Ali was then Bishop of Raiwind, in the Punjab. In 1986, he accepted an offer from the then Archbishop of Canterbury, Robert Runcie, to begin a new ministry in England, where he had studied and taught during the 1970s.

Islamist rabble-rousers have prospered since Nazir-Ali's departure – ever more so since the turn of the millennium. In March 2004, a group of Christian women assembled for prayer at their church in Islamabad's Miskeen Musharaf Colony. There they were harangued and then severely beaten by a hundred-strong Muslim mob, which also vandalised the church building. One of the attackers later justified the crime on the grounds that the church had been built too close to a mosque.[10] Almost exactly a year later (on 28 March 2005), gunmen fired indiscriminately on a crowd of Christians emerging from worship in Lahore, killing Irshad Masih, a man in his twenties, and seriously injuring seven others. Some observers blamed the violence on a land dispute; others have described it as random terrorism. Although a pair of the assailants were arrested, two policemen who should have been guarding the church were absent from their posts when the attack took place. Shortly afterwards, an Evangelical pastor, Babar Samsoun, was found dead in the north-western city of Peshawar alongside his driver, Daniel Emmanuel. They had been kidnapped two days beforehand; the police reported that they were tortured before being shot. Babar Samsoun did not shrink from preaching the gospel to Muslims, and had received numerous death threats over the phone for doing so.

The legal position on religious freedom in Pakistan is straightforward. Article 18 of the 1948 Universal Declaration of Human Rights states: 'Everyone has the right to freedom of thought, conscience and religion; this right includes freedom to change his religion or belief, and freedom, either alone or in community with others and in public or private, to manifest his religion or belief in teaching, practice, worship and observance.' When the declaration was being drafted, the Pakistani representative stated explicitly – contradicting the position of Saudi Arabia – that freedom of religion was consistent with Islam, a view echoing that of Pakistan's founding leader, Muhammad Ali Jinnah.

Pakistan ratified the 1966 International Covenant on Civil and Political Rights (ICCPR) in 2010. Article 18 of this document guarantees that '[e]veryone shall have the right to freedom of thought, conscience and religion'.[11] In a sign of changed circumstances, though, the Pakistani authorities expressed an ominous caveat: 'The Islamic Republic of Pakistan declares that the provisions of Article 8 . . . shall be so applied to the extent that they are not repugnant to the Provisions of the Constitution of Pakistan and the Sharia laws.' This reservation and others have thus given the government the option of taking away with one hand what it has given with the other. An allied ambiguity is evident in Pakistan's constitution, Article 19 of which guarantees freedom of speech.[12]

The ICCPR permits a number of specific restrictions on freedom of expression, relating to the 'respect of the rights or reputations of others', and 'the protection of national security or of public order . . . or of public health or morals'. In the Pakistani context, this is now taken further, as the right is limited 'in the interest of the glory of Islam'. Non-Muslims are thus at an automatic disadvantage and interpretation of the provision varies according to the dominant Islamic theology at any given time.

The blasphemy laws underlie a huge proportion of inter-communal strife in Pakistan. Introduced in stages in 1982 and 1986, this legislation derived from earlier laws, brought in by the British, to combat Hindu–Muslim clashes in 1860. Between Partition in 1947 and the mid-1980s, there was very little religiously motivated violence in Pakistan. In 1982, Zia criminalised the desecration of the Qur'an as a form of blasphemy. Criticism of the Prophet – by now also deemed to be a form of blasphemy – became a capital offence in 1992. Critics of this legislation point out that it contradicts freedom-of-religion clauses in the constitution, and that it can be abused very easily – even a plainly malicious allegation of blasphemy can still be registered by the police under what is known as a First Information Report (FIR).

The fallout of this has been very severe. One hair-raising symptom of the worsening climate involved the suicide of John Joseph, Catholic Bishop of Faisalabad, in May 1998. He shot himself in protest at the death sentence handed down to Ayub Masih, a member of his flock. Mr Masih had been accused and found guilty of blasphemy, but the bishop blamed the conflict on a land dispute between the defendant and his Muslim neighbours. Thousands of Christians marched in support of Bishop Joseph after his death, even though Catholic teaching still holds suicide to be a grave sin. Hundreds of the demonstrators were arrested. Two were themselves indicted for blasphemy.[13]

Comparable tragedies were unfolding over a decade later. Qamar David, a Christian in his fifties, who had owned a paint business in Karachi, was found dead in his prison cell on 15 March 2011. He had remained in jail since being charged with blasphemy five years earlier, all bail requests having been refused. The indictment centred on claims that he had sent text messages making insulting remarks about the Prophet. His accusers were business rivals. A verdict on Qamar David's case was reached on 25 February 2010, when he was sentenced to life imprisonment, while his Muslim co-defendant was acquitted of all charges on the basis of the same evidence. His lawyer, Parvez Choudhry, received regular threats of violence during these years; Qamar David reported being regularly beaten and threatened, both by his warders and by other prisoners. A week before his death, an anonymous caller contacted his wife to announce that her husband would die shortly. The prison authorities claimed that he had succumbed to heart failure, but he had no history of heart problems, and this explanation has been discounted by his family. He has left four children, as well as a widow, who must now be the family's main breadwinner.[14]

Muslims are naturally liable to be accused of blasphemy as well. On 11 January 2011, Muhammad Shafi and Muhammad Aslam, an imam and his son, were sentenced to life imprisonment and fined 200,000 rupees (approximately £1,500) for blasphemy. The pair reportedly tore down a poster from outside their grocery store in Multan, central Pakistan, and were charged because it contained verses from the Qur'an and was advertising an event on the anniversary of the Prophet's birth. Their lawyer has argued that the root of the accusations lies in rivalries between the Deobandi and Barelvi movements within the majority Sunni community. He describes Shafi as a 'practising Muslim . . . the imam of a mosque [who] had recently returned from a pilgrimage to Saudi Arabia'. An appeal was pending at the time of writing.

Naushad Valiyani is a doctor belonging to the Ismaili branch of Shia Islam. He was accused of blasphemy in Hyderabad in December 2010 after he threw away a business card with the name 'Muhammad' written on it. The owner of the card, a visiting medical representative, involved local religious leaders and had Mr Valiyani arrested, despite his apologies. Unusually, he was quickly released after protests from fellow members of the medical profession, and the intervention of another cleric.

The Revd Rashid Emmanuel and his brother Sajid, both Christians from Dawood Nagar, near the Punjabi city of Faisalabad, were accused of blasphemy several years ago on the basis of written insults about the Prophet Muhammad which bore their names. Initial investigations and reports at the time suggested that the allegations were fabricated, but that did not avert protest rallies from local Muslims and immediate calls for the brothers' execution. On 19 July 2010, they were shot dead while in police custody outside court in Faisalabad, just days after handwriting experts dismissed any connection between them and the words they were alleged to have written. A police officer was also wounded in the incident. The President of Pakistan and Chief Justice of Lahore both made statements about the murder; and police officials involved were charged with negligence. Unrest between Muslims and Christians in the affected areas continued for days after the killings.[15]

*

While the position of minorities is important, we can only grasp the real scale of Pakistan's human rights problems by looking at the effects of so-called apostasy. Lifelong members of religious minorities may be viewed with great suspicion in some quarters, but Muslims who have elected to renounce their ancestral faith are widely considered to be guilty of an abomination. A core distinction should be drawn between the Qur'an, which does not prescribe a punishment for apostasy in this life (only in the life to come), and traditional Islamic jurisprudence – texts such as the Hadith and Sunna – which mandate the death penalty for a sane male apostate, and lifelong imprisonment or harsh treatment for a woman in a similar position. It is these post-Qur'anic bodies of teaching that have been used to justify a number of murders of ex-Muslims in Pakistan.

Since religion is always mediated through particular cultural climates, apostasy is best discussed on a country-by-country basis. The observations of Ziya Meral, a Turkish sociologist,[16] give a useful sample of the differences between Muslim polities, as well as the scale of the problem. The apostate is at real risk of death in Saudi Arabia, Mauritania, and Iran, even though the death penalty for apostasy is not codified in those countries. In other places including Bahrain, Jordan, Kuwait, Qatar, Oman, and Yemen, apostates face severe penalties sanctioned by sharia, including the confiscation of identity papers, the loss of property, and the annulment of a marriage. Apostates are also punished under other sorts of law, such as 'insulting Turkishness' in Turkey and 'treason' in Iran, as well as blasphemy in Pakistan. At the time of writing, Sudan and Malaysia have laws prescribing the death penalty for apostasy, and in Egypt legislation allows for the abrogation of an apostate's rights as a citizen. The practical effects of these provisions are extremely disquieting. As Meral writes:

> Apostates are subject to gross and wide-ranging human rights abuses including extra-judicial killings by state-related agents or mobs; honour killings by family members; detention, imprisonment, torture, physical and psychological intimidation by security forces; the denial of access to judicial services and social services; the denial of equal employment or education opportunities; social pressure resulting in loss of housing and employment; and day-to-day discrimination and ostracism in education, finance and social activities.[17]

It goes without saying that the treatment of apostates amounts to a gross abuse of their rights under international law, and a violation of treaties that most Muslim countries have ratified. A growing number of Islamic theologians and jurists in the West have called for reform of laws on apostasy, but liberal voices are still muffled. In Pakistan, the suffering of individual converts has sometimes been grotesque. The following examples set the scene.

Abdul[18] was received into the Church in 1996, after an earlier career as a Muslim preacher or *Maulvi*. He has a job and a family, but spends much of his time and money on caring for other Christian converts from Islam. Experience has taught him that the mainstream Churches can be reluctant to protect converts, because of the likelihood of retaliation from local Muslims. 'No one is willing to give shelter – they'll be killed too,' he told human rights monitors.[19] As a result, Abdul encourages the greatest possible mutual support by converts. Sameera is a girl in her teens who converted to Christianity in 2009. When her parents discovered this, they punished her by pouring petrol on her and setting it alight, causing 40 per cent burns from her neck to her knees. She was advised not to inform the police, because it would alert too many people to her conversion. At the time of writing, she is in hiding and in a state of depression.

Noorjahan and Taleb are a married couple. Noorjahan was born a Christian; her husband converted from Islam in 1996. A number of attempts have been made to threaten and attack them over the years, but when staff from Christian Solidarity Worldwide met the couple in October 2009, they had just been forced into hiding owing to more serious threats after agreeing to shelter Sameera. The couple had not managed to get help from the Church; their children were being looked after by friends. Both had had to leave their jobs temporarily, and Abdul was trying to support them with his own money.

Karim is a convert whose father assaulted him, breaking his arm, on discovering that he had renounced Islam. Karim approached Abdul, who gave him shelter and treatment. A talented artisan specialising in embroidery, Karim had been able to earn a small amount from business that Abdul put his way, working from the home of one of Abdul's friends.

When Bilal became a Christian in 2007, his family reacted by setting him on fire. He left his home in the north-west of Pakistan and moved south, but was abducted by his relatives and taken home. He is alleged to have been pushed off a cliff by his brother-in-law and killed. Police recorded the incident as suicide, claiming that the deceased had mental problems, but this is disputed.

The treatment of Ahmadi Muslims is also iron-handed. They are the only community denied the right of assembly in Pakistan; their faith is not even acknowledged as a form of Islam. Their names are listed on an electoral roll separate from that for other Muslims. Faced with a choice between either accepting that they are not really Muslims or not voting at all, many withdraw from the electoral process altogether. Between the mid-1980s and 2009, about seventy Ahmadi mosques in Pakistan were demolished, closed down, or destroyed; and Ahmadi students have faced regular purges to satisfy the wishes of Sunni clerics. Dozens of Ahmadi trainees were expelled from the Punjab Medical College in 2008, for example; and the following year, all the Ahmadi teachers working at Qurban High School in Lahore were sacked in one go. If anything, the situation declined further after the restoration of democracy four years later. At least ninety-nine Ahmadis were killed in faith-based attacks during 2010, most when two of the community's main mosques in Lahore were destroyed in simultaneous suicide bombings on 28 May of that year.

Sikhs, Hindus, and Shia Muslims have also been targeted. In 2009, suicide bombers killed thirty people, and injured sixty others, during an Ashura procession in Karachi to mark the holy month of Muharram; and on 1 July 2010, 40 were killed, and 175 were injured, when bombers targeted the Sakhi Sarwar shrine in the Dera Ghazi Khan district of Punjab. The culprits' tangled motivation is revealing. The Pakistan Taliban claimed that the attacks had been staged as revenge for the army's crackdown on militants in north-western regions of the country. But a bomber whose explosives failed to detonate confessed that his instructions had simply been 'to kill non-Muslims'.[20]

Outside Pakistan, conventional wisdom has it that the religious schools or madrasas are fertile ground for the spread of extremism. But detailed surveys of education in Pakistan[21] suggest that the greatest problem lies in the mainstream state sector, where textbooks set out a highly tendentious version of history. These teaching materials were devised by the Zia government. They glorify the armed forces and encourage negative stereotypes of non-Muslims. There is some evidence that the current regime, stung by the scale of international outrage over the deaths of Salmaan Taseer and Shahbaz Bhatti, has softened its policies to a degree. For more than a decade before 2011, Pakistan had played a large part in the 'Combating the Defamation of Religion' campaign at the United Nations, a project analogous to the outlawing of blasphemy at the domestic level. But on 24 March 2011, a new resolution, sponsored by Pakistan, was passed by the UN Human Rights Council. It called for 'a global dialogue for the promotion of a culture of tolerance and peace at all levels, based on respect for human rights and diversity of religions and beliefs'. As we have seen, though, fine words alone count for little. In any case, not all of the mood music was positive. Shahbaz Bhatti's successor, Akram Masih Gill, was not given a place in the Cabinet; so the post has effectively been downgraded. This was publicly deplored by churchmen including Joseph Coutts, now the Catholic Archbishop of Karachi.[22]

Yet this is not to deny genuine grounds for hope, still less to question the reality of Shahbaz Bhatti's achievements. His benign legacy survives and blossoms in such groups as the Rawalpindi-based Christian Study Centre (CSC). Christian Solidarity Worldwide notes that most of the centre's work takes place in the Punjab and Khyber Pakhtunkhwa, owing to the higher densities of both Christians and Islamist extremists in these areas. 'Through its partners,' according to a CSW dossier,

CSC has established 660 peace networks in Punjab province and Khyber Pakhtunkhwa, in which both genders are encouraged to participate and minorities represent 44 per cent of participants (41 per cent of these are Christian). CSC has a weekly radio programme on a station broadcast within a 100 mile radius of Islamabad. The session usually includes a message from a religious leader, some discussion, music and a radio play illustrating cooperation between faiths in practical situations. The use of local language press releases and radio programmes has been particularly effective in Khyber Pakhtunkhwa, where interfaith work is still relatively new . . . CSC appears to act on the frontlines of practical, reality-based interfaith work and has much experience to share and is a leader in some sectors. It is telling that Radio Free Europe/Radio Liberty (funded by the US government) also launched a station in January 2010, to counter the broadcasts of religious extremists . . . CSC remains grounded in the knowledge that anti-minority groups are present even in communities where short-term peace has been secured, and its strategies reflect this . . .[23]

So Christians, Muslims, Hindus, Sikhs, and others are still lighting small candles rather than cursing the darkness.

*

Thus far in this chapter we have looked more from the outside in at the agonies suffered by Christians and others. In 2011, I interviewed Christian Pakistanis who had made it to Europe, and a group of young Afghan converts to Christianity, several of whom had lived in the Pakistani city of Peshawar before moving to Delhi. The Afghans were seeking refugee status in India, arguing that they face persecution and likely murder if they return to their homeland. Despite the force of their arguments, they were downhearted about the prospects of a fair hearing from the UNHCR, especially as India is not a signatory to the UN Refugee Convention of 1951.

They felt a sense of liberation in their new faith after the perceived harshness of the form of Islam in which they were raised. It is not my purpose to argue that the Church's message trumps all others: I am naturally aware that many converts to Islam share the zeal of the most enthusiastic born-again Christians. The relevant point is that while freedom of religion should be a right, it is far easier to journey towards Islam than away from it.

All the Afghans I spoke to stand somewhere on the Evangelical spectrum. Azad, an earnest, narrow-faced forty-year-old from Sangeen province, told me that he was brought up to believe that all non-Muslims are satanic, but became drawn to Christianity during the 1990s because of elements in the Christian repertoire that are not heard in Islam: God's self-offering in Christ, the characteristically Christian notion that victory can be won through apparent defeat, and that Christians have the status of God's adoptive children through the Spirit of Jesus.

Azad converted in secret. Then the news leaked out. Faced with the prospect of being killed, he obtained a passport through a middle man and took a truck ride to Kabul. Despite his material poverty, he felt no regret about his conversion. The gospel had freed his conscience and imagination, he assured me, especially through its emphasis on the core principle that forgiveness precedes repentance, not vice versa.

This crucial insight has been incisively summarised by the Catholic theologian Herbert McCabe, who subverted a common assumption (even among some Christians) when he once wrote: 'It is very odd that people should think that when we do good God will reward us and when we do evil he will punish us.'

In other words, Christianity does not teach that we will get our just deserts. McCabe grants that this way of thinking is widespread, 'for God tends to be a great projection into the sky of our moral feelings, especially our guilt feelings'. But for those who have absorbed Jesus's message, Christians confess their sins *because* they are forgiven, not in order to *obtain* forgiveness. Azad grasped this point, and relished it.

His younger friend Raffiq was born in Baghlan province and went as far as to declare his new-found Christian allegiance after converting during the mid-1990s. 'But being a Christian made me a second-class citizen,' he told me, 'and my wife, who is also a convert, was treated especially badly. She was beaten by some of her neighbours, who poured boiling water on her legs.' The couple fled to Iran and lived there for fourteen years before heading for Delhi after a rise of anti-Christian feeling under the Ahmadinejad regime.

Fatima, a self-possessed young woman who has been in Delhi for over five years, married for love and was forced to leave Afghanistan because her family disapproved of the match. Her friend Khadija ran away from a violent husband. Both have declared their Christian faith on YouTube videos; this means that their cards are marked.

The ebullient Mustafa became a Christian in 1999, at the age of nineteen. He moved to Pakistan in 2002 to complete his education, but returned to his native Kabul two years later. Despite his caution, he came to the attention of agents of the Karzai regime, probably because of his relative prominence as a micro-finance facilitator. 'Christians in my country usually operate in cells of five or six or seven,' he said. 'If the secret police find out, the damage is not so bad. I left because I was becoming better known and being sought out for advice by other converts.'

Nur's story was the most pitiable of all. He converted in 2007, fired by a book entitled *Why I Am a Christian*. His two daughters made the same move with his encouragement, but his first wife was horrified and threatened to have him and the girls killed. In the event, Nur escaped to India with one of his daughters, but the other was murdered, as her mother had threatened. A noble-featured but stricken man in early middle age, he stared into the half-distance as he finished addressing me through his interpreter, a fellow refugee and pastor to Delhi's Afghan Christian fellowship: 'In Afghanistan, they don't care how dissolute you are, as long as you're still officially a Muslim. As soon as you say that you are not a Muslim, that's when the problems start. For anyone, whether under the Taliban or Karzai, you're a pagan and under sentence of death.'

Afghanistan plainly stands generations away from accepting freedom of belief. Pakistan, though, should be doing a good deal better. That Nur and his friends have had to take their chances as far afield as Delhi tells us more than many a chart or graph.

5

TURKEY

The murder on 3 June 2010 of Bishop Luigi Padovese, a leader of Turkey's Catholic community, was exceptionally savage. He was stabbed repeatedly at his home in Iskenderun, in the south of his adoptive country, by his driver. The assassin, Murat Altun, then beheaded the victim and cried: 'I killed the Great Satan. *Allahu Akbar*.'

On the day of Bishop Padovese's death, the local government anticipated the post-mortem result by stating that the killing was not politically motivated, merely the act of a deranged individual. As the human rights campaigner John Eibner reported in a disturbing essay on the affair,[1] NTV Turkey wrongly announced that the culprit was a convert to Catholicism rather than a Muslim. After this the police leaked Altun's apparent claim that he had received sexual advances from Bishop Padovese, and had attacked his victim in self-defence. Neither President Abdullah Gül, nor the Prime Minister, Recep Erdoğan, leader of the ruling AK (Justice and Development) Party, expressed public regret over the killing. Elsewhere, the subject was treated evasively. As Eibner puts it: 'If Western diplomats spoke at all about the bishop's murder, it was in the same hushed tones that are used when referring to Turkey's Armenian genocide during World War I, its subsequent use of terror against remnant Christian communities and Kurdish villages, its 1974 invasion of Cyprus and subsequent ethnic cleansing of the occupied Christian population, and its blockade of neighbouring Armenia.'[2]

The reasons for the West's indulgence of Turkey are not hard to find. Ankara's support has counted for much in the battle against al-Qaeda. It is also evident that the AK Party needs to cover its flank: Erdoğan has often been accused by Islamists of selling out the Turkish nation to the West. Pope Benedict himself responded to the murder with great caution. Interviewed on Vatican Radio shortly afterwards, he said that he had 'very little information' about the killing; but to the surprise of many Middle Eastern Christians, accepted the Turkish government's denial of a religious motive: 'We must not attribute the fact [of Bishop Padovese's murder] to Turkey . . . What is certain is that it was not a religious assassination,' the Pope said.[3] By contrast, Archbishop Ruggero Franceschini of Izmir, who was named as caretaker of the dead bishop's diocese, stated that the killing was premeditated and caused by 'religious fanatics and ultra-nationalists'.[4] Bishop Padovese had been 'a man of God . . . dedicated to help the Christian faithful withstand a situation of great difficulty.'[5]

Though chastened by the international outrage that followed the Pope's Regensburg lecture in 2006, Rome can still use blunt language about militant Muslims from time to time. Had he lived, the bishop would have travelled to Cyprus a day later to help launch the Vatican's strategic plan for reviving Middle-Eastern Christianity. Known as an *Instrumentum laboris*, this document argues that Christian–Muslim tensions in the Middle East arise 'principally' because 'Muslims make no distinction between religion and politics, thereby relegating Christians to the precarious position of being considered non-citizens, despite the fact that [their ancestors] were citizens of their countries long before the rise of Islam. The key to harmonious living between Christians and Muslims is to recognize religious freedom and human rights.'[6]

A comment such as this should not be seen in isolation, though the *Instrumentum laboris* is also concerned with bridge-building, and identifies major areas of common ground between the two faiths, including respect for common moral values, opposition to syncretism, materialism, and relativism, and a collective rejection of religious-based violence. But unlike Barack Obama and George W. Bush, who have both saluted Turkey's 'secular' model of government, the Vatican document is clear-eyed about what this really amounts to: an Islamist-tinged nationalism.

Numerous pieces of evidence bear out this claim. On 18 April 2007, for example, two ex-Muslim converts to Christianity, Necati Aydin and Uğur Yüksel, and a German national, Tillman Geske, were tortured and murdered by a group of young men in the office of the Christian publishing company, Zirve Publications, in Malatya, eastern Turkey.[7] On 16 December 2007, a Catholic priest, Fr Adriano Francini, was stabbed in Izmir. Then later that month, on 30 December 2007, police in Antalya prevented an attempt on the life of Pastor Ramazan Arkan, a Christian with a Muslim background.

The following year, on 6 May 2008, an armed assault was launched by three men wearing surgical gloves against the Ankara Kurtulus Protestant Church. The men threatened members of the congregation with guns before running away when they were told by the congregation that the pastor was not in the church. In December of that year, death threats, signed by the Turkish Islam Brigade (Türk Islam Tugayi), were emailed to the website of Taksim Turkish Protestant Church in Istanbul. In two separate attacks on 7 and 12 February 2009, a youth vandalised a Christian bookshop belonging to the Turkish Bible Society in the southern city of Adana. The windows and door of the shop were smashed. The bookshop had received various threats before the attacks. More recently, on 3 August 2009, a young Turkish Christian, Ismail Aydin, was taken hostage in broad daylight in one of the busiest areas of Istanbul. The attacker held Mr Aydin at knife-point, wrapping a Turkish flag over his head, shouting: 'Godless people, they are doing missionary work.'

*

How has a country often viewed as a beacon of the Muslim world come to this? The Turkish republic, founded in 1923 under the Treaty of Lausanne, is the remnant of the Ottoman Empire. Many Ottoman achievements were admirable. When heretics were still being burnt across Europe, the seventeenth-century Huguenot M. de la Motraye maintained that there was 'no country on earth where the exercise of all religions is more free and less subject to being troubled, than in Turkey'. The *millet* system operated by the Ottomans involved conferring limited rights and status on minority communities, but non-Muslims were generally second-class citizens all the same. 'The existence of Christians was always seen by the authorities as a matter of Ottoman forbearance,' as a Turkish Christian who wanted to speak anonymously told me. He went on:

> We are not talking about a widely acknowledged sense that Christians enjoyed inherent rights. The anti-Ottoman rebellion by subject peoples – above all the Greeks in the 1820s and the Bulgarians half a century later – left a deep scar on Ottoman consciousness. It embedded two things above all. A suspicion of non-Turks, and a belief that if you're Turkish, this automatically means that you're a Muslim. Religion and ethnic identity became closely joined.

This comment offers a key to the hounding of Christians in Turkey today – especially of converts with a Muslim background. Hardline readings of the Qur'an are interlaced with a nationalistic mentality that was born out of the collapse of Ottoman rule, and which holds conversion to Christianity or Judaism to be synonymous with treason. Population exchanges between Greece and Turkey took place in 1923 and again in the 1930s. During the Second World War, taxes on Greeks were raised; those who could not pay were sent to labour camps. With the worsening of relations between Turkey and Greece over Cyprus in the 1950s and 1960s, a further exodus of Greeks took place. The demographic evidence now speaks for itself. Christians formed 13 per cent of the Turkish population a century ago, but now only number about a quarter of 1 per cent – that is, between 150,000 and 200,000 out of a population of 72 million.[8]

An observer in the 1920s might well have seen grounds for hope. Mustafa Kemal Atatürk (1881–1938), Turkey's founding President, introduced fundamental reforms including the dissolution of the Caliphate system, the separation of religion from the state, and the outlawing of religious schools and dress codes. It was the defence of Atatürk's programme, known as Kemalism, that prompted three military coups in recent decades. The most recent was in 1997, when the armed forces engineered the ousting of the coalition led by the Islamist Welfare Party. The AK Party (formed from elements of the Welfare Party) won power in 2002, promising to take Turkey on a path to EU membership. Erdoğan assumed power in the following year, having previously been banned from politics after conviction for undermining Turkey's Kemalist character.

On the surface, then, Turkey espouses a strong separation between religion and the state. Yet, as the Vatican document already quoted makes clear, this does not amount to religiously neutral secularism. The government controls all religious activity, heavily monitoring the majority Sunni community on the one hand, and actively discriminating against minority Muslim groups and Christians on the other. The distribution of non-Muslim literature often leads to the arrest of those involved. At least a fifth of Turks are Alevis, a Muslim group considered heretical by many Sunnis for their embrace of certain Shia-inspired practices, and who have suffered systematic discrimination for decades. No mention is made of Alevi beliefs in Turkey's compulsory religious-studies curriculum: Alevis are officially described as a cultural rather than a religious group. Successive governments have ordered the construction of Sunni mosques even in towns and villages where all or virtually all the inhabitants are Alevis. No Alevi has ever been appointed to the Directorate of Religious Affairs.

Conversion from Islam to Christianity can be very costly indeed. Until a decade ago, a Christian convert needed to open a legal case against the state, with witnesses, to declare his or her change of belief. After this had been confirmed by a judge, the convert had to make a formal declaration in a national newspaper. Although the procedure has now been relaxed, the newly professed Christian is still required to make a public statement.

Turkey's Greek Orthodox, Armenian Orthodox, and Jewish populations all come under the aegis of the Foreign Ministry's Aliens' department. As human rights monitors have observed, this implies that ethno-religious minorities are assumed to owe allegiance to Greece, Armenia, and Israel respectively. Turkey's ancient Syrian Orthodox Church is not even acknowledged as a separate Christian community, because the Treaty of Lausanne recognises only four Churches in the country: the Greek Orthodox, the Armenian, the Catholic, and the Anglican.

Before the rise of Islam, the Syrian Orthodox, who are also known as Suriani, were persecuted by the Greek Orthodox because of the split that followed the Council of Chalcedon.[9] The Suriani then retreated to the remote, hilly regions of Turkey close to Syria. Several hundred monasteries survived for centuries in this terrain, but the Suriani population had declined to about 200,000 by the early twentieth century. Many were murdered alongside Armenians during the First World War, and in 1924, their patriarch was exiled to Syria by Atatürk. The local population now numbers only 9,000, served by a small number of monks and nuns based at Mor Gabriel, Deir-al-Zaferan and a few other monasteries.

Overdue light should be shone on the hounding of a peaceful Christian community that has lived in Turkey almost since apostolic times. The tragedy of the Suriani has unfolded incrementally. During the 1960s and 1970s, attacks on Turks in Cyprus led to 'reprisals' against Suriani in the Midyat area of south-east Turkey. Twenty years later, the conflict between the state and the Kurdish separatists of the PKK left Suriani caught in the middle, vulnerable to accusations of partiality with one side or the other. Hundreds were killed or displaced from their homes in towns such as Midyat, Hazagh, and Arkah. Thousands more emigrated to Syria, Western Europe, and North America. The Turkish government 'kept silent' in the face of this tragedy, one of my Suriani contacts insisted. He, too, would only talk anonymously. But in 2000, after the PKK had laid down its arms, some Suriani exiles returned home, only to find that their land had been taken over by local Muslims.

The second major problem faced by the Suriani centres on assaults against Mor Gabriel, one of their ancient monastic communities in the Tur Abdin region. Founded at the end of the fourth century, the monastery currently faces five separate court cases challenging its right to its own property. Four of the cases were launched in 2008, and the fifth in 2010: the plaintiffs are the Ministry of Forestry and the Environment, the State Treasury, and the residents of two local villages. The details of the litigation are complex, but it is not oversimplifying to say that both the state and local Kurdish tribes are intent on a land-grab from a religious minority whose legal position is precarious.

What of other Christian groups? Evangelicals are sometimes described as the most vulnerable minority of all in Turkey. There are under 5,000 at the moment, most of whom are converts from Islam. The state not only refuses to recognise them, but also judges them a threat to national security. Ihsan Ozbek, a house-church pastor, sums up his experience as follows: 'There is a price to be paid for being a Christian in Turkey. And they make you pay it. You're taken in by the police, you get slapped around, you are maligned within society, you can't hold a government job, and your security checks come up negative. Just because you're a Christian, the police come and bother you and your neighbours.'[10]

A recent legislative change has enabled non-traditional Christian congregations to be regulated as 'associations', but still not yet as Churches. The distinction matters a great deal. There are debates in the Turkish media over whether a Turk can be a Christian, and also whether a non-Muslim can be called a Turk. The answers to these questions are evident to the mobs who attack churches and murder Christians in the name of their nation.

For the reasons already sketched, the animosity felt by some Turks towards the Greek Orthodox Church is especially deep.

Consider the treatment of Bartholomew I, the Ecumenical Patriarch, Turkey's most prominent cleric. Istanbul has been the site of what would become Orthodoxy's senior see since the second century. 'Ecumenical' (meaning 'worldwide' in Greek) is an ecclesiastical title dating back to the mid-fifth century, when the Bishop of Constantinople was chosen to be 'first among equals' in the East. This role is still exercised today by the Patriarch. But his position is not juridically structured. The Turkish government continues to reject the title 'Ecumenical' for the Patriarch, arguing that the Patriarchate is a Turkish institution functioning to meet the religious needs of the Greek community living in Turkey. The use of the full title is seen by Turkey as a threat to national unity: over the years there have been demonstrations and attacks by various nationalist groups against the Phanar – headquarters of the Patriarchate, and the nearest thing Orthodoxy has to a Vatican – located near the banks of the Golden Horn in Istanbul.

What is more, the patriarchs of Constantinople/Istanbul are required to be ethnic Greeks, but Turkish citizens by birth – a harsh restriction rendered Orwellian by the closure in 1971 of the nearby seminary on the island of Halki. A principal source of fresh clerical blood was thereby cut off at a stroke. Despite appeals from Western governments and many other bodies, the seminary remains closed. In November 2007, the Chapel of the Transfiguration at Halki was almost totally destroyed by Turkey's forestry authority.

There are a small number of secondary schools in Turkey for minority pupils, but they are strictly vetted. None of these establishments is allowed to teach in any language other than Turkish. All must have a Muslim deputy principal. Only children with minority names and requisite denominational ties may enrol. The restrictions embrace property rights as well. Minority foundations (*vakif*) must be registered as such. The High Court of Appeals ruled in 1974 that the foundations had no right to acquire any properties that had not been registered as far back as 1936. In consequence, minorities have lost significant numbers of properties.

The discrepancies of life in modern Turkey, and the sheer strangeness of official attitudes to Turkish Christians, were laid bare for me by an encounter with a Protestant pastor in Istanbul. Outwardly successful – happily married, youthful-looking for forty-three, and with a good career in business – he has nevertheless suffered severely for converting to Christianity. 'My great-grandfather was an Armenian,' he told me when we met in 2011. In 1915, during the genocide, he was given up for adoption to a Turkish family, and raised as a Muslim.

> I was raised in the Islamic faith as well. But at the age of fifteen I began to read about other philosophies, and became a humanist for a time. At twenty, I met some Christians, read the New Testament, and converted to Christianity in 1987. My family broke off contact with me as a result, although in 1996 I visited my father one final time to introduce my future wife. The government pays lip service to equality here. In practice, there is a file on me, as a Christian leader, in the government's Security Department. And at a job interview, someone is less likely to be successful if the word 'HRİSTİYAN' appears on their identity card.

He views the accession of the AK Party with strong misgivings, pointing out that all senior positions in the Ministry of Religious Affairs are occupied by Sunni clerics. 'The AK describes itself as a counterpart to the Christian democrats in Western Europe, repeating slogans such as "Our Islamic values are human values". This is very inaccurate: the Turkish citizenry is basically sponsoring government-led Sunni propaganda.'

He doubts that Turkey will ever implement sharia law, though. Like the other Turkish Christians I interviewed from across the spectrum, he sees the current government as a throwback to Ottoman times,

> when the understanding was that religious minorities were being granted favours rather than rights. They have benefited from the fact that EU accession talks have not been dominated by questions of religion. Yet they are still clever about pulling the wool over visitors' eyes. In 2003–4, a church, a mosque, and a synagogue were built in a tourist area of Antalya, to show visitors what a tolerant place Turkey is supposed to be. At the same time, 30–40 Christian congregations without worship spaces in Istanbul, Izmir, and Ankara were being told that their 'unofficial' gatherings are illegal.

House churches and other new Christian congregations are by definition made up of Turks not born into the faith – usually because they have decided to set aside their earlier Muslim allegiances. The state's role in creating a climate of fear and recrimination can be seen in the growing vehemence of campaigns against apostasy in recent years. Before then the subject was dealt with only intermittently, albeit via shrill media claims that Christian missionaries were trying to engulf Turkey and lead Muslims astray. In 2005, however, senior politicians began to complain that the alleged 'Christianisation' of the country was posing a threat to national security.

Rahşan Ecevit, widow of the former Prime Minister, Bülent Ecevit, warned that Turkey was in peril because of social reforms designed to promote the country's EU bid: 'Churches have even spread into meeting in flats in residential buildings. Our people are being Christianized through various means. America tops the list of those who await the increase of [the] Christian population in Turkey. America thinks that if the Christian population increases, it would be easier to dismantle Turkey. America dreams to actualize her Grand Middle East Project in this way.'[11]

We might ask why anyone in the public eye would contemplate making such statements, let alone expecting them to be taken seriously, when missionary activity and public expressions of faith are protected by the Turkish Constitution and Penal Code, as well as by international agreements such as the International Covenant on Civil and Political Rights and the European Convention on Human Rights, both of which have been ratified by Turkey. The answer is bound up with the question. Since Turkey is torn between two versions of itself, it suits politicians to play to the religious gallery by massaging the Muslim sense of paranoia over 'apostasy' within, stirred up by mission from without. Knowing that missionaries cannot be charged with a crime, public figures are nevertheless prepared to issue incendiary rallying cries. In an interview with Christian Solidarity Worldwide, a Turkish Christian man with a Muslim background who had joined the army spoke of the distress he felt during a National Security briefing given by intelligence officers. A picture of the man's own pastor, a fellow convert from Islam, was projected onto a screen, and the man was described as a security threat. The new recruits were told that Turkey faced a triple security threat comprising Kurdish militants, Islamists, and Christians.

And on 11 March 2005, the Directorate of Religious Affairs sent the text of a sermon to be read out in mosques around the country that focused especially on the alleged perils posed by the Churches. Mission was likened to the Crusades:

> Some powers, afraid of the incredible expansion of Islam, had formed crusading armies to wipe out Muslims. They failed because the crusaders were fighting a self-confident society

whose members believed in justice. The same powers are trying to sever our people's links to Islam because they see it as the biggest obstacle to their domination. These highly organized forces are using ethnic differences and economic and political hardship to entice our children.[12]

The directorate was pushing at an open door. Mehmet Aydin, a government minister, told the Turkish Parliament on 27 March 2005 that 'the goal of missionary activity is to break up the historical, religious, national, and cultural unity of the people of Turkey', and that the activities of Christian missionaries have 'ulterior political motives'.[13] This all helped stoke up a hectic atmosphere which was not allowed to die down. When the Christian converts Necati Aydin, Uğur Yüksel, and Tillman Geske were murdered at Malatya in 2007, Niyazi Güney, a Ministry of Justice official, told the Justice Commission at the Turkish Grand National Assembly that missionary work in the country was much more dangerous than terrorism, and that parallels were evident between the present time and the final days of the Ottoman Empire.

The Turkish media widely published statements by the murderers claiming that they had acted 'to protect the nation and religion'. Devlet Bahçeli, head of the Turkish Nationalist Party, has summarised the mainstream reaction to the murders: 'We condemn these murders, but missionaries are not innocent.'[14] CSW representatives were present at the burial of Mr Aydin: civilian police officers were seen recording the faces of every attendee. This practice is widespread.

CSW monitored the court proceedings against those accused of murdering the three Christians, repeatedly expressing concern over the prosecutors' 'reluctance to pursue the connections of the accused with official intelligence officers and nationalist party members'. Similarly, the CSW dossier on the case adds, 'lawyers representing the families of the murdered men have regularly drawn attention to the fact that the prosecutor's case file focuses more on the activities of the murdered Christian men and the Christian publication company they work for, rather than on the accused'. Observers complain of 'serious mishandling' of crucial evidence: a series of videotapes recorded during the questioning of one of the accused men during his hospital treatment, which allegedly included a full confession of the crime and planning behind the attack, has been lost. The victims' supporters received a small boost on 18 March 2011, when twenty people allegedly linked to the murders were detained. They included Ruhi Abat, a professor of Muslim theology at Malatya Inönü University, Mehmet Ulger, a retired member of the Malatya Gendarmerie in service at the time of the murders, and other members of the military.

Christian missionaries have continued to be charged more generally in the Turkish media of strong-arming impressionable people by nefarious means – including offers of money and sex. These accusations have never been refuted, still less censured, by Turkey's media watchdog, the Supreme Board of Radio and Television. Human rights campaigners also highlight the venomous character of teaching materials. Religious Culture and Knowledge of Ethics classes, for between one and two hours a week, are compulsory in all primary and secondary schools. The textbooks are prepared and published by the Education Ministry; lessons are heavily based on Sunni Islam. A textbook for eighth-grade pupils has a section called 'Primary Education, History of Republic Reforms and Atatürkism'. It contains the following passage:

Missionary activity is not ordinary propagation of religion. It cannot be considered under freedom of thought and freedom to express opinion. It is a systematic and organized movement that forces people to change their religion. Missionaries have political, cultural, and economic aims in addition to religious aims. They try to fulfil their goals with significant material support from foreign forces, non-governmental organizations and from their own supporters. Missionaries abuse financial difficulties that people experience. They translate texts related to their religion into various languages and distribute them for free and use written and visual media for their propaganda. They constitute a threat to our nation's national unity and wholeness.[15]

*

Though exacerbated by the invasions of Iraq and Afghanistan, hard-edged attitudes towards Christians in Turkey were already apparent beforehand. A wide-angle picture of the hardships faced by the Churches comes in William Dalrymple's *From the Holy Mountain*,[16] an account of the author's journey around the eastern Mediterranean during the mid-1990s. Dalrymple was tracing the route once taken by John Moschos, a sixth-century monk from Mount Athos, but also describes the embattled conditions at the Phanar in Istanbul. These days, it can be a magnet for demonstrators and even for physical attacks by nationalists outraged over Western foreign policy. When Dalrymple was visiting, aggression against Christians was triggered by the massacring of Muslims by Orthodox Serbs in the Balkans. The Phanar's windows were then being broken almost every day, and the perimeter walls spray-painted with threats to murder the Patriarch.

A month before Dalrymple's arrival in July 1994, a large bomb had been placed beside the Phanar's main gate. Had it not been defused, the entire complex would have been destroyed. Nearby, a note from an Islamist group was found that ran as follows:

FROM THE GENERAL HEADQUARTERS
OF THE FIGHTERS OF LIGHT

Our administration has targeted the Patriarchate and its occupying leader, who behind what he considers insurmountable walls takes pleasure in the shedding of the blood of the Muslim people of the East, and to this end he is working on suspect and fiendish plans. We will fight until the Chief Devil and all the occupiers are chased off; until this place, which for years has contrived Byzantine intrigue against the Muslim people of the East, is exterminated. Occupiers disappear! These Lands are ours and will remain ours. We warn you one more time: there is no right to life for those who are occupiers. Until the Greek Patriarchate and the Devil, the ridiculous Bartholomaios [Bartholomew] who wears the robes of the Patriarch, disappears from behind the thick walls where he plans his fiendish intrigues, our fight will continue. Patriarch you will perish!

Long live our Islamic fight! Long live our Islamic Liberation War!

THE CENTRAL HEADQUARTERS OF LIGHT[17]

A Fr Demetrios, one of the priests interviewed in *From the Holy Mountain*, spelt out the implications of life under siege when he was asked whether enough young clergy were coming up through the ranks. He described the closure of the Halki seminary as cutting 'the bloodline of our existence'. A decade from now, he added, 'when the older bishops have all died, there will be no clergy left. After 1,500 years, the Ecumenical Patriarch will have to leave Constantinople. A century ago this was the centre of Greek Instanbul. Today there are no Greeks at all left around here. On a very good Sunday the Patriarch may still get a hundred people in the church. On a bad one he can't even fill the first two rows of pews.'[18]

These forecasts turned out to be too bleak. When I visited the Phanar fifteen years later, the complex had received a facelift funded by the Orthodox diaspora. Worship was well attended. Yet the priest's pessimism cannot be swept aside. The land around the Golden Horn once boasted several hundred churches. All trace of the vast majority has now been extinguished. Evidence of about thirty remain, most rebuilt as mosques. One piece of land, the site of St Polyeuctus's Church, has not been renovated. This extraordinary building, once considered the greatest architectural marvel in the Christian world, is thought to have been the inspiration for the Hagia Sophia itself. Abandoned after the Ottoman conquest, St Polyeuctus's eventually collapsed. Remains of the church were discovered in 1960; archaeologists grew briefly excited by the prospect of excavating a site of profound importance. Yet so far, all efforts to proceed have been thwarted by the government. Buildings that have survived, such as Hagia Eirene (the Church of Holy Peace), are kept locked or, when opened, put to inappropriate uses – including as a setting for beauty pageants.

Dalrymple has gone on to become an effective advocate for the Muslim world since 2001. His shock and anger at uncovering a concerted bid to extinguish evidence of the Christian past across Turkey, as well as in Istanbul, are therefore all the more telling. The discovery prompted him to complain in sharp terms of the Turkish impulse to go 'to any length, however absurd, to annoy their hereditary enemies'.[19] Antioch (Antakya), on Turkey's western border with Syria, provides a clear example of a broader trend. It was once one of the five most important sees in the Christian world, but its Christian population has fallen from 15,000 to less than 10 per cent of that figure within living memory. Most emigrated to Syria, Western Europe, and the Americas. Among those who have remained, many are outwardly Muslim, but practise their faith in secret.[20] A similar story is evident in the cities of Edessa and Diyarbakir, east of Antioch. Shortly after the outbreak of the First World War, Armenians were 'deported' from Edessa, marched into remote parts of the surrounding countryside, and shot. About 2,000 members of the remaining Christian population refused to budge from their homes; most were murdered on the spot. In Diyarbakir, a roughly simultaneous massacre was marked by astonishing sadism. Women were gang-raped and horseshoes were nailed into men's feet. About half a million Christians were killed in the Diyarbakir province at this time.[21]

The reshaping of history has proved an obvious next step for a new generation of nationalist zealot. On an earlier visit to eastern Turkey, Dalrymple had discovered a sculpture garden in the town of Sivas replete with inscriptions in Turkish, Armenian, and Greek. When he returned, the slabs bearing Armenian script had all disappeared. His cousin, an agricultural engineer in Erzerum, later confirmed that Armenian cross-stones or *khatchkars* had been mysteriously removed from the area where he was working. A local confessed to him that this had been a deliberate policy.[22]

One ray of light should be recorded. In August 2011, the Turkish government surprised the Churches and other groups by issuing a decree inviting the country's Jewish and Christian communities to reclaim their long-confiscated properties – hundreds of buildings and parcels of land that had been seized by the state three-quarters of a century earlier. Addressing an audience of non-Muslim religious leaders in Istanbul the Prime Minister said: 'The time when citizens in our country were oppressed for their beliefs, their ethnic heritage or the way they dressed is over.'[23] This was plainly an overstatement, but the announcement was historic all the same. Schools, churches, cemeteries, hospitals, orphanages, and homes would now be returned. Where land had been sold off, Mr Erdoğan added, the rightful owners would be reimbursed at the market rate. The return of such property had long been demanded by Brussels during talks on Turkey's possible EU membership.

*

Can we say more in conclusion than that the Turkish government is unjust towards minorities, partly by dint of its nationalist baggage, and to some degree because it is obliged to look over its shoulder at the forces of Islamism? Yes we can. Some of the evidence suggests that chauvinism prompted by calculations of realpolitik (including the appeal of scapegoating certain groups) shades into something more sinister still: namely, state collusion with the criminal and terrorist underworld. A guide through this very shadowy landscape is naturally unavailable. But it is worth finishing where we started – with the murder of Bishop Padovese – and especially with a look at the reaction of Archbishop Franceschini. On top of the comment already quoted, the archbishop said: 'I believe that with this murder, which has an explicitly religious element, we are faced with something that goes beyond government. It points towards nostalgic, perhaps anarchist groups who want to destabilize the government.'[24]

As John Eibner reveals,[25] the archbishop suspected that the murder was planned by agents of Turkey's so-called deep state – an underworld in which elements of the state, especially the military, cooperate with a mixture of violent extremists (both nationalist and Islamist) and apolitical criminals to serve the interests of the ruling elite. The deep state was once associated with Kemalist secularism. Michael Rubin, among other observers, believes that the AK Party has appropriated the deep state, including a branch known as 'Ergenekon', to promote an Islamist agenda. For the past few years, dozens of government employees have been charged with plotting to bring down the government. Ergenekon is believed to have fomented the oppression of Christians, including the murders of Fr Andrea Santoro, an Italian priest, in the Black Sea town of Trabzon (Trebizond) in February 2006, and of the three Evangelical Christians in Malatya. Fr Santoro's killer also shouted '*Allahu Akbar*' as he approached his victim.

Two other murders are thought to bear the Ergenekon stamp. In January 2007, Hrant Dink, an Armenian Orthodox journalist who had campaigned against official denials of the Armenian genocide, was convicted of article 302 of the penal code, which bans the 'insulting of Turkishness'. Mr Dink was murdered in the same month. Three years later, at around the time of Bishop Padovese's death, Mr Dink's Turkish lawyer, Hakan Karadağ, was found hanged.[26]

It remains unclear whether Ergenekon is genuinely opposed to the government, or an AK device to stoke up paranoia and give the Prime Minister a pretext to clamp down on civil liberties. But Eibner's conclusion seems hard to resist: 'Whoever may be pulling the strings, Kemalists or Islamists, the deep state is no friend of Turkey's Christians.'[27]

6

NIGERIA

An orgy of violence at Christmas 2010, in Plateau state, a deeply troubled region of central Nigeria, is a stark example of the country's chronic sectarian problems. Human Rights Watch and other groups calculated that more than 200 people, including children, were hacked to death, burned alive, 'disappeared', or wrenched off buses and murdered in tit-for-tat crimes.

The violence was triggered by bombings on Christmas Eve at two churches in Jos, the state capital. An Islamist website published a statement by Boko Haram (which roughly translates as 'Western education is sinful'), a militant group based in northern Nigeria, claiming responsibility for the attacks. After that, scores of Muslims and Christians were hunted down on the basis of their ethnic and religious identities. The tension intensified in early 2011. Eight young Muslim men driving to a wedding on 7 January were attacked after taking a wrong turning and arriving in a Christian village, in the Barkin Ladi area. On the following day, the army exhumed five of their bodies from shallow graves nearby. The three others are assumed to have been murdered as well. Muslim youths in Jos went on the rampage as these corpses were being disinterred. They attacked Christians, mostly ethnic Igbo market traders, around the well-known Dilimi market. Witnesses reported that the victims had been butchered with machetes and cutlasses: forty-eight Igbo civilians were killed. In revenge on 8 January, at least fourteen

Muslims were murdered in Jos and surrounding communities. In one instance, the Muslims on an interstate bus were separated from their fellow passengers and hacked to death. Then, on 10 January, gunmen attacked Waren, a mainly Christian village south of Jos, burning homes and killing four women and seven children, among others. During the month that followed, forty-two Muslims and fifty-one Christians disappeared in suspicious circumstances in and around Jos. The response of the authorities to all these crimes, both at state and federal levels, was paltry.

The bloody pattern was repeated a year on. About forty people were killed in a wave of bombings targeting churches in northern and central areas on Christmas Day 2011. Most of the deaths were at St Theresa's Catholic Church in Madalla, Niger state, about 25 miles from Abuja. Thirty-five worshippers were killed when bombs were hurled at them as they emerged from Mass. Christian Solidarity Worldwide disclosed that 'scores more' were injured.[1] The Mountain of Fire Ministries Church in Jos was also attacked; and there were multiple explosions in Damaturu, Yobe state. Boko Haram claimed responsibility for the attacks. Release International, which campaigns for persecuted Christians, said in a statement that its partners in Nigeria believe the Islamists' aim is to tear the country in two to create a separate north ruled by sharia law.[2]

An already tense situation in Jos grew yet more strained on 11 March 2012. Here is how one of my contacts, living very close to the violence, reported events to me in an email:

Dear Rupert, please tell people that there's been another bomb attack on a church in Nigeria – less than two hours ago, and in Jos. The church is called St Finbarr's, and is in a prosperous suburb called Rayfield, where Christians predominate. I was going to Mass there over Christmas while staying with a friend who lives less than a kilometre away. Undoubtedly Boko Haram. Apparently two cars rammed into the gate of the compound; the explosion caused the ceiling of the church to collapse. Up to 20 deaths – and there have been retaliatory killings of Hausas in the area. There may be further trouble in the main part of Jos, so we are not going out.

What my correspondent could not have known at the time was that more Muslims than Christians died in this instance, because the revenge attacks were so brutal.

I visited St Theresa's, Madalla, a few months later – shortly after dozens more Christians had been killed by Boko Haram in Maiduguri, capital of the north-eastern state of Borno, on 29 April – and found a community still living in a state of grief and dread. Madalla is so poor (St Theresa's stands opposite a large shanty town) that evidence of the bombing was at first hard to detect. The signs of recent horrors were indirect: in the presence of heavily armed soldiers; in the scaffolding on adjoining buildings, which were less robust than the church; and in the now surreal-looking Christmas decorations, including a tinsel MERRY CHRISTMAS sign, that were still hanging above the west door. The interior of St Theresa's was hollow apart from the untidy rows of benches and a huge mural depicting the Last Supper, loosely inspired by Leonardo's, filling the space behind the altar.[3] Arriving unannounced, I was warmly received by Fr Isaac Achi, the parish priest. He had the calm of a man whose calling leaves him with no option but to remain among his flock.

*

In some ways Nigeria resembles a bundle of limbs, rather than a body politic as such. Its 140-million-strong population consists of almost 500 ethnic groups, and Muslims and Christians in roughly equal numbers. By agreement between the British and the long-established local emirates, Christian mission in the north was heavily curtailed during colonial times. A small church presence was tolerated for the sake of non-indigenous migrant workers from the south, but evangelism among Muslims was largely banned. These factors help to explain the country's volatility (though large areas of the west and south are relatively calm), as well as its tight interlacing of politics and religion. All the most toxic strands in the postcolonial experience are there, too: military dictatorship for most of the period since independence in 1960, oil wealth that has promoted gigantic inequalities, terrorism in the Niger delta, a general absence of civil society, and widespread female genital mutilation.

More benign or competent rulers would not have had an easy ride. The chief divisions, between the mainly Muslim Hausa in the north, and the predominantly Christian Ebo in the east, mask numerous other conflicts, including that between the Hausa and the substantially Christian Berom in Plateau state. The Yoruba, who occupy much of the south-west, are a mixed community with a Christian majority. Muslim influence rose during the dictatorship of General Sani Abacha between 1993 and 1998 – so much so that the south threatened formal secession. This was averted when the north accepted the presidency of Olusegun Obasanjo – a Christian and former military ruler during the late-1970s – who won the election of 1999.

As a trade-off, northern states introduced sharia law. A dozen had done so by 2006, in defiance of Nigeria's secular constitution. Sharia had long been used to resolve family disputes involving Muslims. Christians were now threatened by an attempt to extend Islamic law into their own communities. In some northern states, Christian girls have been obliged to wear the hijab; and in the north-central state of Kano, for instance, a large body of enforcers frequently break into Christian households in search of alcohol. It is estimated that the expansion of sharia has led to the death of 60,000 people,[4] most of them Christians or adherents of traditional religions. And, as in Pakistan and Egypt, punishment for ex-Muslim converts to Christianity is severe. *Religious Freedom in the World* reports that there are many documented cases in which child abduction has been combined with forced marriage and conversion to Islam in the sharia states. Bauchi, which lies to the east of Kano, is a case in point:

> The State Shar'ia Committee has itself been implicated in these abductions in Bauchi state. Christian women are especially vulnerable in shar'ia states since, according to the Christian Association of Nigeria (CAN), 'a woman [who is] not married, irrespective of her religious background, is seen by Muslim enforcers of the Shari'ah as a prostitute.' In 2003, all girls of Bauchi state above the age of 16 were given 90 days to marry or face arrest on charges of prostitution. Eight women were subsequently arrested, fined, and given 10 lashes for being unmarried.[5]

Antagonism over sharia contributed greatly to interfaith violence in Kaduna during February 2000, in which hundreds died. Hostilities were renewed in the same place three months later: among the casualties was Fr Clement Ozi Bello, the son of Muslim parents in the south-central Kogi state, who was dragged from his home and killed. He had only been ordained for ten months. Other clerical murder victims have included Fr James Iyere, who was fatally attacked in Kaduna in 2006, and Fr Michael Gajere, who in the same year was set on fire at the door of his church in Maiduguri. These men appear to have been targeted for their faith. It is possible that their witness will be formally acknowledged by the Vatican at a later date.

More generally, Christians also complain that only Islam is taught in state schools in sharia states, and that Christian schools are obliged to close for Ramadan in these areas. Hotheads naturally prosper in such confrontational settings. At Eastertide in 2006, a teacher at a Christian school in Bauchi confiscated a Qur'an that one of his pupils had been reading surreptitiously during an English lesson. Two dozen people died in the ensuing mayhem.[6] Furthermore, Christians speak of being denied access to water and electricity in sharia states, and of facing the wrath of Boko Haram and other militant groups such as Al Sunna Wal Jamma. Many pretexts for violence have been used by Islamists apart from the invasions of Afghanistan and Iraq. In the aftermath of international protests against the Danish cartoons of Muhammad in 2005, 50 Christians were killed in Borno state, 57 churches were razed, and 250 Christian-owned businesses were attacked. The cycle of violence has proved exceptionally difficult to break. In retaliation for all this, Christians belonging to the Igbo tribe in southern Nigeria attacked their Muslim neighbours. The following year, a group calling itself the 'Taliban' attacked the police in Kano, killing scores of people.

*

We shall need to note many more such tragedies in this chapter for the record. Seen in isolation, though, they do not necessarily illuminate our central theme. Since both sides feel victimised in Nigeria, it is easy but not necessarily fair to cite one example after another of anti-Christian violence in comparative isolation. The events in Jos already reported show that Muslims have suffered grievously at the hands of Christians as well; and while there is merit in the Christian claim that the cycle of violence often begins with a provocation by Islamists, Muslims can also point out with justice that even more members of their own community have died in inter-communal conflict overall. In other words, is it self-evident that 'Who started it?' – the question most posed by Christians – trumps 'Who has suffered most?' – the preferred focus of Muslims?

Some observers conclude that both communities must accept a more or less equal share of blame for the violence. Those who take this view often stress the implications of Nigeria's topography. The south is swampy, the north is far more arid. One reason for poor interfaith relations is that Islam and Christianity confront one another in the country's Middle Belt, a fertile area 200 miles in width, between the seventh and tenth parallels. Since 9/11, tens of thousands of people have died in this region because of fighting that is widely seen as faith-based. But most of the disputes spring from conflict over jobs and resources, election results, or indignation among Muslims at the treatment of their fellow believers. As a Human Rights Watch dossier puts it, local political elites 'have long battled for power and control of limited resources and have stoked religious tensions to those ends'.

These differences have in turn been intensified by government policies that discriminate against members of ethnicities known as 'non-indigene' – namely those who are unable to trace their ancestry from the region's original inhabitants. Non-indigenes are not allowed to apply for state and local-government posts. In Jos, the largest ethnic groups are the Hausa-Fulani and Berom. The Hausa-Fulani, most of whom are Muslim, form the largest community in northern Nigeria. Even though many have been in Middle Belt areas such as Jos for generations, they are classed as non-indigenes. The predominantly Christian Berom are indigenes. We can thus draw a very important distinction between the Middle Belt, with its layers of conflict, and the north, where Muslims are the majority and have done more to shape the dynamics of conflict.

This is not to suggest that people are coy about donning the mantle of religion when it suits them. A town such as Yelwa in the south-eastern part of Plateau state, reflects the broader problem as much as Jos. Though Muslims have formed a majority of the 30,000-strong population for most of the past century, their dominance is under threat, because many adherents of traditional religions have converted to Christianity. When the two candidates in a local election assembled for hustings at a football ground in May 2002, the atmosphere was heavy with tension. The clash that ensued is described by Eliza Griswold in her book *The Tenth Parallel: Dispatches from the Faultline Between Christianity and Islam*.[7] 'No one knows what happened first. Someone shouted *arna* ('infidel') at the Christians. Someone spat the word *jihadi* at the Muslims. Someone picked up a stone. Chaos ensued, as young people on each side began to throw rocks. The candidates ran for their lives, and mobs set fire to the surrounding houses.'[8] That was the day when 'ethnicity disappeared entirely and the conflict became just about religion', a Muslim community leader told Griswold. The comment was probably an overstatement: as merchants and herders, the Muslims of Yelwa are richer than their neighbours, and evangelists such as Pastor Sunday Wuyep told Griswold that Muslims were trying to sap the Christian population through intermarriage with Christian women. 'If a woman gets caught with a Muslim man,' Wuyep said, 'she must be forcibly brought back.'

The atmosphere in Yelwa remained fraught thereafter. In February 2004, about seventy members of an Evangelical group in the town, the Church of Christ in Nigeria, were worshipping one morning when they heard cries of '*Allahu Akhbar!*, let us go for jihad!' from the neighbouring mosque. The church was set on fire; people who tried to escape were killed. In all, at least 300 Christians perished. For Pastor Wuyep, who lost seven members of his family, the disaster was a sign of the end-times. 'The Bible says in Matthew 24, the time will come when they will pursue us in our churches,' he suggested to Griswold when they discussed what had happened.[9]

So it was not hard for misguided Christians to harness a scriptural warrant to their plans for bloody revenge – though their own crimes are more accurately seen as an expression of hysteria and mob rule. Two months later, a throng of men and boys surrounded Yelwa, many reportedly wearing Christian Association of Nigeria name tags. Human Rights Watch estimated that 660 Muslims were murdered over the following two days; a dozen mosques were set on fire and hundreds of Muslim-owned homes were destroyed. A national state of emergency was declared at about this time. Young Muslim women were marched out of Yelwa and imprisoned in a camp. Many were forced to drink alcohol and eat pork; fifty were killed. Reflecting later on her ordeal, one of the survivors, a woman named Danladi, revealed that Muslims were no strangers to apocalyptic speculation when she predicted the imminent end of the world and the conversion of all to Islam. 'According to our *ulamas* [teachers],' she declared, 'there is no way that the whole world will not be Muslim.'[10]

A second striking feature is the poor leadership offered in parts of the Christian community in recent years – a notable example being Peter Akinola, Anglican Archbishop of Nigeria from 2000 to 2010. Given that this book is saturated with examples of heroic forbearance among Christians, and recognises the value of non-Western readings of the Bible, it is also important to

115

see ignorance and irresponsibility as they are. When confronted over Christian involvement in the death of Muslims at Yelwa, Akinola was uncompromising: 'When you have this attack on Christians . . . and there are no arrests, Christians become *dhimmi*, the status within Islam that allows Christians and Jews to be seen as second-class citizens. You are subject to the Muslims. You have no rights.'[11] When asked about the CAN name tags, the archbishop grinned:

> No comment. No Christian would pray for violence, but it would be utterly naive to sweep this issue of Islam under the carpet . . . I'm not out to combat anybody. I'm only doing what the Holy Spirit tells me to do. I'm living my faith, practising and preaching that Jesus Christ is the one and only way to God, and they respect me for it. They know where we stand. I've said before: let no Muslim think they have the monopoly on violence.[12]

Akinola is known for his hostility to homosexuality in particular – he once compared gay people unfavourably with animals – and to liberal theology in general. Asked in 2003 why he appeared obsessed about gay sex to the exclusion of war, corruption, HIV and poverty in Africa, he replied: 'I didn't create poverty. This Church didn't create poverty. Poverty is not an issue. Human suffering is not an issue at all.'[13]

A different perspective on interfaith rivalries was supplied by another Anglican leader – Benjamin Kwashi, appointed Archbishop of Jos in 2008. When he was abroad in early 2006, Islamists broke into his home, temporarily blinding his wife and beating his two sons. During the 1980s, when he was ministering in the north, Muslims burnt his house down. He ascribes such violence to the rising popularity of Christianity, seeing a proxy conflict between Islam and the West playing itself out in Africa:

'The Islamic world wants to counter the Christian West. They don't understand that Christianity isn't the West. The church is just a scapegoat for the West, and nobody wants to come to its help.'[14] Some will judge Kwashi's picture to be simplistic. But it nevertheless encapsulates a widely held view linked to 'African' readings of Scripture: that Nigerian Christians must first confront their liberal co-religionists in rich countries if they are also to resist Muslims on their own doorsteps.

A third noteworthy area takes us beyond religious competition and recrimination. Two clerics, Imam Muhammad Nurayn Ashafa and Pastor James Movel Wuye, are dedicated to community bridge-building in the very violent city of Kaduna. The pair have travelled far. They were once sworn enemies: Ashafa's supporters even cut off Wuye's right arm with a machete during the late-1990s. As a young man during the previous decade, Wuye had led Christian militia dedicated to protecting churches from Islamist-inspired violence. He justified his conduct by saying that 'We've been beaten on both cheeks, there's no other cheek to turn.'[15] He was also fond of deploying Jesus's command to the disciples just before the crucifixion, as recorded in Luke 22:36: 'And if you don't have a sword, sell your cloak and buy one.' At one point, Wuye was part of a Christian group fighting for control of a market. They were outnumbered by local Muslims. Twenty of his friends died in the conflict; he himself was knocked out. When the pastor regained consciousness, his arm had been severed.

As Haruna Yakubu, another former militant, explained to Griswold, Muslims, too, are strongly divided about their future path. Hardliners argue for a 'return to Medina' (that is, an emphasis on more hard-edged material in the Qur'an relating to the later part of Muhammad's ministry, in contrast to the more tolerant phase in Mecca); strict Sunnis disapprove of the Sufi majority (those who lay greater stress on the mystical elements in Islam); and both these communities are wary of Shia elements who are supported by Hezbollah in Lebanon. 'Even the Prophet lived with Christians: why can't we?' Yakubu asked. 'If we call ourselves true Muslims, why can't we do that?' Ashafa was raised to associate Christianity with colonialism. His dim view of the Church was confirmed when Christian paramilitaries stabbed and killed a Sufi hermit whom he had come to revere. But reading the Qur'an (notably Muhammad's magnanimous words at Ta-if, where the angel Gabriel is represented as asking the Prophet whether he wants revenge after being attacked, and Muhammad replies, 'Lord, forgive thy people, they do not know') released him from the vortex of hate and set him on his current path. Pastor Wuye and Imam Ashafa now share platforms on television and at churches and mosques, where they stress the peace-building messages of their respective traditions. It is no derogation of this achievement to say that the scale of their task is huge.

A more sensitive matter concerns the apportioning of blame. Eliza Griswold (the daughter of Frank Griswold, a former Presiding Bishop of the Episcopal Church in the United States) does not flinch from exposing cruelty and intolerance among Christians where appropriate. But while it is quite true to say that Christians often behave at least as provocatively as Muslims in the Middle Belt, or that gospel teaching on self-sacrificial love has only permeated parts of Nigerian society to a limited degree – a fact as true of Europe, of course, especially viewed over the past century, as of countless other societies – this does not mean that Christian–Muslim tension in Nigeria can be summed up as six of one and half a dozen of the other.

We have seen that Islamist self-assertiveness is especially evident in the north, where it is easier to trace a faith-influenced element at work, less tied to other forces. Take the attack by Islamists on Damaturu, the capital of the north-eastern state of Yobe, which began in the late afternoon of 4 November 2011. The attackers entered the town like a swarm of bees, as one observer put it. At the end of their four-hour rampage, up to 150 people had been killed, mostly Christians. At least 10 churches were destroyed. The militants, 200 of them, belonged to Boko Haram.

The incursion was meticulously planned. First, all four major roads into the town were blocked off. Then Boko Haram members stormed the police headquarters, killing all the officers on duty, and broke into two banks. Their final destination was the main Christian neighbourhood, New Jerusalem. They shot dead anyone they met who couldn't recite the Muslim creed. The Revd Idris Garba, chairman of the Yobe state chapter of CAN, told human rights monitors that the attack was a 'jihad' against the Church: 'When Boko Haram members and other Muslims here attacked us on that 4th of November, it was like the end had come for Christians in this settlement,' he said a few days afterwards. 'Bullets were fired indiscriminately into our houses. I and my family locked ourselves in my house. Bullets were dropping on rooftops like ice blocks from a rainstorm. The trauma my ten-year-old son had as a result of sounds from guns and explosions has not left him, as he has refused to eat ever since the attack.'[16] Mr Garba, who also pastors the Evangelical Church of West Africa's Good News Church in the New Jerusalem area of Damaturu, complained that his 500-member church had dwindled. 'We could not have had more than a hundred worshippers on the Sunday after the attack,' he said. 'Most Christians are either missing or have left the town.'

A week before the Damaturu outrage, Zonkwa, a town in Kaduna state, fell victim to an Islamist gang not linked with

Boko Haram. The prime target was St Joseph's Catholic Church: Emmanuel Mallam, the seminarian leading worship at the time of the attack, said it was miraculous that only two people – Justina Zugwai Isaac and Hassana Luka, both mothers in their twenties – were killed. A dozen more were wounded. Speaking shortly afterwards, Mallam added that the church had suspended both morning and evening services, because his parishioners feared another attack. 'It appears that there is no government in Nigeria,' he stated. 'If not, how can Christians be slaughtered in northern Nigeria and the government is unable to stop this carnage?' Fulani herdsmen (a nomadic Muslim group) have been blamed for the attack; they in turn see their action as revenge for earlier, Christian-inspired violence against them. Boko Haram also staged an attack in Madalla on 27 September 2011. Militants marched into Christian-owned shops and ordered those inside to recite verses from the Qur'an. Five who were unable to do so were shot dead.[17]

*

As in many other Muslim societies, hardliners are vehemently opposed to conversion to Christianity, even when the decision is made freely after due preparation. Hannatu Musa, from Yauri in the north-western state of Kebbi, had been a Christian for six years when her parents were converted to Islam by Muslim missionaries in 2008, and were instructed to convert their immediate family also. When the children refused to renounce their faith, their father, Musa Ashika, was ordered to arrange marriages with Muslim men for his daughters. Once she realised that the village headman and her parents were planning a marriage for her without her consent, Hannatu informed her pastor, Manu Makeri, that she could not cope, and would either kill herself or run away. Pastor Makeri advised her to speak to her parents about her feelings. He also tried to speak to them himself. But when they continued to ignore her wishes, Hannatu fled the area in March of 2009. The family blamed the pastor; after tracking down Hannatu with Manu Makeri's assistance, they brought him before the sharia court in Birnin Yauri the following month, even though this cannot happen officially unless the people concerned have given their consent in writing.

The pastor was sentenced to twelve lashes – which were administered – and obliged to choose between either a jail sentence or a fine of 10,000 nairas (£40) to the court, and 30,000 nairas in compensation to the family. His relatives had no option but to raise the money. Hannatu was forcibly converted and married to a Muslim man against her will. She fled again soon afterwards. The pastor was brought before an Islamic court once more, this time the Upper Sharia Court of Yauri, where he was charged with abduction.[18]

In the north-eastern state of Borno, Christians are still coming to terms with the violence unleashed by Boko Haram in 2009, when more than 2,000 people are thought to have died and 26 churches were damaged or destroyed.[19] In Maiduguri, a source reported that corpses had been piled four feet high at the hospital alone, and that three mass graves had been created. The testimony of Victoria Orji, widow of an Evangelical pastor, George Orji, stands out among many that I have read. Pastor George was held as a human shield at Boko Haram's camp in the city, refusing all efforts to convert him forcibly to Islam. He called on his captors to repent, then began singing praises just before being beheaded. Some of his final words (subsequently circulated around the world) were addressed to a fellow captive: 'If you survive, tell my brothers I died well and am living with Christ. And if we all die, we know we die for the Lord.'[20]

The testimony given to human rights monitors by two Boko Haram hostages – Christina, then aged twenty-three, and Mary, a thirteen-year-old,[21] is no less searing. They were confined in their church on the evening it was attacked by forces loyal to Muhammad Yusuf, a senior Boko Haram commander, because Mary was unwell and could not travel home. Christina stayed to help her. When the Islamists stormed the compound, they killed the watchman, beheading him 'as though they were cutting meat', Mary recalls. Other men were murdered before the girls were taken separately to the Boko Haram camp, where they were to witness further atrocities. Some of the attackers spoke Hausa, but were clearly not from Maiduguri, as they were asking fellow militants where churches were located so as to destroy them. More seriously, and in an indication of foreign involvement in the violence, the girls informed CSW that several Boko Haram members who could not speak Hausa communicated in Arabic. Later, a captured militant confessed to receiving training overseas.

Once in the camp, male and female hostages were separated and held in different places. Christian men were given the option of conversion or death; women and children were obliged to choose between conversion and perpetual slavery. But in the event, most male hostages were killed outright, whether or not they chose to convert. Survivors state that the Boko Haram leader personally oversaw the forcible conversions. He also decided at random who lived or died.

At first, Christina and Mary were accused of insulting Islam and saying that Christianity was best. They denied these claims. To buy time, Christina maintained that she and Mary could not embrace a set of beliefs they did not understand; one of the militants then took it upon himself to teach them. At one point, the girls were able to avoid taking part in a conversion ceremony because of heavy rainfall. In the meantime, as punishment for their insistence on remaining Christian, they were taken to an area in the camp where they saw around thirty corpses. There they were given a small packet of soap powder and told to wash blood-marked clothes until they were clean, but without finishing the powder. As they scrubbed the garments, more and more women were brought into the compound. 'One was crying that her husband had been killed in front of her face. We tried to comfort her,' Mary told CSW monitors.

The girls also met Muhammad Yusuf himself, whose tactics were laid bare when they heard him ordering his men to set fire to police stations in the area, steal weapons, and obtain police uniforms where possible 'to fool others'. Christina and Mary were given back their mobile phones after three days: their captors had immersed the devices in water and assumed that they no longer worked. But not all of them were unusable. And since one of the women captives had hidden a SIM card in her bra, the group were able to contact the police. The authorities were already planning an assault on the compound. When it took place, Muhammad Yusuf and his henchmen got away, but Christina and Mary also managed to escape. They almost fell prey to Boko Haram sympathisers at first, but were eventually rescued by an elderly Muslim man in the adjoining area.

Another case revealing a different dimension of the problem involves a former Muslim, now treasurer of the Evangelical Church of West Africa in Kano, and widely known as Mr Ali. Censured by an Islamic judge for his conversion, he migrated east, to Gombe state, for a spell. He was reconciled with his father in 2008, who apologised in tears for his past actions. During interviews with CSW in 2009–2010, Mr Ali began by reiterating the fact that in areas of Kano where indigenous Christians are in the majority, such as Rogo, Tudun Wada, and Sumaila, they still faced 'severe and deliberate marginalization'.[22] Education in particular was paralysed, he said; there were no schools for Christians. He added that the state government in Kano effectively abandoned Christian areas. In addition, when Christian children did receive placements in schools, false accusations of desecrating or insulting the Qur'an, Islam, or Muhammad were often made against them. Violence ensued. The students were forced out of school, even though the accusations remained unproven. Ali said that many children could not gain access to higher education once they were found to come from Christian homes. In response, CAN Kano has set up a school in the town of Sabon Gari to help students who cannot afford fees or have faced other difficulties in obtaining education. This foundation currently caters for 300 boys and 70 girls from Kano's majority-Christian areas. Mr Ali is personally involved in the setting up of eleven primary and secondary schools, but many more are needed.

The *Hisba* (sharia-enforcement) force in Kano continues to harass converts from Islam more systematically. One recent case involved a young businessman who converted to Christianity. His uncle threatened him with death unless he reverted to Islam, but died himself very shortly after. Harassed at every turn, his nephew lost everything and had to flee to Abuja for his own safety. During one incident, the Kano *Hisba* locked him up for a week and told him to 'come back [to Islam] or we will know what to do with you'. His in-laws also took away his wife and children, although the children were eventually returned to him. In another case, a forty-year-old man was forced to flee to Borno to escape pressure from the *Hisba*. In yet another, an eighteen-year-old convert was taunted so badly that he went into hiding. His family took to the airwaves to try to track him down, announcing repeatedly that their son was 'lost'.[23]

As elsewhere, Christians complain both that they are not allowed to build new churches and that their access to resources is restricted. Roads to Christian villages are not repaired; boreholes are not supplied.[24] Kano's Christians feel particular indignation over an evident violation of children's rights. Christian religious knowledge classes are not allowed in the state – a ban that breaches Nigeria's undertakings in international law. Many Christian children adopt Muslim names simply to gain school admission, but can still suffer adverse consequences (such as the withholding of their exam results, which stops students from proceeding through the system) if they come clean about their religious identity.

And all the while, some Muslims are prepared to raise the stakes by playing the blasphemy card, which usually involves differences of view. A recent CSW report on Nigeria cites a case that occurred at the Sumaila Secondary School in Kano in January 2008. Papers deemed defamatory of Muslims or Islam were discovered, a Christian student was blamed.

> Muslim students and townsfolk armed themselves and began to hunt down Christian students. A policeman died in the violence, the police station was set on fire, and a student was almost beheaded, but was rescued and rushed to hospital, where he later recovered. A similar incident occurred at another secondary school on 22 January 2009, and in November, children at Rimi Secondary School faced similar accusations after a paper containing defamatory words was put under a prayer mat in a mosque. Eight Christian children were expelled, briefly reinstated, then expelled again two days later. When representatives of the local chapter of CAN visited the school to enquire about the expulsions, the principal informed them that the children were expelled following a directive from the zone educational office. At the time of the CSW visit, the eight children were at home, unable to attend school.[25]

Jigawa state, north-east of Kano, displays a similar clutch of problems. Sometimes permission to build a church will be given, only for the congregation to be told at a later date that a mistake had been made in the allocation of land, and the building must be pulled down. One pastor described the *Catch-22* situation in which he and others find themselves. Land can be purchased only by individuals, and not by the Church as a body. But when buildings are erected for worship, congregations in due course receive a message along the lines of 'You cannot build a church on Muslim land.'[26] Educational restrictions similar to those operating across Kano have been reported in Jigawa; Christians also complain of discrimination in employment.

Nigeria's elections in April 2011 were a further spur to violence. The victory of the Christian candidate, Goodluck Jonathan of the People's Democratic Party (PDP), was immediately disputed by supporters of the opposition candidate, Muhammad Buhari of the Congress for Progressive Change (CPC). Violence in the northern states left more than 800 people dead; relief agencies estimated that 65,000 were displaced; about 350 churches were razed.[27] In mainly Christian areas of Kaduna state, Christian mobs retaliated by murdering Muslims and destroying mosques.

The following month, President Jonathan appointed a new twenty-two-member panel to investigate the causes and extent of the post-election violence. A police spokesman in Kaduna state told Human Rights Watch that more than 500 people had been arrested in connection with the mayhem. But previous moves of this kind have not led to successful prosecutions on any scale. As one Christian leader put it, 'There have been . . . inquiries set up in the past, but I don't know what they did; that is why we are really sceptical.'[28]

The ills charted in this chapter are clearly much exacerbated by a near-breakdown of law and order across many parts of Nigeria. CSW has issued this rallying cry on the subject:

No effort must be spared in pursuing, capturing and prosecuting funders and perpetrators of this violence, no matter how highly placed they may be . . . This has rarely been the case in the past: the vast majority of those arrested for such violence have been quietly released once news of their crimes is no longer in the headlines, much to the distress and annoyance of survivors and friends and family of their victims . . . Impunity and lawlessness will only end when the rule of law is upheld in every instance and religion-related crimes are treated as crimes under the law . . .[29]

A final point deserves underscoring. As signposted in the Preface to this book, my prime aim is to record the voices of Christians. But it cannot be overstated that the violence they have suffered is as repugnant to a vast proportion of Muslims as it is to all other fair-minded people. After the Christmas Day attacks chronicled at the start of this chapter, three British Muslim groups spoke for many others in describing the suffering of Christians as 'outrageous' and 'heinous'. One statement insisted that '[t]here is nothing in our faith of Islam that can condone attacks on places of worship or on Christians as we have seen today.'[30] The co-chairmen of the Christian–Muslim forum, Bishop Richard Cheetham and Shaykh Ibrahim Mogra, said: 'We reiterate that attacks on people of other faiths are not part of either Christianity or Islam and that both religions seek to increase [mutual] understanding . . . and to work for peace.'[31]

This was more than an expression of pious sentiment. On the ground in Nigeria, Christians have been protecting mosques, and Muslims protecting churches, as young people, above all, have harnessed the Internet to thwart extremists in a number of cases. When I visited the National Mosque in Abuja and talked to worshippers, their detestation of Boko Haram was readily apparent. At an official level, two of the country's spiritual leaders, Sultan Muhammad Sa'ad Abubakar and the Catholic Archbishop of Abuja, John Onaiyekan, have built many interfaith bridges. Needless to say, the stability of these structures can never be taken for granted.

7

INDONESIA

The instances of Islamist violence against Christians in Indonesia since the mid-1990s are legion. Ten Protestant churches were destroyed by Muslim rioters in Surabaya, eastern Java, on 9 June 1996. Four months later, twenty-five more churches were razed in the area, as well as a church-run orphanage and two Christian schools. Pastor Ishah Christian, a Pentecostal minister, and his wife, daughter, and niece, were burnt to death.[1] Thirteen churches were set on fire or otherwise damaged by Islamist mobs in Jakarta on 22 November 1998. The following year, on the island of Ambon (north of East Timor and west of New Guinea), Christian–Muslim communal conflict resulted in thousands of deaths. In 2000, friction spread to the surrounding archipelago, stirred up by gunmen affiliated to the Laskar Jihad militant group, who had been trained in camps in Java. 'These fighters transformed what had been communal violence into massacres and forced conversions of Christians,' according to Religious Freedom in the World.[2] Its report also details a case of unimaginable horror in Sulawesi. On 29 October 2005, three teenage schoolgirls, all of them cousins, were beheaded as they walked to their Christian-run school in Poso district, central Sulawesi. The head of one of the murdered girls was put in a plastic bag and left on the steps of a local church. A fourth girl, Noviana Malewa, also a cousin of the other three, was critically injured with lacerations to her face and neck. A few days later, terrorists shot two other high school students in Poso. Seven Islamists later confessed to the beheadings, which were fiercely condemned by mainstream Muslim groups.

The disaster is all the more pitiable because religious pluralism in the world's largest Muslim-majority country runs deep. During the second half of the first millennium, two societies – the Hindu Mataram kingdom, which ruled Java, and the Buddhist Srivijaya empire, centred on Sumatra and much of the Malay Peninsula – emerged to dominate their respective patches of this giant archipelago covering 17,000 islands. Java, Bali, and other neighbouring islands were controlled by Hindu rulers until the thirteenth century, when Islam spread rapidly across the region. Christianity was introduced by colonisers: first the Portuguese, who vanquished the Muslim kingdom of Malacca in 1511 (a decisive moment in the rise of Western power); and later the Dutch, who had taken over much of what is now Indonesia by the beginning of the eighteenth century. The Dutch are especially associated with manipulating Christian mission to sideline Islam. Aware that Muslim communities tended to be solidly rooted in coastal areas, they concentrated on gaining converts among the tribal communities inland. Sometimes Muslims were paid to be baptised.[3]

After Indonesia gained independence from the Netherlands in 1945, the inaugural President, Sukarno, sought to consolidate his country's tradition of interfaith diversity by enshrining the notion of *Pancasila* – a guiding philosophical principle or article of civic religion – in law. A definition of *Pancasila* ('five pillars') appears in the preamble to Indonesia's Constitution: 'Belief in a monotheistic god, just and civilized humanity, the unity of Indonesia, democracy guided by the wisdom of deliberations of representatives, and social justice for all the Indonesian people.' Five faiths – Islam, Buddhism, Hinduism, Catholicism, and

Protestantism – are recognised under Indonesian law, though adherents of other creeds are allowed to worship as long as they identify themselves with one of the officially sanctioned traditions. Interfaith conversion is permitted, but proselytising is a source of acute controversy. Twelve per cent (about 28.5 million) of Indonesia's population of 242 million are Christian; 79 per cent are Muslim. Given this balance, there is a de facto need for senior public office-holders to be Muslim, with all that this implies about glass ceilings for minorities.

The largest division in the majority community is not between Sunnis and Shias (there are only 1–3 million of the latter), but between what might loosely be called modernisers and conservatives. Many Muslim supporters of *Pancasila* take pride in what one veteran voice calls a 'very harmonious' arrangement. Others who had fought for liberation from the Dutch were outraged by *Pancasila*, seeing it as involving too great a concession to 'Western' values. When the militants of groups such as Jemaah Islamiyah attack churches, injure or kill Christians, and demand that Indonesia, Malaysia, the Southern Philippines, Singapore, and Brunei be united in a Muslim megastate, they also cite *Pancasila* as a source of their grievances.

It is no easier to disentangle politics from religion here than in many other places. The Islamist rallying cry against 'Christianisation' is as much a mark of factors ranging from local turf wars to globalisation as it is of matters theological. During the late 1960s, the dictatorial government of Sukarno's successor, President Suharto, clamped down on Confucians, most of whom were ethnic Chinese, as part of a drive against Communism. A significant proportion of this group then converted to Christianity. This meant that essentially ethnic tensions could now be mapped onto older Muslim–Christian animosities. Another major challenge has followed from the government's policy of reducing overpopulation on Java by helping people to move to other islands. Rivalries have grown as new Muslim communities have sprung up in what were previously Christian-majority areas, especially as Christians suspect the government of ulterior motives based on an 'Islamisation' agenda.[4]

These problems are in turn aggravated by poor governance, including a gap between the government's public support for interfaith toleration and its failure to put its rhetoric into practice. Despite economic progress, post-independence Indonesia was deeply marked by corruption, especially during the Suharto period, lasting for three decades from 1968. Suharto was replaced by Abdurrahman Wahid and, after his ejection from power in 2001, by Megawati Sukarnoputri, who was also in power for three years before the election of Susilo Bambang Yudhoyono. The 2004 elections were generally judged to be free and fair, betokening significant advances for a country that had witnessed colossal violence under Suharto – not just during the 1960s against 500,000 suspected members of the Indonesian Communist Party, but also 100,000 Christian civilians in East Timor between the 1970s and 1990s. Cronyism is still endemic, however. Even the country's Attorney General, Abdul Rahman Saleh, declared recently that justice was still typically awarded to the highest bidder.[5]

According to Dr Musdah Mulia, who chairs the Indonesian Conference on Religions for Peace (ICRP), there are at least 147 'discriminative laws and public policies in regards to religion'. He argues that 'as long as those laws are permitted to prevail, there is always a strong potential for violence in society. There need to be efforts for reforms and also to create new laws that are more [accommodating] towards the principles of human rights, the principles of democracy, tolerance and pluralism.'[6] He is also very worried about what he and others see as the draconian provisions – including severe restrictions on building places of worship and religious education – in proposed new 'Religious Tolerance' laws.

The Revd Gomar Gultom, General Secretary of the Communion of Churches in Indonesia, is chiefly concerned by what he terms the 'absence' of the state: 'In various acts of violence . . . it looked as if the police were helpless and even tended to let the violence occur in front of them.' At least three court cases have been won by churches in the state administrative courts, which have ruled that the congregations involved are all allowed to build and use their places of worship without hindrance, but in all three cases the court rulings have been disregarded.[7] The point is powerfully made by Fr Franz Magnis-Suseno, a highly regarded German-born Catholic priest who has ministered in Indonesia for fifty years:

> The government seems to let religiously motivated violence go by. Local politicians seem to calculate opportunistically that a hard attitude towards minorities will pay a dividend at the next elections. The national leadership, while occasionally condemning violence, close their eyes. They have never spoken out in favour of minorities . . . The one that does not do its duty is the state. It is the state that does not take action when minorities are threatened. Both the executive, the legislative and the [judicial] branches of state power do not show courage and character. We notice an unpleasant mix of cowardice, opportunism and narrow-mindedness. If the state surrenders its mandate to carry out the rule of law, to make the constitution and *Pancasila* effective, this will not only have bad consequences for minorities, but also for state and society in general.[8]

Islamist hardliners are especially quick to take advantage of legislation passed since 1998 that devolves power to the regions. For example, sharia law has been introduced at a local level in Sulawesi, Sumatra, Eastern Java, Banten, Flores, Sumba, and the Bandung area. In practice, this has meant that women are forced to wear the hijab, alcohol vendors have been attacked, and stones have been hurled at those failing to stop work or park their cars at Muslim prayer times.

Dissension is partly stirred up from overseas – Saudi Arabia and Iran especially. The extremist Hizb-ut-Tahrir Indonesia (HTI), for example, has roots in the Middle East. Wahhabis are taking up positions in local government and at mosques, threatening the influence of Nahdlatul Ulama (NU) and Muhammadiyah, still Indonesia's two largest organisations, and both traditional bastions of tolerance. Wahhabi influence is also reflected in the country's Justice and Welfare Party (PKS), a body whose constitution in key respects matches that of the Muslim Brotherhood in Egypt. Ibnu Ahmad, a jihadi fighter interviewed at length by Eliza Griswold for her book *The Tenth Parallel*, comes from a family battle-hardened by generations of fighting – first against colonisers, then for Indonesia to become an Islamic state. In the late 1980s and 1990s, his views were buttressed by a move to al-Qaeda's al-Sadda camp in Afghanistan. At least four Cabinet ministers responsible respectively for Religious Affairs, Social Affairs, Agriculture, and Information, are Islamists, representing the Justice and Welfare Party and the Renewal Democratic Party (PDP).

*

The violence illustrated by the attacks on Noviana Malewa and her cousins did not grow uniformly after 2005, though some of it has obviously been associated with 9/11, and the Bali nightclub bombing of 2002, in which more than 200 people lost their lives. Directed against tourists, the Bali attack was explicitly billed as revenge against 'crusaders' – in this case Australians, whose armed forces, backed by the UN, had played a leading role in rescuing Christian civilians in East Timor from Jakarta's death squads. Despite the febrile international atmosphere that followed the invasion of Iraq, the frequency of attacks on religious minorities – Ahmadiyya (or Ahmadi) Muslims, as well as Christians – in fact eased somewhat during the middle of the 2000s, before increasing in around 2008–2009. Other symptoms of the problem include the abuse of Indonesia's blasphemy law, a joint ministerial decree of 2008 banning the distribution of Ahmadiyya teachings, and controls on the building of places of worship – a move that has in effect forced churches to close. Nor have Buddhists avoided the storm. In April 2011,[9] the Ministry of Religious Affairs ordered the removal of a large statue at the Tri Ratna Buddhist monastery in Tanjun Balai, in northern Sumatra.

Church-building is a source of bad blood through being a common phenomenon – a product both of growth and of the tendency of newer Evangelical and Pentecostal groups to splinter, or to attract recruits from more established Christian bodies. Under revised rules introduced in 2006 across Indonesia, an application must be supported by at least ninety members of a congregation, with signatures, and by sixty other people of different faiths in the local area. It must also be supported with a recommendation by the Forum of Religious Harmony (FKUB), a government-backed body operating across Indonesia. In some instances, even when churches have obtained the necessary permissions, the authorities have withdrawn permits under pressure from Islamists. As we have seen, even in cases where the Supreme Court has ruled in favour of a given church, a ban on its opening has remained in place.

A number of recent examples of church closures and related violence have prompted international attention, particularly that of the Gereja Kristen Indonesia (GKI) Yasmin Church in Bogor, West Java. The mayor of Bogor issued a decree granting GKI Yasmin a building permit in 2006. Three months later, however, bureaucrats ordered construction to stop and the church to move to another location. The building has been targeted by Muslims in a series of demonstrations, but GKI Yasmin leaders have continued to press their case. On Christmas Day in 2010, the authorities attempted to stop the church from holding a service; in response the congregation set up a tent in front of the newly re-sealed building and began impromptu worship. On 14 January 2011, the Supreme Court ordered that the church be reopened, and ruled against the revocation of its permit. The city authorities have not complied with the judgment.

Objectors are clearly motivated by more than one consideration. The alarm felt by Muslims and others in response to aggressive Christian missionaries may be warranted in some cases. As often, though, the complaint can also be a fig leaf for people who will not concede the principle of freedom of belief. Muslim civil-society groups in Indonesia are among those who see Islamist arguments as opportunistic. A report by the International Crisis Group in late 2010, 'Indonesia: "Christianisation" and Intolerance',[10] concluded that the majority of churches were not guilty of using strong-arm tactics, though missionaries were warned about showing due sensitivity to local cultures. The warning reflects a division between Catholics and mainline Protestants on the one hand, who have jettisoned the approaches of earlier eras in favour of seeing mission much more as a matter of witness; and, on the other, fundamentalist Christians with less subtle beliefs and a more hostile attitude to other faiths. The document also argues that many Muslims do not understand why a town may typically contain several churches rather than just one, because they are unaware of Christianity's denominational structure.

As noted, some cases of anti-Christian discrimination or harassment also involve ethnicity – especially in the case of Indonesia's largest Reformed grouping, the Huria Kristen Batak Protestant (HKBP) Church, which consists for the most part of ethnic Batak members whose forebears moved from Sumatra to Java. Take the testimony of pastors in places such as Cikarang, Bandung, Bekasi, and Ciketing: 'Our struggle started in 2007 when we tried to build [our] church,' the pastor and elders at the HKBP Citra Indah church in Cikarang told Christian Solidarity Worldwide representatives in 2011.[11] 'Our church congregation started on 20 April 2003 with thirty to forty members. We started here in this village, with an ethnic Batak congregation, who were working in the local area, many as teachers. There was a lot of new real estate, and many Christians lived here.' Several other Protestant congregations had taken root in the locality by this time, but Bataks felt much more at home worshipping with those of their own ethnicity. To start with, their Sunday gatherings took place in a business centre, but when the congregation outgrew this space, an application was made to build a church. Eventually, several churches sprang up together on one patch of land, because Catholics, Pentecostals, and Seventh-Day Adventists also needed new worship spaces of their own. A portent of worsening times came in 2005, when the local mayor's re-election campaign foundered amid claims by his critics that he was allowing 'Christianisation' to develop on his watch. A mosque council described by a local Christian source as 'more radical, less tolerant' was elected in 2006, after which the new mayor told the HKBP community that its church should be closed. The pastor picks up the story:

> We had several meetings with the local government, developers, local church leaders and Muslim leaders, but the result was always the same: we were told we could not build the church. The local government was not neutral – it sided with the Muslim community. The developers were ambiguous, and were afraid that if they defended the rights of Christians, radical Muslim groups would destroy their business. The radicals demanded that the building must stop and came close to saying it should be destroyed. The developer protected the licence for the building, but the only option was to limit the construction to two churches – one Protestant, one Catholic. The Muslim community complained that they are the majority but they only have one mosque. They told us that we were only 2 per cent [sic] of the population in Indonesia, and asked why we had so many churches. They don't understand that . . . there are many denominations [within Protestantism]. Furthermore, every cluster has a mosque, so in fact they have more places of worship than Christians.
>
> In 2008, at a meeting between local government, the developer, and Muslim and Christian leaders, we were told we must destroy the church building, which was 60 per cent complete. There was a big demonstration by the Muslim community every Sunday, with shouts of: 'The church must be destroyed.' When the HKBP and Catholic church buildings were destroyed, a representative of the developer came and informed us that this was the day for the buildings to be torn down. The developer himself agreed to the decision, but refused to come and participate. We could do nothing, except demand that the money used to build the church, which had come from church members, would be returned to us. We signed a memorandum of understanding to get our money back from the developer.[12]

The dispute's aftermath has been complex. In essence, the HKBP and Catholic churches were destroyed, and one church remained, which is now shared by seven Protestant congregations. The Catholics celebrate Mass in a separate building, but do not have permission to do so. All congregations are growing, and now gather in what the HKBP pastor describes as very hot and cramped conditions. 'We want to build a new church building to give us more space, even if that involves further struggle. We don't have equal rights.'[13]

The Christians in Cikarang are on the whole well educated. They shun violence and have the patience and wherewithal to lobby the authorities through mainstream channels of protest. But they also refuse to apologise either for their growing congregations or for the fluidity in employment that is driving significant demographic shifts in this part of the world. The pastor's concluding remarks apply well beyond his own patch:

In Europe too many churches are empty, while here, we need churches. The regulations from the Ministry of Religious Affairs and the Ministry of Home Affairs contradict Chapter 29 of the Indonesian Constitution, which protects religious freedom. We don't feel free. We urge the Indonesian government to withdraw this regulation. Christians played an active role in the struggle for independence from the Dutch. We built this nation together. We don't want Indonesia to be divided, like Sudan, between Muslims and Christians, but if Indonesia continues on this path and becomes an Islamic state, we are afraid that Christians will decide they don't want to take part. The government says it will implement human rights, but in reality they don't. Why don't we have equal rights? We don't demand too much – we just demand our basic rights. If Muslims can build mosques, why can't we build churches?[14]

The pastor at HKBP church at Bandung, in western Java, tells of a comparable situation. 'HKBP started here in Bandung in 1999, in a rented house. However, the local community rejected it and so the church moved to another place. In 2004, the church bought a building and began to worship there.'[15] The arrangement did not last long. After protests by local Muslims, members of the congregation began to meet in each other's homes. Then, when the dust appeared to have settled, they returned to the church as discreetly as possible, and continued to use it from 2005 till 2010. After this, as the pastor recounts, the situation worsened suddenly:

> On 14 November 2010, during a Sunday service, a demonstration was held by Muslims demanding that we stop. The pastor was not there. The elders tried to discuss with the demonstrators but found no solution, so they went to the local government to discuss. On 16 November, we decided to send a letter to the local elected representatives, in the name of the Christian community here, asking for a solution. Until now we have received no answer.
>
> The local government suggested we move to another place, but it is not easy because in 2006 we had to pay for the building. To rent another building would be more than $100. It is not easy – we don't have a lot of money. The local government said that they had obtained permission from the director of a government building for us to use the building for services, but when we called the director he told us no permission had been given. So we decided to keep worshipping in our building, even if there are demonstrations, if there is no alternative place. On one occasion, there was a demonstration and the pastor asked the mob to give us one hour for a meeting with church members. We had silent worship, without singing or prayer, to make it seem like a meeting. After this, the local government sent us a letter, informing us we must not use the building.

In December there was a meeting with the district level government, but still no solution. On 11 December, words were written on the wall of the church building: 'This building cannot be used for worship, and must only be used for residential purposes.' SMS text messages were sent to many people inviting all Muslims to come and close the church, accusing it of being involved in prostitution. The police took no action.[16]

On 12 December, the church asked for police protection at seven in the morning; two hours later, a 300-strong mob marched from the local mosque to the church demanding its closure. They tried to force the pastor to sign a document assenting to their demands, but he declared himself unable to do so. Some members of the crowd went on to seven other local churches, removing crosses and other objects, and interrupting worship. Then they returned to the scene of the main demonstration, where a cordon was created by local government officials and signs erected declaring that worship at the church in question was now banned.[17] 'I feel that there are rules only for Christians, not for Muslims,' Pastor Badia concludes. 'I have reported the case to the national human rights commission . . . and they informed the local government that we should be permitted to use the church again, but still no permission has been granted. I want the world to know that although Indonesia is a democratic country, it does not feel like it to me.'[18]

Religious enthusiasm is often used as a front for crime. Take the evidence of a woman pastor, Obertina M. Johanis, of Gereja Kristen Pasundan (GKP) Deyeuj Kolot, Kabupaten Bandung, in West Java. Her church moved to a new location in 1995; the congregation functioned without hindrance for a decade. Yet in August 2005, demonstrators came to the church and claimed that it should close, because it had no licence and no permission to operate. Tensions simmered – for a time the congregation moved to a nearby hospital chapel – and on 18 November 2008, a crowd returned to the church and 'took all the chairs out, broke the organ, the cross, lamps, fans, and threw everything outside', Pastor Johanis reports. She was not there, but her husband and one-year-old child were. Her husband called the police, who did not come for two or three hours and then took no action. 'The government is too weak,' she insists. 'During Ramadan, three or four times, [the mob] threw stones at the pastor's house. One week they came and were very angry at us, and tried to intimidate us. However, the people doing this are outsiders, radical groups from other areas, who come and ask local Muslims to act against us.'

At various times of hardship in recent years, she adds, many Muslims came to the church for help – for food, medicine, shelter. In this community, Christians regularly provide their Muslim neighbours with medicines and free medical check-ups. But in 2008, churches in Bandung received a letter from one leader of a radical group, asking for money. 'He was blackmailing us,' recalls Pastor Johanis,

> offering to ensure our safety if we paid. Some churches do pay gangsters to secure their churches, but not all churches can pay. There are 153 churches without a licence in my district alone. We are no longer fighting to get a licence. We have tried four times since 1998, and it requires a lot of time. We recognize that the building is not everything – the church is community.
>
> The radicals accuse the church of 'Christianization', but this term is becoming similar to the Communist Party in the 1960s in terms of the stigma it carries. Even if we are carrying a Bible, we are accused of 'Christianization'.[19]

The HKBP Filadelfia Church at Bekasi, in West Java, has endured a familiar saga involving a legal battle to establish its right to worship, along with repeated obstruction from the local mayor. The pastor, the Revd Palti Panjaitan, emphasises that Christians are by no means the only victims. Local Muslims supporting their Christian neighbours have faced intimidation and economic reprisals. The church has worked hard to develop good relationships with local Muslims, 'and that is why local Muslims have been supportive', Pastor Panjaitan comments. 'For example, members of the church helped the Muslim community build their mosque, helped to fix the road, and regularly join in Islamic festivals and celebrations. *We see Muslims as brothers*.'(my italics)[20] But he added this warning:

> I hope that the Christian community can survive and does not become radicalized itself. I have seen some brothers react badly to the situation, treat Muslims badly, in Papua and Maluku in the past, and I hope that does not happen any more. We understand there is a limit, though, to what people can take. We hope the international community will be more active in protecting minority rights. If there is no help from the international community, we are hopeless here. If there is no help, we will be destroyed. We still love our country, but one day Christians and Ahmadiyyas will decide we want to separate from Indonesia, if the situation does not change. It is only a matter of time before there is Sudanization – a separation of Indonesia between Muslim and minorities, like the separation of north and south Sudan. We don't want that.[21]

Catholics in Indonesia are no strangers to the Islamist menace, even though they have been praised by the Minister for Religious Affairs, Suryadharma Ali, as key partners with Muslims in boosting education and development.[22] In July

2009, Muslim groups stopped the building of a Catholic-owned home for disabled children in Junrejo, on the outskirts of Batu in Malang, East Java, alleging that it might be used for missionary activity. Sr Chatarina Sulasti of the Institut Sekulir Alma, a secular women's institution supporting the project, rejected all allegations of proselytising. Two churches had building permits cancelled after protests by Muslim groups in March 2010. Fr Peter Kurniawan Subagyo of Santa Maria Immaculata's Church in Citra Garden, West Jakarta, said he had received a permit for a new church after the large congregation outgrew their existing building. A few weeks after construction had started, Islamist groups began demonstrations. The permit was subsequently revoked by officials.[23] And in May 2010, a website posting material that was blasphemous to Muslims led members of the Islamic Defenders Front to attack St Bellarminus School in Bekasi district, West Java. The posting appeared on a blog, allegedly run by the school, and was accompanied by a photograph of a copy of the Qur'an in a toilet. Sr Ignatio Nudek, a spokeswoman for St Bellarminus's, said: '[We do] not have such a blog. We never disgrace other religions. In fact we have Muslim students at the school.'[24]

Violence against Christians has increased in the recent past. During the first nine months of 2011, for example, at least thirty churches were attacked around the country. The most severe example was the suicide bombing of a church in Solo, Central Java, on 25 September of that year: more than twenty people were injured. The thirty-one-year-old culprit, Pino Damayanto, otherwise known as Ahmad Yosepa Hayat, reportedly claimed that it was his religious duty to kill 'the enemies of Islam'. Police believe he was linked to the Jamaah Ansharut Tauhid ('Partisans of the Oneness of God' or JAT), a terrorist group thought to have been founded by Abu Bakar Bashir, who is currently serving a prison sentence on charges of terrorism.[25] Other examples from 2011 include the burning of some of the buildings belonging to two churches in East Luwu, South Sulawesi, on 2 June; an attack on a church in Klaten, Central Java, in which Molotov cocktails were thrown early in the morning of the same day; the burning of two churches in Kuantan Singingi, Riau, on 1 August; and attacks on two churches in Tangerang on 5 September, resulting in injuries to one of the pastors.[26]

Several further cases in 2011 highlighted Indonesia's twin problems of religious intolerance and an absence of the rule of law. The first was the trial of the perpetrators of an attack on an Ahmadiyya community in Cikeusik, West Java, in which three people were killed, and others were severely beaten and injured. One man told CSW, 'When the attackers caught me, they stripped me naked on the road, dragged me through a river, beat me with sticks and machetes and tried to cut off my penis. They bashed stones on my head, and dragged me around the village. One man used a bamboo spear to hit my eye. They shouted that I was an "infidel" and should be killed. I lost consciousness.'[27] The mob responsible for the attack numbered more than a thousand people, yet only three of the perpetrators were arrested. The trio eventually received sentences of between three and six months in prison, and one Ahmadiyya man, Deden Darmawan Sudjana, was jailed for six months for disobeying police orders to leave his home.[28] Similarly, in March 2011, nine people who had attacked a pastor with a club and stabbed a church elder at a church in West Java were sentenced to between five and seven months.[29]

In October 2011, CSW observers returned to Bogor, West Java, to monitor the GKI Yasmin Church discussed earlier in this chapter. On Sunday 16 October, a crowd of about a hundred people armed with bamboo sticks held a demonstration against the Church. A fortnight later, members of Forkami (Forum Komunikasi Muslim Indonesia – the Indonesia Muslim Communication Forum) threatened to attack, 'hurling verbal abuse at the Christians'.[30] It was also reported, although CSW was not able to verify this, that most of the demonstrators were from outside West Bogor sub-district where the church has been built, and were paid 200,000 rupiah ($2.20) each. They were thought not even to know what they were protesting against.

Church representatives told the human rights monitors that there were approximately 300 Christian families in the Yasmin area of Bogor, and at least 1,000 individual Christians – more than enough to warrant the presence of a church. Moreover, the congregation is supported by most local Muslims. A *kyai* (Islamic cleric), who is a member of the National Commission on Violence Against Women, attended the Sunday service to demonstrate his support. Radical groups such as Hizb-ut-Tahrir Indonesia (HTI) and Forkami are likely to have been behind the strife.[31]

*

We have already noted that inter-religious tensions in Indonesia are rising because of population transfers from Java to other parts of the country. West Papua is a case in point. Human rights observers believe that if the marginalisation of Papuans is not addressed, the tensions have the potential to develop along religious as well as ethnic, social, and economic lines. 'It is very dangerous,' said one church leader. 'The Muslims are increasing rapidly. This is an Indonesian programme to establish Papua as part of an Islamic state. It could lead to extremism – after they become more and more in number, they will become more radical, and they will burn churches, close churches.' Another source confirmed that 'Islam is getting stronger in numbers and in influence, in government, politics, in the economy.'[32]

While militants have not yet taken up arms in West Papua, a Kuwaiti-based organisation with links to extremists, the Revival of Islamic Heritage Society, has been sponsoring missionary activity or *dakwah* in the region. 'Papua is seen as a big frontier for Islamic *dakwah* groups,' said one respected international expert. 'Radical networks are ready . . . and if tensions increase they could act.'[33]

Any discussion of this field would be far from complete without a glance at East Timor's recent history. This former colony was taken over by Indonesia in 1975. During a struggle for independence from Jakarta lasting nearly a quarter of a century, about one-sixth of the Timorese population (100,000 people) were massacred. Although the conflict was essentially political, East Timor's population is overwhelmingly Catholic. Suharto famously described the territory as 'a pimple on Indonesia's face'.[34]

Some Timorese engaged in a guerrilla campaign against the Indonesian army, but most activists opted for non-violent resistance. Many were attacked in their beds at night by so-called Ninja gangs – thugs in the pay of Suharto's forces.[35] The victims' struggle eventually received international recognition in the award of the 1996 Nobel Peace Prize to José Ramos-Horta and Bishop Carlos Felipe Ximenes Belo of Dili. Aware of the Church's importance as a rallying point for dissenters, the Indonesian army defaced crucifixes and other Christian monuments. In the words of George Aditjondro, an Indonesian observer of great experience, 'The military have been in growing confrontation with the Catholic Church, since the Church is the only institution in Timor that it cannot control.'[36]

The tragedy of East Timor was often highlighted internationally by Christian campaigners and secular NGOs. But to my knowledge there was never a violent backlash against Muslims elsewhere. The double standard reflected by this contrast is revealing.

8

INDIA

Between August and October of 2008, the eastern state of Orissa in India saw the worst outbreak of brutality against Christians since Independence. Hindu extremists murdered at least ninety people, displaced at least 50,000 more from their homes, and attacked about 170 churches and chapels. The victims included Hindus who had tried to defend their Christian neighbours. Most of the attacks took place in Kandhamal, but violence raged in thirteen surrounding districts as well. Among other targets was a Catholic priest, Fr Bernard Digal, who was killed, and Sr Meena Barwa, who worked in the Divyajyoti Pastoral Centre in Konjamendi. Hunted down by the mob, she was publicly stripped and gang-raped before eventually escaping and seeking police help. She has nevertheless rebuilt her life, returning to her studies and taking her final religious vows.

News of this disaster may have surprised people who associate Hinduism with nothing but spiritual serenity – and think that crimes such as the murder of Dr Graham Staines (the Australian missionary and medic burnt to death in 1999 along with his two young sons in the Keonjhar district of Orissa) are exceptions that prove a peaceful rule. But it is a mistake to see the trauma suffered by the Staines family as exceptional: 1999 was neither the best nor worst of times. In the previous year, the Delhi-based

United Christian Forum for Human Rights recorded more than 120 attacks against Christians in India, including the torching of 30 churches in Gujarat.[1] Nor is the problem of recent origin. Hindu resistance to Christian mission has deep roots.

The Orissa tragedy of 2008 was sparked by the assassination of Swami Lakshmanananda Saraswati, a local figurehead of the Hindu nationalist VJP party, on 23 August. Most neutral observers believe that the culprits were Maoist insurgents. As Saraswati's body was being carried around Kandhamal on the following day, crowds of hardline Hindu activists set up roadblocks, blamed Christians for the killing, and called for revenge attacks against the alleged perpetrators. In testimony given later, a group of twenty-eight Christians said that they had been forced to flee to the surrounding hills after their homes had been destroyed. The assailants, who were from their own village, contacted them four days later to set up what they called a 'peace committee'. Spokesmen for the Christians reluctantly agreed. On returning to the village, they found hundreds of people gathered around a bonfire. In the presence of a Brahmin priest, the Christians were tonsured and submitted to a yagna ceremony 'reconverting' them to Hinduism. They were then told that the process would be sealed by the ceremonial burning of their Bibles on the following day. After nightfall, they fled.[2]

The significance of this sequence should not be missed. In the view of a close observer of the scene such as the human rights activist David Griffiths, what started as vengeance over Lakshmanananda's murder turned into a wider effort to force Christians to renounce their faith. Christians not only faced accusations of murder, they later explained, but cries of: 'Hindu, Hindu, *bhai*, *bhai*!' (Hindus are brothers!); 'This is a Hindu land and foreign religions don't belong here!'; and 'Become Hindus or leave!'. A Christian in the Raikia relief camp revealed that even so-called peace committees posed grave threats: 'If you don't reconvert, we will kill you,' he was told. The militants were successful in some cases. For example, a Catholic priest has described how his father, a catechist, had an axe held to his neck as he was told to reconvert. He was escorted to a local temple every day for a period thereafter. Clerics at Balliguda, another village in Kandhamal, have given evidence of how 'reconverted' Hindus were forced to carry out extensive rituals as proof of their changed allegiance.

We shall return to the Orissa attacks, which form one of the central exhibits in this chapter. What, though, of the broader background? Misconceptions about the alleged other-worldliness of Hinduism have been noted. A larger fallacy springs from an ignorance in the West and elsewhere of India's Christian past. The European or North American secularist is likely to agree with hardline Hindu nationalists – the advocates of Hindutva – in holding that Christianity is nothing more than an unwelcome cultural import to the subcontinent. In fact, church roots in India have been traced to the apostolic period via the Acts of Thomas (an apocryphal document) and through ancient oral traditions among the country's Syrian Orthodox populations. As Robert Eric Frykenberg has recorded in his major study *Christianity in India*,[3] these Orthodox communities – who belong to one of the world's most ancient family of Churches – became assimilated into Indian society many centuries ago, avoiding missionary activity and observing Hindu practices in areas including ritual purity and marriage.

Hindutva activists are admittedly less concerned with such discreet (not to say idiosyncratic) expressions of Christianity – including collusion in the caste system. Their fire is chiefly aimed at those with a stronger commitment to gospel teaching on the equality of all, and whose message has long drawn converts from among the Dalit (Untouchable) and Adivasi (aboriginal) sections of Indian society. Yet the record here is also knotty. It is obviously true that Western commercial operations – Portuguese, Dutch, British, and now, especially, American – brought preachers in their wake, most of whom would not have apologised for opposing a religious pyramid which has inflicted almost incredible levels of cruelty against about a quarter of the populace. This is not to defend the record of Western Christians without qualification. The grim social legacy of nineteenth-century Evangelicalism, in particular, is a matter of record.[4] But it is also important to recognise that there was never a large number of missionaries relative to India's immense size. Neglect of this point has in turn caused some commentators to downplay the role of Indian-born evangelists. Frykenberg maintains that where Christianity took wing, it was largely with the consent of converts and through a process of inculturation. He describes the work of pioneers such as the Tamil poet Vedanayagam Sastriar (1774–1864). But Frykenberg also gives due weight to the mainly low-born preachers especially well placed to reframe Jesus's message of freedom for the captive. Even in the twentieth century, Church growth tended to take place on India's geographical margins, especially in the north-eastern states of Nagaland and Mizoram, rather than in centres of expatriate British life.

Frykenberg's work is studded with other pieces of apparently counter-intuitive information – for example, that the British Raj tended to display religious pragmatism in its dealings with Indians. The economic logic often argued far more in favour of interfaith toleration than of an uncompromising assertion of Christian standards. In the nineteenth century, it was the British Evangelicals who felt more aggrieved about this than the East India Company or members of any other religious group; and even though Lord Bentinck's attempt to ban infanticide and *sati* (widow-burning) in 1827 was prompted by Evangelical pressure, high-caste Hindus often guarded their traditions with zeal.

The two elements in this equation were mutually reinforcing. External pressure led to the crystallising of a Hindu identity that had previously been a good deal more diffuse. 'Hinduism' is not the age-old entity of Hindutva imagination. Rather, it is a patchwork stitched together in the eighteenth and nineteenth centuries by Indian and European scholars seeking to tabulate and summarise an enormous variety of religious belief and practice known as *sanathana dharma* (literally 'eternal religion') which had come to light as the British Empire expanded.

Thus the Christianising of many Dalits and Adivasis prompted retaliatory campaigns by proponents of Hindutva to win these converts back to a faith that they had never really professed in the first place. The mutiny of 1857 was in part prompted by fears over the place of Christianity in the Raj, after which the East India Company took further steps to distance itself from controversy by commending greater neutrality in matters theological. The results of this stance were mixed. On the one hand, it helped to provide one of the foundations for independent India's secular tradition, but on the other the growing muscle of the Church of England during the period of Crown rule from 1858 to 1947 (both culturally and in terms of revenues raised from the Empire) lent substance to Hindu defensiveness.

So today's aggression has been fed by perceived weakness. In 1909, the Hindu scholar U.N. Mukherji published a monograph entitled *Hindus: A Dying Race*, which forecast the long-term decline of his co-religionists relative to their Muslim neighbours. The Hindu nationalist ideology that has arisen over the past century begins with a conception that India is a Hindu nation, in which Hinduism is the default way of life for Indians.

This model entails a distinction between conversions away from Hinduism, which are seen as a threat to the national integrity of India and a key contributor to the alleged decline of Hinduism, and conversions *to* Hinduism, which are described by the term *ghar vapsi*, translated as 'homecoming', or 'reconversion'.

Related terms helpful for appreciating this subject in the round include 'communalism' – the fomenting of interfaith tension out of a sense that the interests of one religious community are unavoidably in conflict with those of another. In other words, relations between religious communities are seen as a zero-sum game, in which one community's gain inevitably involves another's loss. This view has in turn been yoked to the assumption that religious conflict is inevitable – all the more so when the perpetrators feel that police investigation of their crimes will be lenient or even non-existent.

The term 'Hindutva' was coined by V.D. Savarkar (1883–1966). He contrasted Hindus, who regard India as 'Holy-Land', with Muslims and Christians, for whom India could not be more than their 'Father-Land'. Adherents of these minority faiths by definition possessed a split loyalty: 'Their holy land is far off in Arabia or Palestine. Their mythology and Godmen, ideas and heroes are not the children of this soil. Consequently their names and their outlooks smack of foreign origin. Their love is divided.'[5] Savarkar's words were echoed by another significant figure, M.S. Golwalkar (1906–73), who declared that 'All those not belonging to the national i.e. Hindu Race, Religion, Culture and Language, naturally fall out of the pale of the real "National Life".'[6]

The more militant forces of Hindu nationalism are known collectively as the Sangh Parivar. Its chief organ is the Rashtriya Swayamsevak Sangh (RSS), which has spawned numerous subsidiary groups. The Vishwa Hindu Parishad (VHP) is the religious wing of the Sangh Parivar, and was heavily implicated in the anti-Christian attacks in Orissa. The VHP's youth wing, known as the Bajrang Dal, is also often behind violence against Muslims and Christians. Associated with the Sangh Parivar are the Akhil Bharatiya Vidyarthi Parishad (ABVP), a mainly student body, and the Vanvasi Kalyan Ashram (VKA), set up after Independence to counter the influence of Christian missionaries. The Sangh Parivar's principal political arm is the Bharatiya Janata Party (BJP), India's main governing party between 1998 and 2004, but still a major force in regional government. It holds power on its own in Chhattisgarh, Gujarat, Himachal Pradesh, Karnataka, and Madhya Pradesh; and in coalition with other parties in Bihar, Jharkhand, Nagaland, Punjab, and Uttarakhand.

India's political currents naturally do not all flow in the same direction: the country has an impressive constitution replete with pledges to uphold freedom of religion and belief, as well as other liberties.[7] The problem is that this and other relevant pieces of legislation are ambiguous in places. Dalits who convert to religions other than Hinduism, Sikhism, or Buddhism – usually Islam and Christianity – lose their status as Scheduled Castes, and thus their eligibility for remedial measures. Among the consequences of this are that many Christian and Muslim Dalits conceal their religious identity for fear of reprisals; and that those who attack members of these two communities know that they cannot be prosecuted under the Scheduled Castes and Scheduled Tribes (Prevention of Atrocities) Act. A challenge to this position is under way in India's Supreme Court; adherents of Hindutva naturally support the status quo.

The state-level anti-conversion laws are formally known as Freedom of Religion Acts. Although these pieces of legislation are strongly endorsed by the BJP, it was the Indian National

Congress-appointed 'Niyogi Committee Report on Christian Missionary Activities in Madhya Pradesh' in 1956 which paved the way for the earliest anti-conversion laws; and the Orissa, Madhya Pradesh, and Himachal Pradesh laws were passed by non-BJP governments. The Niyogi Committee Report alleges that 'Evangelization in India appears to be part of the uniform world policy to revive Christendom for re-establishing Western supremacy', and that 'Conversions are mostly brought about by undue influence, misrepresentation, etc., or in other words not by conviction but by various inducements offered for proselytization in various forms.'[8]

This is to beg the question. Mission of all kinds can be conducted insensitively on occasion. But the problems that arise when people convert to Christianity are more social than theological. If some members of a given village change their religion, the result can be traumatic – especially if the move involves inter-generational clashes. Networks of solidarity break down; converts are liable to be shunned. Established power relationships can be challenged. Even though some Western secularists see Christian mission as disruptive or imperialistic, these people are often among the first to commend multiculturalism in their own societies with greatest vigour. The double standard here is obvious, and prompts an equally obvious question: shouldn't law-abiding religious minorities be tolerated everywhere, and not just in places such as Europe and North America?[9]

*

Worry about India's human rights record is widespread. In the report of her 2008 visit to the country, the UN Special Rapporteur on freedom of religion or belief wrote that she was 'deeply concerned that laws and bills on religious conversion in several Indian states are being used to vilify Christians and Muslims'. She added that these 'should be reconsidered since they raise serious human rights concerns'.[10] A recent snapshot of these laws in a range of states revealed that those of Orissa (1967), Madhya Pradesh (1968), Chhattisgarh (1968), Gujarat (2003), and Himachal Pradesh (2006) are in force, while Arunachal Pradesh's was introduced in 1978 but not implemented, and Rajasthan's was introduced thirty years later, but has not yet been brought into force. Each of these pieces of legislation bans conversions achieved through the use of 'force', 'fraud', or 'inducement'. But 'victims' and 'perpetrators' have changed places here: the legislation simply makes it easier for Hindus to attack Muslims and Christians because they can claim that the communities concerned were seeking to proselytise others. In the document just cited, the Rapporteur found that 'such laws or even draft legislation have had adverse consequences for religious minorities and have reportedly fostered mob violence against them'.[11]

The picture painted so far may appear startling to readers familiar with the secular Indian tradition already referred to. But during the 2004 elections, the Congress party leader, Sonia Gandhi, a Catholic by background, campaigned against the maltreatment of Christians and Muslims under the BJP. A Congress-led coalition emerged to form a majority in parliament: Manmohan Singh became the first Sikh Prime Minister, and repeated Mrs Gandhi's pledge that violence against Christians would cease.[12]

This is not the place for a comprehensive account of all the legislative to and fro that has unfolded over recent years, both at national and state levels. The essential points are that after a halting start, the Congress-led UPA government has made tackling communal violence a priority, but India still has a long way to go before a suitably balanced law gets onto the statute book. As in many other spheres of Indian life, sources of redress are theoretically strong. One of the main problems lies with absent, ineffective, or corrupt police forces. As the Rapporteur noted in her report, 'the system of impunity in India emboldens forces of intolerance'.[13]

The strategy of Hindutva propagandists becomes clearer when we look more closely at Orissa's history. It became a province in 1936, uniting most of the Oriya-speaking territories. Sindh was created as a mainly Muslim province at the same time, a move feeding the sense that Orissa had been formed as a sop to Hindus. But as David Griffiths, among others, has pointed out,[14] the idea that Orissa forms a Hindu holy land is wishful: Jainism and then Buddhism had once flourished in what became a complex religious ecology, while the Adivasis had an animist belief system that included shamanism.

Historically, Orissa's Kandhamal district has been populated by two tribal groups, the Kandhs and the Panas. The Kandhs have tended to predominate. Christian missionaries came to the region in the mid-nineteenth century and achieved some notable successes, especially among the Panas. (Missionary energy often involved efforts to end the local practice of *meriah* – human sacrifice.) After Independence, the Kandhs were classified as Scheduled Tribes, and the Panas as Scheduled Castes. Kandhamal was designated a 'Scheduled Area' and thus social benefits were apportioned to the Scheduled Tribes. This included land ownership, so historic power relations between the two groups were reinforced. As observers have noted, Pana efforts to improve themselves tended to be seen as a threat by the Kandhs. These essentially ethnic tensions were transposed into a religious key from the late 1960s onwards, when

Lakshmanananda Saraswati was dispatched to Kandhamal by the VHP to instil a sense of Hindu identity among the Kandhs as a buttress against the Christian presence. But the Kandhs were not primarily Hindus: their traditional world view, like that of the Panas, is more accurately termed animist. The BJP strategy was thus to designate this cluster of beliefs as a form of Hinduism, then to charge this process with political significance by portraying Christianity as a destabilising foreign force. In the words of Angana Chatterji, a leading expert on Orissa, 'Minorities [have become] the foil for manufacturing a monolithic Hindu identity.'[15]

As might be expected, Christian Panas did badly from this process. They lost their status as Scheduled Castes, since (as we have seen) only Hindus qualify for this designation and the benefits that go with it. In the event, though, the victims of the communal violence in 2007 and 2008 were from both Kandh and Pana stock. What united them was their Christian faith. As I saw on a trip through the region with a CSW team in 2011, the rebuilding of shattered communities is a patchy process. This is India's deep interior: poor, isolated, removed even from Orissa's relatively developed coastline. The infrastructure is pitiable. Material shortages mean that the rebuilding of homes and lives has been haphazard at best. Most relief camps had closed by the beginning of 2010, but many victims could not go back to their villages, owing to the hostility of their Hindu neighbours.

Between 2,000 and 3,000 families were still without homes when I visited. They were surviving in tents, or in the ruins of their former homes. Small amounts of government compensation have been paid out, but homeless Christians have consistently voiced two sorts of complaint. Firstly, that damages were unjustly assessed. For example, houses with little more than a wall left standing had been classed as merely 'partially damaged', with the result that their former occupants have qualified for a lower level of compensation, which falls well short of the cost of rebuilding. In a large proportion of damaged villages, victims said that 'all' homes had been destroyed, but only a small proportion had been considered worthy of full compensation. The second complaint was that help for Christians to rebuild their homes has not been accompanied by any form of welfare assistance – a disastrous outcome for people already facing ostracism because of their faith. Inevitably, victims have tended to spend initial tranches of compensation on food and other necessities rather than on rebuilding their homes. But by not showing evidence of reconstruction, villages have failed to qualify for later instalments of their money.

The need to rebuild churches is also an obvious priority in a landscape still blighted by architectural carcasses on land once used for worship. Even the Catholic pastoral centre where I stayed, though sturdy-looking from the outside, was a skeletal place within. During the 2008 attacks, the extremists had piled the furniture into the middle of every room in the compound before setting light to it. The structure survived, but all walls and ceilings were left severely charred. Having taken part in vespers Indian style (prayer mats, joss-sticks, and a very Indian, vibrato-laden rendering of the Psalms), I joined the chaplain and other residents for dhal and rotis on plastic chairs in the corner of a refectory that had until recently fed more than a hundred people at a sitting.

What has become of the culprits? Most have evaded justice, as have the majority of those responsible for violence against religious minorities across India. In Kandhamal, a pair of fast-track courts was set up to concentrate on cases linked to communal violence. The conviction rate, while higher than the national average, is still low. Statistics from the All India

Christian Council (AICC) and the Human Rights Law Network (HRLN) indicate that by May 2011, of the 115 cases dealt with, 87 had resulted in acquittals and only 28 in convictions. Yet even these bleak statistics give an unduly positive picture, because a high proportion of cases never resulted in litigation in the first place. (In 2009, lawyers in Kandhamal said that of the 3,223 complaints submitted to the police, only 831 had been formally registered – a necessary first step in the legal process.) Observers have also pointed out that conviction rates for the most serious crimes, especially murder and rape, are much lower than for lesser charges. CSW's verdict on the strengths and drawbacks of the legal system is worth quoting, not least for what it tells us about India's bumpy path towards implementing the rule of law:

> While the judicial system in place has been partially successful, it has not addressed adequately the needs created by the contingencies of the situation, including the poverty, illiteracy and fear that are widespread among the victims, and the politically fraught nature of the cases. Many victims or witnesses are reluctant to testify in court for fear of retribution and lack of confidence in the efficacy of the system, or because they have been intimidated, sometimes by mobs outside courtrooms. Some judges have refused to order the protection of witnesses, instead merely notifying the police of alleged cases of intimidation. Lawyers working in the area believe that courts need to be more sympathetic to these problems and that many cases have been thrown out for arbitrary reasons or without taking into account the situation of victims. In practice, many victims and witnesses are heavily dependent on the small number of organisations providing legal aid in Orissa, and cases are much more likely to result in a conviction if the victim or witness is assisted in every step of the process.[16]

Among the results is an abiding climate of fear. The Christians I met in settlements across Kandhamal were almost all scared – several had witnessed the murder of friends or relatives, and all were acquainted with fellow believers who had lost loved ones. A majority said that there were no mechanisms in place to promote reconciliation with Hindus, and that they would in due course face further pressure to abandon their Christian faith. In one village, Christian victims of violence claim that their Hindu neighbours were being trained as paramilitaries by the Sangh Parivar. This allegation could not be verified, but it can justly be described as symptomatic of the baleful conditions faced by a peaceful, upright group of people who ask for little more than the freedom to earn a living and worship unhindered. We squatted down outside a two-room house on a smallholding to hear the story of one woman, a cowed-looking widow in her thirties, whose husband had been fatally stabbed in front of her. By now weeping quietly, she went on to explain the absence of her only son, whom she had felt obliged to send to a boarding school on the other side of India for his safety.

Attempts at reconciliation are nonetheless not wanting. Two bodies, especially, have a remit that includes healing of communal tensions: the National Human Rights Commission and the Orissa State Human Rights Commission. From a Christian point of view, though, these groups need to campaign with more vigour, especially given the leniency towards extremists displayed by the Orissa courts. (A specific case in point centred on the granting of bail in July 2010 to Manoj Pradhan, a BJP member of Orissa's Legislative Assembly, even after his conviction for rioting and causing grievous bodily harm in a fracas involving the death of a local Christian, Bikram Nayak, in August 2008.)

Unsurprisingly, Christians feel they have done their best. Having returned from Orissa's rural interior to the city of Bhubaneswar, our party managed to interview the then Catholic Archbishop, Raphael Cheenath, a heavy, owlish man on the verge of retirement. Leaving me with a sense that his frustration was contained by a complicated mixture of world-weariness and wisdom, he stressed the repugnance felt by many Hindus for the recent communal conflict, and even the regret expressed by some who had stirred it up. The Churches, he suggested, were doing a creditable job of 'de-poisoning the minds of the people by good, healthy contact with them'. The archbishop had long defended the general conduct of mission. 'It is absolutely wrong to assume every conversion to Christianity is by force,' he wrote in 2007. Missionaries are entitled to preach the word of God, he added, and not merely to dispense food aid or medicines. But they have no licence to strong-arm others: 'Our Christian spirituality should be open and welcoming [to] all so that communal harmony can be fostered.' These high-minded sentiments match the findings of the Indian People's Tribunal, an independent human rights group, in 2005: 'The Tribunal's investigations in Phulbani reveal that, overwhelmingly, conversions to Christianity do not occur with the intent to destabilise the Hindu community, or other communities, and that the content and program of church-based education does not foster communal hatred or divisiveness in thought or deed.'[17]

Nevertheless, the challenges are enormous. Attacks on Christians have persisted at a steady rate. In 2010, at the Mondakia relief camp in Kandhamal district, a Hindu extremist attempted to rape a Christian woman, Afasari Nayak. Other Christian refugees managed to rescue her, but her assailant returned with four others that evening (8 February), threatening the Christians with severe consequences if they filed a complaint. The Christians did not report the incident, feeling that they would not be helped by the police, but eventually passed on what had happened to human rights observers. On 20 February, at Bhawanipatna, in Kalahandi district, Hindu extremists objected as a local minister preached in public, and took him to the police station. Although the preacher had previously obtained police permission for his activities, the extremists filed a formal complaint against him. He was then sent to the district jail. On 8 June in Nuapada, extremists forced their way into the home of a Christian, Bhakta Bivar. They removed four Bibles from the building and forced their victim into a local Hindu temple. There they burnt the Bibles, said they would murder him if he did not reconvert to Hinduism, and forced him to eat food that had been sacrificed to Hindu gods. They then dressed him in a saffron robe and allowed him to return home while threatening to kill his family if they remained Christians. In this instance, a complaint to the police led to the arrest of the perpetrators. On 14 October, at a village called Paikamara in Puri district, militants confined three Christian converts in a house, assaulted them, and ordered them to reconvert to Hinduism. The victims, Aswini Sahu, Sanatana Jena, and Amulya Swain, had fled the village several months before the attack amid a tide of anti-Christian feeling after their conversion. They had returned after being told that the atmosphere had improved. The police helped to secure their eventual release from the house.[18]

*

At about the same time as the 2008 attacks in Orissa were unfolding, another tide of violence directed against minorities was flowing through the Dakshina Kannada district of Karnataka, the western Indian state abutting Goa. The targets included all sorts of churchpeople, who were blamed for 'insulting' Hindu deities in a pamphlet allegedly produced by an organisation called the New Life Fellowship Trust (NLFT). This publication was probably a malign hoax. The name 'New Life' on the front cover appeared to have been printed independently; the publisher turned out to be based a long way away in Andra Pradesh; the NLFT denied producing it.

The police responded with a mix of heavy-handedness – a common alternative to indifference – and partiality. Christian protesters against the bloodshed were charged under non-bailable sections of the relevant legislation, while Mahendra Kumar, state convener of the Bajrang Dal, was bailed within a few days. A team from the aid organisation Nazarene Compassionate Ministries visited the region in September of 2008; its report concluded that the violence had been 'well planned'. The document went on to criticise the government for failing to take preventive measures after the violence of the previous month, and the police for clamping down on the legitimate activities of Christian demonstrators.[19]

The Indian government acquitted itself no better than the police. A single-member body, the Justice B.K. Somasekhara Commission of Inquiry, was set up to examine the affair. Its report drew praise from Hindu nationalists – who were absolved of responsibility for the violence – and heavy criticism (including charges of incoherence) from others. For instance, the document concludes that 'there is no basis to the apprehension of Christian practitioners that politicians, BJP, mainstream Sangh Parivar, and State Govt., directly or indirectly, are involved in the attacks', yet it names the Bajrang Dal and other groups, whose membership of the Sangh Parivar is well established, as being responsible for several acts of violence. As CSW notes, 'It also finds that police and district administration were guilty of considerable excesses in a number of cases, but fails to attribute any liability to the state government. Nobody from the state government, and only one member of a Sangh Parivar organisation, was examined by the commission.'[20]

The report also infers that the violence involved retaliation for Christian mission among Hindus – an echo of the general Hindutva narrative. Another senior lawyer, Justice Michael Saldanha, conducted an independent inquiry and delivered a verdict sharply at odds with that of Justice Somasekhara.[21] Saldanha was clear not only that the attacks were pre-planned, and that assaults on churches had taken place in parallel with similar action against Muslim-owned property, but also that the police colluded with Sangh Parivar groups in allowing the mayhem to take place.

Karnataka has recently seen the highest number of attacks on Christians and church property in India. Scores of incidents took place in 2010. On 22 January, for example, at Mundolli village in the Uttara Kannada district, Hindu extremists desecrated a cross next to St Lourdes' Catholic Church. Two days later, at Bidarikere, in the Davangere district, extremists forcibly entered a church rented by the Indian Evangelical Mission during a service. They set light to Christian literature, attacked a pastor, H. Raju, and accused him of forcible conversions. A First Information Report or FIR (the document triggering legal proceedings) was filed at a local police station on 27 January; and three of the perpetrators were arrested. At the same time, in the village of Dudda, in Hassan district, a complaint was filed against two Christians, Sekhar Chandra and his wife, Kala, who had led worship services in their home under the auspices of Calvary Gospel Church. The police reacted by stopping the services; later, the couple were ejected from their house by their landlord with the assistance of Hindutva activists. The Jesus Loves Holy Temple Church was burnt down in the town of Chitradurga on 28 January.

At Gokula, in the Mysore district, over 300 Hindu extremists forcibly entered twenty-two Christian households on 17 February. The intruders physically attacked the occupants, and tried to force them to declare in writing that they had converted to Christianity under duress. Several of the victims required hospital treatment. Some were denied medical attention, however, because the police removed them to the local police station by force. Officers, including an Inspector Nameraj, told the Christians that they should renounce their faith and yield to the extremists' demands. A case has since been registered against the attackers.[22] On 28 February, in Karwar, part of the Uttara Kannada district, a further group of extremists allegedly led by a municipal councillor, Raja Gowda, forced their way into the New Life Fellowship Church. They falsely accused two local Christians, David Lambani and Satish Ambedkar, of forcible conversions. The two men suffered grievous bodily harm and needed hospitalisation. The police registered an FIR against the attackers; no arrests were made.[23]

On 8 August, at Kanakgiri, in Koppal district, around sixty extremists disrupted a prayer meeting led by Pastor John Harris. Members of the congregation were driven out of doors, accused of forcible conversions, and verbally abused in front of a group of journalists. The Christians were then taken to the nearby police station, where their assailants urged that they be detained. In the event, the police released the Christians, but ordered them to stop 'all Christian activities' in the area or risk future arrest. At Mahalingpur, in Bagalkot district, around 200

RSS extremists disrupted the screening of a Christian film on 19 August. They confiscated electronic equipment belonging to a local pastor, Hanok Mahadev Inachi, of the New Apostolic Church. Pastor Inachi was taken to the local police station and not released until the following morning, when he was made to sign a pledge that he would never enter the village again. Several weeks later, at Byappanahalli, in the Bengaluru district, a mob attacked a half-built church. Police arrived in time to prevent the building's complete destruction, but the culprits filed a report accusing Pastor John Babu and other local Christians of engaging in forcible conversion. At the urging of the assailants, the police issued a notice halting construction work on the church and served arrest warrants for the pastor and seven members of his congregation. The Christians have petitioned the courts to clamp down on further attacks of this kind, but building work on the church was suspended.

Karnataka is no more of an isolated case than Orissa. Take the situation in Rajasthan. On 16 January 2010, at Tidi, in Udaipur district, Hindutva activists, allegedly from RSS, marched into a prayer meeting held in a private house. They kicked and punched the Christians present, including women, children, and the pastor, Surajjth Bhagari. Seven Christians needed urgent medical treatment, which the Faith Calvary Ministry arranged at a local private hospital after the government hospital refused to treat them.[24] Extremists then burnt down the Memorial Gypsy Church at Hyderabad, Andhra Pradesh, on 22 January. The pastor, Kumara Nayak, suffered severe burns attempting to put out the blaze. And on the following day, in the town of Shahdol, in Madhya Pradesh, militants interrupted another Christian prayer meeting and took thirty-five members of the congregation to the local police station. There they were harangued and beaten until they agreed to sign false statements alleging that Pastor S.K. Ashawan had bribed them into becoming Christians and forced them to eat beef. The police summoned Pastor Ashawan at midnight and threatened to detain him and cause him physical harm if he did not pay them 100,000 rupees ($2,000). Members of his flock rallied to the pastor's defence and took the case to a higher authority. Mr Ashawan was in due course granted police protection at his church on Sundays.[25]

Another state to have seen sustained problems is Chhattisgarh, west of Orissa. In Dinapur, a town in the Raipur district, around twenty-five militants forced their way into a service at the Believers Church of India on 21 March. They insulted the congregation and confiscated piles of Christian literature, threatening violence if the church members did not leave the area. One member of the congregation, a government worker, was told that she would lose her job unless she returned to the Hindu faith. Police detained the Christians for about three hours and endorsed the extremists' threats.[26]

On 17 April, at Betul in Madhya Pradesh, a dozen or so extremists entered an evening prayer meeting organised by the Evangelical Lutheran Church. Members of the congregation were physically assaulted. Many of them fled, but later realised that their pastor, Amit Gilbert, had not escaped with them. A search was launched; Mr Gilbert's body was later found in the village well. His congregation believe that he had been killed earlier, because there was a large wound on the back of his head and no water in his lungs or stomach. This case has been taken to court.[27] On 6 May, around fifty extremists, apparently from the Bajrang Dal, forced their way into a church in Kanpur, Uttar Pradesh. They attacked Pastor Dalayu Sonam and his wife Shanti, threatened to kill their one-year-old son, and accused them of using the church as cover for a brothel.

The congregation attempted to file an FIR, but were persuaded to desist.[28]

At Haridwar, in Uttarakhand, for several days in mid-August 2010, about 1,500 extremists partially destroyed the 150-year-old Reformed Presbyterian Church despite protestations from Christians that the building had been legally erected. Accompanied by local policemen, the attackers used a bulldozer. They returned on 20 August to destroy the remainder of the building. But by this stage the minister, the Revd Wilson Masih, and a team of his supporters were able to prevent further damage. Police refused to file an FIR for the incident.[29]

As is widely recognised, Muslims have been the chief victims of communal violence in post-Independence India: hundreds of thousands were killed during Partition; and 2,000 people, most of them Muslims, died in riots at Ahmedabad in 2002 after fifty-nine Hindu pilgrims had been burnt to death on a train in Godhra. Muslims are also among the perpetrators of anti-Christian violence in pockets of India. On 4 June 2010, at Muvattupuzha, in the Ernakulam district of Kerala, eight Islamists stopped a car containing a Christian, Professor T.J. Joseph, who was returning from church with his family. They threatened his mother and sister, before amputating Professor Joseph's hand, in retaliation for a question paper he had prepared which contained a reference to the Prophet Muhammad that they judged to be offensive. The policemen investigating this attack themselves received death threats, but six suspects were eventually arrested.[30]

In the summer of 2010, at Shivpora in Kashmir, the Foreigners Registration Officer for Jammu and Kashmir issued a notice to a Catholic priest, Fr Jim Borst, who had run the Good Shepherd Community School there. Fr Borst (a member of the Mill Hill Missionaries, a London-based order) had a valid visa lasting until 2014, and had lived in the area since 1963, but local Muslims accused him of forcible conversions.[31]

The year 2011 saw a repeat of this pattern almost ad nauseam. Ramesh Devda, a 30-year-old pastor, was beaten up by Hindu extremists on 22 April in the Meghnagar district of Madhya Pradesh. The Compass Direct News agency published a photo of Mr Devda on his sickbed with obvious injuries to his face and wrist.[32] A few months later, Christians at Grace Church, in the Dhamtari district of Chhattisgarh, were ordered to stop holding services after complaints from Hindu hardliners. The congregation was warned that the local authorities could not be held responsible for any violence that might arise from its non-compliance.[33] Several similar developments took place at almost the same time in parts of Uttar Pradesh and Karnataka.[34]

Bibles, hymn books, crucifixes and vestments were set on fire during an attack on St Mary's Church, Secunderabad, in Hyderabad, central India, in August 2011.[35] Responding to this assault – directed at the Syro-Malankara community, which is in communion with Rome – the parish priest, Fr John Felix, stated in an open letter to the state authorities that it had all been made possible by 'the inactivity and neglect of the police'.[36] He wrote that proceedings connected with similar attacks between 2004 and 2008 had also been quietly dropped by the security forces. (In July 2004, a mob had abused and threatened to kill a priest and parishioners helping out during the building of their church. In July 2008, two years after the structure had been completed, 250 people, including children and the elderly, were locked inside the building for several hours by a group of pro-Hindutva demonstrators.) Fr Felix added: 'In order to avoid further conflicts . . . we practised forgiveness and love of enemies.' But he also warned that his flock could not be expected to carry on living under constant threat.[37]

The distance Orissa still has to travel became plainer still as the third anniversary of the 2008 attacks drew near. A Baptist pastor, Minoketan (or Michael) Nayak, of Midiakia-Kutipada village in Baliguda, a south-western area of the state, was murdered on the evening of 26 July 2011. He never returned after giving two men a lift by motorbike to a nearby village. His body was found in a pit, with a hole-like wound beneath his ear. When Pastor Nayak's brothers came to collect his corpse, they were told by a village elder that their brother had met with an accident. This struck them as obviously untrue. Yet the police refused to investigate the matter further.[38]

Amid continuing tension across the province, Raphael Cheenath's successor as Archbishop of Bhubaneswar-Cuttack, John Barwa, announced that the anniversary would not be marked publicly. 'Over the past three years, a lot has happened towards reconstruction and dialogue,' the new archbishop told monitors from Aid to the Church in Need. 'My message is clear: we need peace and tranquillity – no more violence, no killing. The Christian faithful have the right to be in Kandhamal. They are growing in faith.' A measure of justice had been obtained over the events of 2008, he said, but 'we are a little discouraged. Lower-ranking officials disturb us, but the higher-ranking ones are trying their best.'[39]

The core argument of many Indian Christians can be readily guessed at. They are not claiming to be blameless in every respect. But they reject allegations that they are predators who force vulnerable people to renounce their religion. Such a model allows no space for seeing a change of faith allegiance as a positive choice. The plangent words of a Catholic priest attacked in Kandhamal in 2008 take us to the heart of the matter: 'I am local. I was born here. I studied here. But now I have become a foreigner.'[40]

9
BURMA

Burma's by-elections in early 2012 are widely judged to have marked a step forward for a country dubbed only shortly beforehand a giant prison without walls. The poll should also be seen in perspective. The National League for Democracy (NLD) won almost all of the 45 contested seats, but there are 664 places in the Burmese Parliament altogether. The ruling party and armed forces remain firmly in control.

This much is familiar to the large audience aware of the country's history of dictatorship, its catastrophic human rights record, and the extremely harsh penalties dealt out to Aung San Suu Kyi and other pro-democracy activists. The treatment of tribal peoples such as the Karen has also drawn international censure. Less widely appreciated is the targeting of people specifically for their religion – although valuable studies of the oppression of Muslims and Buddhists have appeared in recent years.[1] Anti-Christian discrimination has perhaps been the least-noticed problem of all – though in Britain the writer and human rights campaigner Benedict Rogers has done much to adjust the balance, notably through his ground-breaking report 'Carrying the Cross'.[2] Rogers's findings are based on extensive first-hand research among the Chin people on the India–Burma border, the Kachin people on the China–Burma border, the Karen and Karenni on the Thailand–Burma border, and in Rangoon and Mandalay, Burma's two major cities.[3]

In an overview of the country, Rogers notes a paradox about the situation faced by Christians. On the one hand, churches appear to function normally in certain areas. On the other hand, the regime – known by the Orwellian title of the State Peace and Development Council (SPDC) – displays a high level of anti-Christian bias. The main explanation lies in the interlacing of religion and ethnicity. As one Chin Christian woman put it: 'If you are double C – being a Chin and being a Christian – you have nothing in Burma, not a bright future at all.'[4] The statistics bear out her complaint. About 90 per cent of the Chin are Christian, according to the Chin Human Rights Organization (CHRO). The Chin population is reckoned to stand at 1.2 million, but CHRO believes that less than half of this community live in Chin state. About 100,000 reside in Rangoon, while 300,000 are in Kalaymyo, Sagaing Division, and a further 150,000 are clustered in other parts of the same region. At least 100,000 refugees live in India.

Christians form a significant proportion of the population in Kachin, Karen, and Karenni states, and some have taken up arms against the regime. Where this has happened, government clampdowns have been draconian. In cities, the curbing of Christian activity is usually less direct. There may be restrictions on the building of new churches, on the renovation or extension of existing church buildings, and on the setting up of house churches. Openly professing Christians employed in government service find it virtually impossible to get promotion.

The matter has been memorably summed up by Johann Candelin, Goodwill Ambassador of the World Evangelical Fellowship, in a comment recorded by Benedict Rogers that applies to religious oppression in many contexts besides Burma's:

Persecution seems to pass through three phases. The first is disinformation. Disinformation begins more often than not in the media. Through printed articles, radio, television, and other means, Christians are robbed of their good reputation and their right to answer accusations made against them. Without trial, they are found guilty of all kinds of misdemeanours.

The public opinion that easily results from being constantly fed such disinformation will not protect Christians from the next step, which is discrimination. Discrimination relegates Christians to a second-class citizenship with poorer legal, social, political, and economic standing than the majority in the country.

The third stage is persecution, which, once the first two steps have been crossed, can be practised with impunity without normal protective measures taking place. Persecution can arise from the state, the police or military, extreme organisations, mobs, paramilitary groups, or representatives of other religions.[5]

Hostility to Christians does not derive only from secular intolerance. Besides straitjacketing the population in other ways, Burma's rulers also try to impose Buddhism on adherents of other faiths. Since the standard view of Buddhism in the West tends to be even more rose-tinted than that of Hinduism, it will shock many to learn that Buddhism has a darker side – a side that supports and even provokes violence on occasion. The full range of the Buddhist repertoire is well understood by contemporary historians such as Michael Jerryson and Mark Juergensmeyer, editors of the scholarly collection *Buddhist Warfare*.[6] They quote the seventeenth-century Zen Master Takuan:

The uplifted sword has no will of its own, it is all of emptiness. It is like a flash of lightning. The man who is about to be struck down is also of emptiness, and so is the one who wields the sword. None of them [is] possessed of a mind that has any substantiality. As each of them is of emptiness and has no 'mind', the striking man is not a man, the sword in his hands is not a sword and the 'I' who is about to be struck down is like the splitting of the spring breeze in a flash of lighting.[7]

In the same book another scholar, Brian Daizen Victoria, traces a direct link between Takuan's writings and the 'Soldier-Zen' model used for military training during the Second Sino-Japanese War (1937–1945) in which the genocide of 20 million Chinese took place. Victoria also points a finger of blame at D.T. Suzuki (1870–1966), the leading exponent of Zen to Western audiences during the past century, who endorsed the 'unity of Zen and the sword'.

The militarism of Takuan and Suzuki is not to be dismissed as exceptional. Among the more striking pieces of evidence for this are the texts that reanimate and transplant the Buddha into startling situations – including the *Heap of Jewels* sutra, in which he is threatened with a sword by his disciple, Manjushri. The Buddha is represented as praising his acolyte on the grounds that 'there isn't any more of me than there is of anyone else. If Manjushri were to kill the Buddha it would have been a right killing.' There is also the notorious case of the ninth-century Chinese monk Yi-hiuan, who urged those he addressed to 'kill everything you encounter, internally as well as externally! Kill the Buddha! Kill your father and mother! Kill your closest friends!'.

None of this it to imply for a moment that Buddhists speak with one voice. (To cite two obvious examples: the non-violent witness of Aung San Suu Kyi has been deeply informed by her Buddhist faith, and large numbers of monks have taken heroic stands against the regime.) A central conclusion of *Buddhist Warfare* is that principles such as 'emptiness' have been abused for a long time, and that Buddhist opinion-formers bear a heavy responsibility for allowing the rot to spread. Buddhist chauvinism is evidently an exploitable factor in Burma's troubles. It has been appropriated with relative ease by the generals in their drive for uniformity.

They have this much in common with the preachers of Hindutva in India. But unlike Hindutva activists, Burma's leaders are not trying to erase evidence of a long Christian history. Maung Nao, probably Burma's first convert, sought baptism in 1819. Tantalisingly, the first generation of Karen Christians testified that certain biblical passages resembled stories that had survived for generations through oral transmission, and which they ascribed to a lost document known as the 'Golden Book'. Some of these stories bear a marked resemblance to parts of Genesis: the Karen believed in a monotheistic deity whom they called Y'wa – a name reminiscent of Yahweh, one of the Hebrew words for God. They even held that human beings had become alienated from their maker by eating forbidden fruit. As an old Karen poem puts it:

> Y'wa formed the world originally.
> He appointed food and drink.
> He appointed the 'fruit of trial'.
> He gave detailed orders.
> Mu-kaw-lee deceived two persons.
> He caused them to eat the fruit of the tree of trial.
> They obeyed not; they believed not Y'wa ...
> When they ate the fruit of trial,
> They became subject to sickness, ageing and death.[8]

The first Karen convert was Ko Tha Byn, a reformed criminal, who was baptised in 1828 and went on to exert a profound influence over his tribe. By the middle of the nineteenth century, about 12,000 Karen had become Christians and were launching missions of their own among neighbouring tribes. Subsequent persecutions are marks of their success, as well as of the anti-colonial sentiment stoked up by the three Anglo-Burmese wars of the 1820s, 1850s, and 1880s.

The extensive maltreatment of Christians during this period is set out by Courtney Anderson in *To the Golden Shore*, his biography of Adoniram Judson, one of the first missionaries in Burma. Judson died in 1850, leaving sixty-three churches and solid foundations for the charitable and educational ventures of his successors. Missionaries developed a roman script for the Chin language and translated the Bible into several Burmese dialects, besides engaging in philanthropy. Dr San C. Po, a prominent Karen leader of the early twentieth century, wrote: 'The educational, social, and spiritual progress of the Karen has been due, to a very large extent, to the missionaries who have so faithfully and sympathetically worked among and with them. The Karen are not ashamed or afraid to proclaim to the world publicly or in private that they owe what progress and advancement they have made to the missionaries.'[9] Much the same could be said of the Chin people.

The hostility of Burma's rulers towards Christians persisted after independence in 1948, when the country enjoyed a period of fragile democracy. On Christmas Eve 1948, a congregation of eighty people was slaughtered, reportedly by Burmese militias, when hand grenades were thrown into a church at Palaw, Mergui district, in the south-east of the country. Gifts that had been hung on Christmas trees were looted by hostile villagers, and as attacks on the Karen began in some places on 23 December, many of the victims were unable to celebrate Christmas at all. At least 200–300 Karens were killed in neighbouring villages. Further attacks occurred in January 1949. Fighting broke out on the streets of Insein, the Karen quarter in Rangoon, and homes were destroyed. By 1949, the Karens' uprising had begun in earnest.[10]

U Nu, the country's leader at that time, sought to make Buddhism the official state religion in 1961 – a move that sharply increased nationalistic feeling among Christians. The Kachin, for example, founded the Kachin Independence Organisation (KIO), beginning an armed struggle that ended with a ceasefire in 1994. Burma succumbed to military dictatorship after a coup in 1962. Rejecting federalism for ethnic nationalities, the new ruler, General Ne Win, cracked down on church life. All foreign missionaries were expelled four years later.

The UN Special Rapporteur for human rights in Burma has accused the SPDC of crimes against humanity and war crimes during the intervening decades. In the east of the country, the regime has been waging offensives against civilians leading to the displacement of hundreds of thousands of people, and also involving rape, torture, and forced labour.

The Chin people, who remain very poor materially, still face persecution for their political activism, ethnicity and religion. A variety of organisations – the UN, Human Rights Watch, the US State Department, and the Chin Human Rights Organization – have given chapter and verse on the most egregious crimes against the Chin.[11] At the same time, these people are also denied access to basic health and education. The broader situation is better known: on 7 November 2010, the government staged elections that Burma's population and the international community widely saw as a charade. Aung San Suu Kyi, who had by then spent fifteen years in detention, was barred from taking part, and her party, the National League for Democracy (NLD), was declared illegal after its decision not to contest the poll.

Some of the destruction of churches in Karen and Karenni states can be ascribed to Burma's wider ethnic conflicts. But observers have also uncovered evidence that churches can be targets, while Buddhist pagodas or monasteries are left standing. In 1996, the Karen Human Rights Group published a collection of interviews exposing the regime's anti-Christian agenda. One interviewee said:

> In our village, there are no problems between Karen and Burmese [civilians], but all are afraid of the SLORC [the previous name for the SPDC]. The SLORC is trying to divide Karen and Burmese, Christian and Buddhist . . . A SLORC major went into every village [in the area] and ordered the villagers to donate money to build a pagoda in each village, and he said 'Christians must disappear'. Also, there is a village called Padauk Gone which is completely Christian, and there a pagoda was built just in front of the church, only about ten yards from the church building. At the ceremony to mount the pagoda with the *hti* [the ceremonial umbrella-shaped ornament crowning every pagoda] the Christians had to dance *doan* [a popular Karen traditional dance]. There is not a single Buddhist in that village. If a Christian church seeks to make repairs, it must ask permission from [the authorities], and construction of new church buildings is not permitted. As for the [regional] Christian convention, previously anybody could go but now only five people per village are permitted.[12]

This example is representative of many collected by human rights groups, as are tales of the destruction of churches. On 5 May 1995, for example, soldiers of the SPDC and members of a militia, the DKBA, burnt down the church at Bwa Der village, south of the south-eastern town of Papun. Witnesses reported that the church's bell was removed and taken to a nearby pagoda. Two years later, villagers said that at least ten churches had been burnt down in the region. In 1998, DKBA troops posted signs in Karen in front of the village churches of Pah Dta Lah, Hee Po Der, and Mah Bpee in Ler Doh township, reading 'Anyone who comes to this church on Sunday we will shoot dead.' According to the Karen Human Rights Group, 'as a result none of the Christians in these three villages worship any longer on Sundays'.[13]

Further attacks took place in Karen state around the turn of the millennium – at Tee Tha Blu in Dooplaya district, in 2002, for instance, and at Kwe Doh Kaw, in Mon township, in 2003.[14] The year 2006 brought forth the worst offensive against the Karen in nearly a decade. More than 25,000 people were internally displaced; civilians were shot at point-blank range; some were beheaded. A similar pattern of events has unfolded in Karenni state, where many villagers live in temporary camps because of forced population movements. Many of these people are Catholics. Their clergy have tried hard to supply them with food, medicines, and blankets. Yet time and again, the authorities have thwarted such humanitarian work, forbidding the construction of makeshift churches.[15]

One of the state's leading Baptist pastors, Saw Stephen, has also paid an extremely costly price for his witness. He puts his finger on the source of the problem as follows:

> The Burmese government is anti-Christian. They are afraid that Christianity will bring in the Western ways to Burma. It will ruin the Burmese culture, they say. They see Christianity as a Western religion. It is the main religion of the West, they say, which is why they hate it and are afraid of it. We have been told by the junta leaders that the people of Burma have to be careful about Christians; the Western policies can come in and overtake us, they say.[16]

The SPDC destroyed Saw Stephen's church in 1999. 'They captured me and took me to their military office,' he reported. 'They put me under house arrest for four months in a small room. I could not contact my family.' After his release, he was sent to another church, with a 600-strong congregation: this, too, was closed down by the SPDC. 'On 5 November 2002,' he said, 'the military government came into the village and ordered us to move . . . The soldiers [then] destroyed our church.' Saw Stephen has spent much of the past few years on the run.

In Chin state, life is harder for Christians than anywhere else in Burma. Pastors report that it is almost impossible to build a church. Places of worship have been destroyed systematically; crosses – long erected on hilltops and beside roads by local people as emblems of Christianity – have been pulled down. The destruction of crosses began in around 1990. Since then, in the words of a Chin campaigner, Salai Bawi Lian Mang, 'almost every cross in all of the nine townships in Chin state has been destroyed by the regime'.[17] Many of these crosses have been replaced with Buddhist pagodas and statues of Buddhist monks. Other tactics repeatedly deployed against Christians by the SPDC include the disruption of church services, assaults on pastors, and the use of clerics and other senior members of the community as forced labourers – especially on Sundays – to build pagodas and other monuments. Benedict Rogers gives many examples of this practice. In February 2005, he writes that twenty villages in Chin state were forced by the SPDC to contribute funds and labour for the construction of a Buddhist monastery. Each household had to donate 5,000 kyats ($3.95), though most were Christian.[18]

Rogers charts further aspects of 'cultural genocide' faced by the Chin. His prime exhibit is 'OB', a mixture of methyl and ethyl alcohol that the SPDC brought to Chin state in large quantities from the early 1990s onwards. Highly addictive, this drink would be too toxic to sell in the West; it is also extremely cheap. As people became hooked on OB, they also turned to crime, leading to what one Chin Christian described as 'the breakdown of body, mind, spirit, and society'. Church attendance among the young has fallen in consequence.

Many of the examples of strife cited in this chapter date from slightly further back in time. That Christians have continued to feel the heat of harassment and persecution is sharply illustrated by the testimony of a Chin pastor in 2010:

In Matupi, in southern Chin State, the people are uneducated. They dress very simply. As most are not educated, the soldiers force us to do whatever they want. The government does not allow us to construct new churches, but they also don't allow us to have meetings outside the church. I want to establish a children's home. The government has a children's home but it is only for Buddhists. There is no chance for Christians. I am now helping some orphans – most of them are children whose parents cannot take care of them, they are busy with their farm work, so they left their kids at home. Some give them to the Buddhist children's home. But at the Buddhist children's home, the monks ask the parents for an agreement that the children become Buddhist. Then they force the parents also to become Buddhist. They enrol them into Buddhism. The monks are connected with the military. The government wants to extend Buddhism. I would like to have a children's home providing children with Christian guidance, but I cannot get financial assistance.

I was arrested three times. The first time was in 2005. I was at home when the military came. They didn't tell me anything. They just took me to the jungle, for three days, made me work as a porter in the jungle, carrying their arms, and then released me. They asked me what I was doing, and I just told them about my church work. In February 2008, I was arrested a second time and held in a military camp. I had gone to the next village for a funeral, and got into a discussion with some monks about the Bible. An argument began and people reported it to the authorities, and I was arrested. I was held for one week, then released by the help of others. In November 2008, I was arrested again, while preaching in a village. The military were trying to catch Chin National Front (CNF) soldiers, and they entered the village, saw me, were suspicious because I was the only stranger in the village, and arrested me. They asked me questions and beat me three times with bamboo, and then handcuffed me and took me to Matupi District Prison.

In June 2009, my wife was arrested while I was away. She was held for two days, handcuffed, along with one other lady and a man. She was given no reason. I have a lot of experience of forced portering. Sometimes the military comes during a church meeting and asks us to do portering, or to give them chickens or pigs. Currently many villages are contributing forced labour for the construction of a road from the village to Matupi, which is 25 miles [long] and at least 6ft wide. They have to work three months a year, provide their own food, and all the materials for the road construction.[19]

Christians and their churches continued to be attacked in 2011, even as the regime spoke of reform. Two illustrations from Kachin state are symptomatic of an abiding problem. On 16 October, troops seized control of a Catholic church in Namsan Yang village, Waimaw township, where twenty-three people had gathered for worship. Live rounds were fired at some of those who took refuge in the Lady chapel. Jamgma Awng Li, the parish priest's forty-nine-year-old assistant, tried to negotiate with the soldiers, but was beaten to the ground with a rifle butt. Both the Catholic church, and the Baptist chapel on the other side of the village, were destroyed.[20] A few weeks later, on 6 November, soldiers attacked the Assemblies of God Church in Muk Chyik village, also in the Waimaw township. The congregation were ejected from the building; donation boxes were reportedly looted. At least fifty members of the congregation were taken away to work as forced porters for the army. Worse still, the pastor, the Revd Yajawng Hkawng, was tortured and later admitted to hospital.[21]

And in mid-March 2012, troops in the Bhamo District ransacked the Baptist chapel in Pang Mu village, claiming that the building was being used by the Kachin Independence Army.[22] At the same time, a conference of 1,000 Evangelical Christians in the Matupi township was disrupted by soldiers. Delegates were threatened at gunpoint, even though the organisers had obtained official permission for the gathering.

*

As in India and elsewhere, a small amount of evidence exists to suggest that Christians do not always help themselves. House-church congregations have been known to antagonise their Buddhist neighbours by an overenthusiastic style of worship. When the Full Gospel Church and its network of daughter churches were closed down in Rangoon in 2005, a Baptist pastor based in that city told CSW:

> The problem over the past two or three years has been that the Full Gospel Church, which does not have its own buildings, but rents buildings from other people, worships very loudly. They play drums, jump and dance – and so many neighbours have complained. They have held all-night prayer meetings where they pray and worship very loudly. Almost the whole city complained. When people complain, the authorities acted and closed these churches down.[23]

Rogers is nevertheless surely right in inferring that 'the pressure on Christians from the regime is overwhelmingly part of the regime's deliberate policy. And it is time for the international community – political bodies, media organisations, and the Church – to recognise this and respond.'[24]

The regime's anti-church policies can be ascribed to causes we have already identified – the internationalist outlook of Christians, their commitment to education and good works – and, of course, their proclamation of a kingdom not of this world. We have now noted many times that hardship can simply strengthen the resolve of the oppressed. A Chin pastor who recently chose to return to his people, despite the danger, said: 'Please let the world know we want freedom. Freedom, just freedom. Freedom to speak, freedom to worship, freedom to praise God, freedom to work, freedom to learn, freedom to write. Just freedom.'[25]

10

CHINA

I remained in the prison in Haifeng until August of that year. Nineteen of us prisoners were transported by truck to the Municipal Prison #2. We were held there for a month while waiting to be transferred to northeastern China, in Manchuria. There were one thousand two hundred of us prisoners, all packed into a special train that brought us directly to the province of Liaoning, to a place near Dairen. I was shut up in a cattle car, together with so many prisoners that there was no place to sit. The only ventilation possible came through a few little holes. The wagon was sealed from the outside. For the four days and nights that it took to reach the northeast, we never saw the sun. In Jingzhou, a city of the province of Liaoning, they made six hundred prisoners get off the train, while the other six hundred continued the journey to another labour camp. I was in the first group, and my new prison was a machine factory. In my section there were around two thousand prisoners. We had to produce screws, metal plates and tires. I was rather lucky, if I can say so, that I had been sent to an industrial prison and not to the agricultural labor camps.

In the farming camps the living conditions were primitive; the inmates lived in straw huts without any necessities at all. Moreover the work was grueling and the hours simply incredible. Someone who was sentenced to more than twelve years of hard labour was not sent to the farming camps, because he would be dead before completing his sentence. In the farming camps there was only cold water for bathing and a little sponge, whereas in the industrial labour camps there was hot water for a bath every two weeks. And so I was quite set, condemned to a life sentence from which only death would free me, condemned for my whole life to an endless punishment in the cold of northeastern China, far from the balmy climate of my home in the south of the country.

A terrible sensation went through me. While I was a prisoner in Haifeng, awaiting trial, I used to think about the sentence which they would have inflicted on me. I wanted the trial to be concluded quickly, because I thought that at most they would give me three or four years in prison. Instead the verdict was the death penalty. Then, when this sentence was commuted to long-term imprisonment, I understood that the Communist Party had devised their plan to exterminate the Church once and for all and that I was a victim of that plan. The real reason for my sentence was precisely the extermination of the Catholic Church and not the crimes of which they were accusing me.[1]

These words, at once tender and searing, come from the pen of Fr John Huang Yongmu, a Catholic priest who began a twenty-year prison term in 1958 and later produced a diary of the ordeal. As the quoted extract suggests, his is the work of an uncommonly generous spirit: clear-eyed about the maelstrom into which China was plunged by Mao, yet free of rancour. Nor is the document unique. Fr John's memoirs are similar in tone to those of other venerated figures, including Fr Francis Tan Tiande from Canton, who was sentenced to an indefinite period of hard labour in 1953, and did not regain his freedom for three decades.[2]

A giant of a slightly later generation is Matthias Duan, one of the longest-serving bishops of the twentieth century, who oversaw the diocese of Wangxian, on the Upper Yangtze, from

1945 until his death in 2001. During the Cultural Revolution, he was jailed, paraded through the streets, and sent to forced labour in the river docks for several years. At one point, some Red Guards dragged a statue of Mary from his cathedral and demanded that he hack it with a hammer. He refused, and for a time it looked as though they would kill him.

As China itself has changed so, too, has the shape of Chinese Christianophobia. It is almost a truism that memories of the Church's near demise during the Cultural Revolution must now be supplemented by a grasp of this process in reverse: a spiritual renaissance since Mao's death sometimes called the greatest religious revival in history.[3] The swinging pendulum points in turn to clashing official perceptions of Christianity and its representatives as both cherished and unwelcome influences.

The impact of the West for both good and ill has been momentous in this large corner of the world. After the Tiananmen Square massacre in 1989, the Chinese government introduced its Patriotic Education Campaign to reinculcate school pupils with ideas about the crimes of Western imperialist 'devils'. Though hardly objective, the producers of this material had deep seams to mine. In 1832, officers of the East India Company had marched into the regional administrator's office in Shanghai, demanding that the terms of trade between China and Europe be freed up. Several years later, Britain provoked the First Opium War, terrorising Shanghai's civilian population in the process. Similar atrocities followed in the Second Opium War of 1856–60, and during the crushing of the Boxer rebellion by a large international alliance forty years after.[4]

Less widely recognised is the staggering capacity of the Chinese for harming one another – about 20 million people perished during the Taiping Rebellion of 1850–64, for example, when the followers of Hong Xiuquan, self-styled younger brother of

Christ, rose up in support of their leader. The benign effects of the Christian presence in China are equally disregarded. During the late sixteenth and early seventeenth centuries, Matteo Ricci and other Jesuit pioneers revolutionised the Chinese understanding of mathematics, astronomy, and geography. Three hundred years later, British missionaries in the so-called treaty ports immunised the inhabitants on a wide scale, just as British engineers laid China's first telegraph lines and railways.

These and other pieces of evidence are well marshalled by Victor Goossaert and David A. Palmer in their 2011 study *The Religious Question in Modern China*.[5] Of special relevance are the examples of Sun Yat-sen (1866–1925), the revolutionary founder of the first Chinese Republic, and his successor, Chiang Kai-shek (1887–1975), both of whom were Christian converts. For men such as these, 'superstition' in the form of Buddhism, Taoism, and practices such as feng shui and divination, was to be swept away, but the new rulers' targets did not include Christianity, which they considered to be compatible with science and a unifying political force. (Many in Sun's and Chiang's circles were strongly anti-Christian, but the spiritual allegiance of the two men was striking nonetheless.)

Some elements in China's early twentieth-century transformation were clearly cultural. Astrology-based techniques for measuring time were replaced by the Gregorian calendar in 1912. A host of traditional practices were abolished. But Goossaert and Palmer are clear that in the eyes of figures such as Sun and Chiang, 'the decline and decay of China were due to idolatry, while the strength, prosperity, and higher civilization of America were due to the Christian religion. Christianity, for them, could bring dignity and equality to China.'[6] Church life blossomed steadily during this period, notably across the indigenous bodies, especially the True Jesus Church, the Jesus family, and the Little Flock. It is thought that between 1906 and 1949, the Protestant community swelled from 180,000 to almost 1 million; the Catholic community from 500,000 to 3 million.

After 1949, the chief aim of the Communists was to neuter church life, rather than abolish it entirely. To start with, they sought to do away with Confucianism, temple-cults, and other practices they judged to be relics of a feudal mindset. Foreign missionaries were told to leave, and the main faith groups – Buddhists, Taoists, Muslims, and Christians – categorised under the so-called Three-Self basis (self-governing, self-financing, self-propagating). Then as now, Protestantism and Catholicism were counted as separate religions. As well as the Protestant–Catholic divide, a further subdivision would later develop between registered (or official) Churches and unregistered (underground) Churches that refused to accept participation within the Three-Self structures.

The scale of the cataclysm that engulfed China under Mao is now widely grasped: Jasper Becker (author of *Hungry Ghosts*) and Frank Dikötter (in *Mao's Famine*) estimate that 45 million people died between 1958 and 1962 alone. The Dalai Lama fled to India in 1959, after the Chinese abrogated an agreement allowing religious autonomy in Tibet. Religion was proclaimed to be a matter of class struggle during the Cultural Revolution. Christian clergy were purged. Re-education officers were sent to villages across the country to wipe out practices deemed 'capitalistic' (an umbrella term that included religious rituals); then came the 'Smash the Four Olds' campaign – the quartet in question being old customs, culture, habits, and ideas.

Some observers concluded from this that the apparatus of faith had been entirely swept away in the world's most populous nation.[7] Others, including Goossaert and Palmer, identify 'a parallel trend of political sacralization' in Communist policies.[8] Others again judge that religious activity spread below the radar on a substantial scale, despite all appearances to the contrary. Whatever the exact truth of this, water returned to the desert during the reigns of Deng Xiaoping and his successors, Jiang Zemin and Hu Jintao. Registered Catholics now number about 5.7 million; the Vatican puts the number of underground Catholics at 8 million. About 23 million Protestants belong to state-registered bodies, while unregistered Protestants are the largest Christian group of all – perhaps numbering between 50 million and 60 million.[9] Looser institutional structures have worked to Protestantism's advantage in this regard. Religious entrepreneurs running their own show and already offering hope, faith, and healing to the religiously unenfranchised from Peru to Manila could now set their sights on Beijing, Shanghai, and other Chinese cities. Even non-Pentecostals have been inspired by that tradition's emphasis on what the Christian writer Lian Xi, author of *Redeemed by Fire*, has called 'a potent mix of evangelistic fervor, biblical literalism, charismatic ecstasies, and a fiery eschatology not infrequently tinged with nationalistic exuberance'.

The volatility of this mixture helps to account for the harsher conditions that Christians are facing once more, particularly since the 2008 Olympics, in the lead up to which the Chinese Communist Party (CCP) had talked the talk about progress on human rights in the face of international criticism. On the one hand, Communist high-ups believe as clearly as their early twentieth-century forebears that the mixture of industry and stability common in Protestant societies, can be harnessed to boost wealth and social cohesion – Christianity is seen as both the medicine and the opium of the people. On the other hand, the authorities have an uneasy sense that Christian activism can bring down the mighty from their seats.

The CCP is particularly nervous about the extensive contacts between Chinese Christians and Christians in other countries. Thousands of missionaries from overseas operate in China, most of them putative students or language teachers, and many – Americans, above all – see the upcoming superpower as a potential recruit in the battle of ideas against radical Islam. The CCP's current aversion to Catholicism springs from the Vatican's demand to control the appointment of bishops, and its recognition of Taiwan. (In fairness, the antipathy also dates back to the 1930s and 1940s, when Catholic bishops aligned themselves strongly with Chiang Kai-shek's Kuomintang Party during the Civil War against the Communists, excommunicated Catholics who joined the CCP, recognised the Japanese annexation of Manchuria, and continued to support the 'unequal treaties' that were relics of the Opium Wars.) In a letter to Chinese Catholics in 2007,[10] Pope Benedict called on the underground and official Churches to unite, so that all Catholics in China could come into communion with Rome. He was seeking to pour balm on a wound: tensions between parts of the two Catholic communities have been simmering for decades, though the situation cannot be summed up easily. In practice, the difference between the two groups is blurred, especially given the beginnings of an understanding between the Vatican and the Chinese government, evident from around the turn of the millennium, whereby the Holy See's tacit approval of episcopal appointments in the Chinese Catholic Patriotic Association (CCPA) was sought. As we shall see, however, modest steps forward can easily be reversed.

The background to relations between underground and official Catholics is complicated. During the 1950s, the Communists tried to force all Catholics to renounce their allegiance to Rome. A few went over to the government side. The great majority refused to do so. It was this stance that caused so many to be jailed or martyred. Yet when religious policy was relaxed around 1980, the government reconciled itself to the fact that congregations in reopened churches were publicly praying for the Pope. (Few, if any, Catholic churches omit these prayers today.) Certainly, the government-recognised Catholic bishops' conference affirms the status of popes as spiritual heads of the Church on earth. While the government allows such a view to be expressed, however, it still jibs at the direct exercise of papal authority on Chinese soil. The situation was summed up by Audrey Donnithorne, a veteran China-watcher, in an article published around the turn of the millennium arguing that there can be legitimate differences of opinion among Catholics over the best course of conduct:

> In the 1950s, the choice was clear-cut. In the last two decades it has not been so simple. Is it preferable to reach an accommodation with the Government and maximise the pastoral opportunities thus provided, or to oppose the Government and choose a riskier but perhaps less complicated life? It is a matter on which good Catholics can disagree and on which decisions can rightly be made one way or the other in the light of local conditions – and, in a country as large as China, local conditions vary enormously. This explains why in some parts of the country both 'open' [official] and 'underground' Catholics are found while in others, such as south-west China, most Catholics worship publicly.[11]

Tensions remain, however. I cannot say anything that might shed light on the identities of my underground Catholic interviewees, but the testimony of one young man in particular is representative. Events had chiselled him into early maturity: he didn't just weigh his words because we were speaking in

English. 'My grandfather was baptised in Ho Pei province in the 1940s,' he told me.

> During my childhood [the 1980s], we could only go to Mass five or six times a year – usually at midnight or very, very early in the morning at a neighbour's house. By the early 1990s, there were more priests to serve us. These men tended to be strong in faith but not well trained. . .
>
> The basic problem with many bishops in the official Church is that they don't have the courage to defend the interests of the Church. An example is Bishop Paul Jiang Tao-ran [of Shijiazhuang, south-west of Beijing], whose diocese owned valuable land around his cathedral. The government wanted this land, and the bishop sold it for a low price. My own bishop, Augustine Kia, has now been in prison for many years. Nearly twenty! Some of the official bishops are very different – they seem weak and ambitious . . .
>
> I am not very optimistic about the near future. Evangelisation has only recently been made a priority by the official bishops, and inter-Catholic tensions have consumed too much of our energy.

Beijing's nervousness has been heightened by the resolution of other oppressed communities, notably Buddhists in Tibet, who continue to demonstrate against Han colonisation; Uighur Muslims in the western province of Xinjiang; and members of Falungong, the movement based on a *qigong* form of meditation, who have evolved into anti-corruption campaigners and faced ferocious sanctions for their pains. Taoists and Buddhists, who collectively number about a quarter of the Chinese population, have both experienced large-scale revivals marked by the rebuilding of temples and the reintroduction of pilgrimages.

Goossaert and Palmer conclude that China is 'a huge religious laboratory in which all kinds of spirituality . . . have become possible in a massive cauldron, an expanding grey area that largely falls beyond direct legal and institutional control'.[12] They go on to propose three avenues along which China might develop: those of Western-style secularism; a reassertion of the Qing model under which the state was arbiter of religious orthodoxy; and official atheism, with religion harnessed to promote patriotism. In fact, as the journalist Simon Scott Plummer has observed in a magisterial essay on Chinese religion,[13] all three tendencies are already in evidence.

*

So much for the general picture. Two points that should stand out from a more detailed discussion are that the treatment of Christians and other faith groups can still involve gross abuses of their human rights, and an obvious breach of Article 36 of the Chinese constitution, which stipulates that 'citizens of the People's Republic of China enjoy freedom of religious belief'. The reality is that beliefs may be manifested only in particular ways, as spelt out in recent fresh blueprints, the Regulations on Religious Affairs (2005) and the National Human Rights Plan (2009). The other broad consideration of note is that religious freedoms vary considerably from region to region.

There are still five officially recognised faiths (Buddhism, Taoism, Islam, Protestantism, and Catholicism). Yet only citizens engaging in 'normal religious activities' are guaranteed liberty to practise their religion, leading to an arbitrary definition of what constitutes 'normal' activities.[14] Each faith group has a state-sanctioned body under which it is governed. For Protestants, this remains the Three-Self Patriotic Movement (TSPM); for Catholics, the Catholic Patriotic Association; and for Muslims, the Islamic Association of China (IAC). These groups are subject to varying restrictions – over the selection and training of religious personnel; the location, purchase, and renovation of venues; publications; finances; teaching on certain topics; relations with co-religionists abroad; and other matters. Restrictions are placed on working with certain classes of persons, including those aged under eighteen. Anyone publicly professing religious beliefs that do not match those of the five recognised faith traditions is therefore deemed to be in breach of the law. This automatically means that certain forms of peaceful activity are off-limits.

Official bodies lack the resources to cater for their membership. In Beijing, with its population of more than 17 million, there were only a dozen state-approved Protestant churches in 2010–2011. What is more, while in the capital many, but not all, unofficial house churches are able to function with little interference from the authorities, in other areas, members of unofficial groups face harassment, fines, confiscation of property, detention, and, in some cases, imprisonment or torture. Fresh regulations introduced in 2005 renewed the drive to enforce registration of all congregations, although in practice it is extremely difficult, if not impossible, for a Protestant church to register outside the TSPM system. The printing and distribution of religious literature is tightly controlled. The government allows the production of a limited number of Bibles, for example, but this is not enough to keep up with demand, particularly in the rural house churches. Christians who have produced their own Bibles or religious materials have been arrested, fined, and imprisoned.

The idea of a correspondence between economic progress and progress on human rights thus requires heavy qualification. More Christians are imprisoned in China than in any other country in the world. It is estimated that almost 2,000 members of house churches were arrested during the twelve months after May 2004 alone.[15] 'Troublemakers' typically still face several years' labour in 're-education' camps without anything remotely resembling due process, because public security officials have the right to imprison people for up to three years without trial.

And China's general human rights record remains very poor. The bravest critics of the regime include the Nobel Prize-winning activist Liu Xiaobo, who was given an eleven-year prison sentence in 2009 for 'inciting subversion of state power'. A rather less well known but also exceptionally courageous campaigner is the human rights lawyer Gao Zhisheng. Though hailed as 'one of the country's ten best lawyers' in 2001 by China's Ministry of Justice, he has since been sent to jail and tortured by the secret police for taking on human rights cases, especially those involving medical malpractice and dispossessed landowners seeking compensation. He has also defended Falungong practitioners and underground Christians. In his memoirs, *A China More Just*, he criticised the Communist Party for employing 'the most savage, most immoral, and most illegal means to torture our mothers, torture our wives, torture our children, and torture our brothers and sisters'. Renouncing his membership of the party had been the proudest day of his life, he added. In December 2011, he received a three-year prison sentence for 'violating the terms of his probation',[16] despite having been in custody for much of the previous period. He was not seen in public at this time, feeding fears that the episodes of torture he had already faced during earlier spells in prison were being repeated.

Further views of a dark landscape are easy to come by. A highly respected Catholic bishop, James Su Zhimin, who had already endured almost three decades of imprisonment, was incarcerated in October 1997 after appealing for freedom of worship for his fellow Christians. His whereabouts remained unknown for six years until he was seen under guard in a hospital in Hebei province at the end of 2003. Underground Christians are most at risk of torture. Gong Shenglang, a leading Protestant pastor who heads the large South China Church, was repeatedly tortured after his arrest in 2001. More than 300 members of his flock were detained in 2004. At about the same time (18 June 2004), Jiang Zongxiu, a thirty-four-year-old Protestant woman, died of her injuries under police interrogation.[17] On 4 July 2006, Zhang Rongliang, leader of the 10 million-strong China for Christ Church, an umbrella house-church body, was sentenced to seven and a half years in prison. His 'crime' was to have owned devotional literature and videos.

As mentioned, the situation became a little easier under Jiang Zemin. The deteriorating climate now in evidence owes a good deal to the more hardline attitudes of Hu Jintao (in office from 2005 to 2012). The backward move has been especially notable on the Catholic front. We have already noted that episcopal appointments were more or less jointly recognised by the Vatican and the Chinese government between 2000 and 2010. But in December 2010, state-registered bishops were forced to elect Fr Joseph Guo Jincai as Bishop of Chengde and president of the country's college of Catholic bishops. Before the ordination ceremony, which was conducted without papal approval, underground bishops and clergy were forcibly taken from their homes to take part. Some were offered financial incentives to attend. (This situation echoed earlier crises in relations between Beijing and the Vatican, including that of November 2006, when the Chinese Catholic Patriotic Association (CCPA) ordained two bishops: Joseph Ma Yinglin in the south-western province of Yunan, and Joseph Liu Xinhong in Wuhu, Anhui province.) The move was condemned as 'very disloyal' to Rome by the Archbishop of Hong Kong, Cardinal Joseph Zen Ze-kiun, in an interview with the BBC Chinese service. In mid-2012, several

Catholic priests were still being held in prison or forced labour camps. Up to six bishops were under house arrest. Of these, the whereabouts of two are still unknown after many years – seventy-six-year-old Bishop James Su Zhimin of Bading, who disappeared in 1996, and Bishop Cosmas Shi Enxiang, eighty-seven, of Yixian, who vanished from view in 2001.

Among many other notable cases is that of seventy-five-year-old Bishop Julius Jia Zhiguo, Bishop of Zhending, in Hebei province. Revered by his fellow underground Catholics, he has spent over two decades in prison for his consistent refusal to join the CCPA. In what is thought to be retaliation for this, an orphanage for a hundred disabled children that the bishop set up in his diocese has been threatened with closure. In December 2010, the police tried to force him to sign a document authorising handover of the orphans to the district. He refused and is reported to be under constant harassment from the authorities in consequence. He remains under 'residential detention', namely house arrest, in which his movements, visitors, and communications are severely limited.

Recent editions of *Persecuted and Forgotten?* give numerous examples of human rights abuses reflecting China's journey backwards. In March 2009, Fr Francis Gao Jianli, forty, of the Catholic diocese of Fengxiang in the northern province of Shaanxi, was beaten in connection with comments he made about a plot of land containing a former church which was seized by the authorities. The mayor had invited Fr Gao to visit the town hall to discuss the land in Xiangong parish. After a heated debate, the mayor called in two men, who beat up the priest so badly that he had to be taken to hospital. The land had been seized during the Cultural Revolution to build a factory. The plant closed down some years ago, and under Chinese law those who have rightful title to property can claim it back if it is not being used. There had been positive discussions between the Church and the district government's Property Management Office until the mayor decided to take the land and turn it into a garden.[18]

In the eastern province of Shandong in August 2009, a registered church in Rizhao City had a graduation ceremony disrupted by officials from the City Bureau of Religious Affairs and the Dongang police department. After seizing Bibles, computers, and other items, they revoked the church's registration.[19] The following month in the province of Shaanxi, up to 400 police officers and others descended on the Gold Lamp Church, built to hold nearly 50,000 worshippers. They broke doors and windows, seized Bibles, removed computers, caused dozens of worshippers to be hospitalised, and jailed the church's pastors. Officially, the crackdown was the result of a land dispute, but the church was unregistered. Five church leaders were convicted of illegally occupying agricultural land and assembling a crowd to disrupt traffic. A lawyer for the defendants said the church had applied for building permits, but had not received any reply.[20]

At the end of 2009, another senior Catholic cleric in Hebei province, Leo Yao Liang, coadjutor Bishop of Xiwanzi – that is, the named successor to the incumbent bishop – died in hospital at the age of eighty-six. Even though the police were deployed to keep members of his (underground) diocese away from the funeral, and there had been heavy snowfall, at least 5,000 people attended. The local authorities tried to force the funeral organisers not to refer to Bishop Yao's episcopal rank and simply call him 'Pastor Yao'. During the burial, however, many mourners openly prayed for 'Bishop Yao', and some placed his episcopal insignia in his coffin. His death came a year after he had been released from a three-year prison sentence.[21]

The unregistered Shouwang Christian Church, a Protestant fellowship, had its website forcibly shut down in April 2009 for being the product of 'an illegal Christian organization'. After the rental agreement of the restaurant used by worshippers ended in April 2011, they began to meet in public spaces. The pastor, Jin Tianming, and senior elders were placed under house arrest. Members of their congregation had prayed outside a commercial building in Zhongguancun district on Sunday 10 April, so the following Sunday police detained 169 worshippers, and the Sunday after that a further 39 people. Most were released within twenty-four hours, but more than thirty were stopped from leaving their houses on subsequent Sundays. Pastor Jin remained under extended house arrest in mid 2012. The church, which attracts a high number of professional people, has been repeatedly prevented from occupying space in a Beijing office building which it had bought for 27 million yuan (£2.5 million) in 2009. News organisations, including Reuters and ChinaAid, have suggested that the crackdown against the Shouwang Church is a sign that the government will not allow such churches to get too large.[22]

The impact of Bishop Guo's irregular status was felt sharply in the summer of 2011. Despite subsequent episcopal ordinations in March and May, in which candidates had the joint approval of the Vatican and Chinese government, Church–state tensions continued to increase. Guo's illegal status in the eyes of many Chinese Catholics meant that religious officials' insistence on his concelebrating at subsequent ordinations further divided the Catholic community. The diocese of Handan (in Hebei province) made secret arrangements on 21 June to ordain Fr Sun Jigen as coadjutor bishop to prevent the participation of Bishop Guo. Despite receiving prior approval from the Vatican and Beijing, Bishop Sun was subsequently detained by officials together with two diocesan priests. They have since been released.

On 29 June, Fr Paul Lei Shiyin was ordained Bishop of Leshan in the southern province of Sichuan. The ceremony was conducted by Bishop Johan Fang Xingyao of the CCPA, even though the Vatican had made it clear that Fr Lei was an unacceptable candidate 'for proven and very grave reasons'.[23] Bishop Fang had been in communion with Rome, as were the seven concelebrating bishops. A Vatican communiqué on 4 July said that Fr Lei had been excommunicated for flouting canon law.

Fr Huang Bingzhang was ordained Bishop of Shantou, in south-eastern Guangdong, on 14 July. Reports suggest that Fr Huang had already been informed by the Vatican that he was not a suitable candidate for episcopal office. He is a delegate to the National People's Congress and is regarded by many in the diocese as being 'too political'. Moreover, Shantou diocese already has an underground bishop recognised by the Vatican, but not by the Chinese authorities. Bishop Fang again presided at the ceremony. The Vatican issued a further declaration that Huang Bingzhang had incurred excommunication as a result of his actions.

Statements issued by the Holy See after the Chengde and Shantou ordinations recognised that some of the consecrating bishops tried to avoid being strong-armed into taking part, and praised the efforts of laypeople 'who had defended their pastors'. The bishops of Shenyang and Xiamen resisted taking part altogether, but both subsequently faced official sanctions, and were told they could not receive visitors. 'The pressure faced by many bishops is severe,' comments Lawrence Braschi, a British China specialist. 'They are usually removed from their dioceses several days prior to the ordination ceremony, their phones are removed and officials remain with them day and night, even following them to the bathroom.'[24]

Fr Yang Yu, a spokesman for the CCPA, said in June 2011 that there were 'urgent' preparations for electing and ordaining bishops in forty more Chinese dioceses. Ordinations would continue 'without delay', and Fr Joseph Yue Fusheng was the next in line to succeed in the Harbin diocese. On 25 July, officials for the State Administration for Religious Affairs called the 'so-called excommunication' of Chinese bishops by the Vatican a 'gross interference' in Chinese religious freedom and an 'extremely unreasonable' act. Archbishop Savio Hon, writing in the Italian daily *La Stampa* on 12 July, suggested that the dispute risks returning the Chinese Church to the situation of the 1950s.[25]

*

The evidence of the past few pages is of great significance to China-watchers. More general readers are likely to be interested in the prospects for progress on religious freedom, and human rights in general, across China. Where Christians are concerned, the short answer is that they have travelled a long way, but will remain on an arduous path for some time to come.

Even so, given the Communist Party's goal of self-preservation, it is not surprising that it seeks to keep Christians and other people of faith under a very tight rein. On 29 July 2011, the authorities sentenced Shi Enhao, deputy leader of the Chinese House Church Alliance, to two years' 're-education through labour' – a sentence requiring no trial.[26] Mr Shi was officially charged with holding 'illegal meetings and [of] illegal organizing of . . . religious meetings' by dint of his role as pastor to thousands of house-church members around Beijing. His congregations were then ordered to stop meeting for worship; robes, musical instruments, and cash from collection boxes totalling nearly $22,000 were confiscated. Especially instructive was an article by a government adviser, Ma Hucheng, published by the China Social Sciences Press, connecting the growth of Protestant Christianity with political dissidence. 'Western powers, with America at their head, deliberately export Christianity to China and carry out all kinds of illegal evangelistic activities,' he wrote. 'Their basic aim is to use Christianity to change the character of the regime . . . in China and overturn it.'[27]

These words are no less informative for being intemperate. It would be hard to improve on Simon Scott Plummer's verdict on the irresistible forces and immovable objects described in this chapter. He begins by noting that the sheer variety of the elements – communal societies, Buddhist and Taoist temples, official and underground church congregations – makes it hard to imagine their uniting to mount a serious challenge to secular authority. 'A second factor', he goes on,

> is that there is, as yet, no indication that they would like to. Buddhism may have the largest number of followers but, outside Tibet, has not defied the state in the way . . . that the monks have in Burma under the junta. Christianity's links with the outside world may make it suspect but the number of faithful, perhaps around 80 million, while impressive in absolute terms, is only a small percentage of China's total population of 1.3 billion. And the indigenous churches have generally shunned political engagement. Finally, there is the Communist Party's determination to crush any dissent which poses even a whiff of existential threat.[28]

11

VIETNAM AND NORTH KOREA

The maltreatment of Christians has been flagrant in Vietnam's cowardly new world. As I researched this book, it was my Vietnamese interviewees – above all, the seminarian who told me that his great-aunt had been buried alive during the 1970s – who moved me to tears most quickly.[1] Though it is unlikely that torture and murder as grotesque as this could take place today, Vietnamese Christians are still suffering for their faith, despite the government's denials and (we've been here before, of course) its notional commitment to freedom of belief. That Christians are barred from professions such as medicine, teaching, and the police force tells its own wintry story – as does Marxism's status as a compulsory subject for university students.

The familiar Communist complaint that Christianity was a legacy of empire in Vietnam is odd, as well as misleading: Marxism was certainly a European import, but Christian – and Buddhist – missions preceded the colonial period. Earlier still, during the first millennium AD, Vietnam's elite were converted to Confucianism by their Chinese overlords. From the foundations established by Alexandre de Rhodes (1591–1660), the renowned French Jesuit who gave Vietnam its Westernised alphabet and baptised about 6,000 people between 1627 and his expulsion from the country three years later, Vietnamese Catholics saw their fortunes rise and fall according to the attitudes of the secular power. Far greater instability was to follow. During the five decades before Vietnam acquired the status of a French protectorate in 1883, up to 300,000 Catholics were persecuted or killed. Attitudes towards Christianity remained polarised thereafter, as the Church was linked to French hegemony in nationalist eyes. Nevertheless, large numbers were converted. There were about 1.5 million Catholics and a small contingent of Protestants by the 1930s.

When Vietnam was partitioned under the General Armistice Agreements of 1954, two-thirds of Catholics fell under the aegis of Ho Chi Minh in the Communist North. Faced with the overwhelming likelihood of a violent crackdown, about 670,000 of them fled to the South. Of those who remained, many were imprisoned immediately,[2] even though they were supposed to have ten months in which to decide whether to stay or go. Others travelled south across the countryside or down canals. More prominent members of the community who remained – clerics, especially – were imprisoned. After the fall of Saigon in 1975, a further exodus involving 1.5 million people, this time to the wider world, took place from the South.

Samples of the horror endured by Christians in the North are given by Robert Thomas Dooley in his book *Deliver Us from Evil: The Story of Vietnam's Flight to Freedom*.[3] At the village of Haiduong, for example, Communist forces went into a school and accused pupils and their teachers of a conspiracy, because they were talking about religion. The punishments for this 'crime' were unspeakably sadistic. Children had chopsticks stuck so far into their ears that they lost their hearing for good. Their teacher's tongue was held out with pliers and then cut off with a bayonet so that he would never be able to speak again. Despite this, the victims escaped to the South shortly afterwards.[4]

Comparable examples of extreme brutality are cited by Robert Royal in *The Catholic Martyrs of the Twentieth*

Century.[5] A priest apparently left at liberty in the North found himself arrested one evening, hung by his feet, and beaten with bamboo 'to drive the evil out of him'. He also survived, and was smuggled to the South by a group of his parishioners. Another cleric had eight nails hammered into his head as an act of 're-education'. Members of his congregation removed them; then they got him to the South for medical treatment. He eventually returned to the North to resume his duties.[6]

Further atrocities occurred in the South after the American withdrawal. One of the outstanding Catholic victims of persecution in Vietnam has been a remarkable churchman (now a Rome-based cardinal), François-Xavier Nguyen Van Thuan. The scion of an old Vietnamese Catholic family and very active as a preacher and broadcaster, he was named Archbishop-designate of Saigon in 1975. When the Communists assumed control of the whole country, they forbade him from taking up the appointment, describing it as 'a conspiracy between the Vatican and the imperialists'. The archbishop was at first placed under house arrest. Then he was forced to join other clergy and laypeople in so-called re-education camps. He spent the next thirteen years in prison, a term that included long periods of solitary confinement.

Despite the fearful conditions in which he was kept – his cell in Phu-Khanh prison was windowless, forcing him to spend his waking hours pressing his nose against a small hole in the wall to get fresh air – this saintly man has never displayed any public animosity towards his tormentors. His only expressions of regret centred on his inability to help and minister to other people during his incarceration. 'I wanted to do so many things,' he later wrote, 'to serve my people, but I could not. Then I came to think about Jesus on the cross: that he was immobilized, he could neither preach nor administer any sacraments – he, too, was "helpless". Nevertheless, it was from there that he performed his greatest deed: he redeemed us sinners. Thanks to his help, I have never regretted my destiny.'[7]

This reflection and many others were smuggled out of jail and circulated to console Catholics who remained in Vietnam, and the so-called Boat People who had escaped. The archbishop's captors were in time won over by his noble nature: at least one converted to Christianity and another allowed Nguyen Van Thuan to make a cross and chain from some wood and wire. This became his pectoral cross after his release. He wrote that he wears it every day, 'not because they are reminders of prison, but because they indicate my profound conviction, a constant reference point for me: only Christian love can change hearts, not weapons, threats, or the media.'[8]

Fr Thaddeus Nguyen Van Ly is perhaps the most prominent Christian witness in Vietnam today. Beatings, imprisonment, and health problems, including several strokes, have not stopped him from denouncing human rights abuses and campaigning for freedom of conscience. Notoriously, he was gagged in court to stop him from speaking out against the government. In recent years, he has been released from prison, and then re-arrested, in rotation. Among many other initiatives, he co-wrote the 'Manifesto on Freedom and Democracy for Vietnam', published on 8 April 2006. The signatories later became known as 'Bloc 8406', with reference to the date of the document's release.

Fr Thaddeus has at least benefited from the diplomatic muscle of the world's largest organisation. Though sentenced to fifteen years' imprisonment in 2001 for supporting freedom of expression, he was set free in 2004 thanks to Vatican pressure, and placed under house arrest. In early 2012, however, he was back in prison, despite having suffered several strokes and developing a brain tumour. A corollary of this is that the

Vietnamese government can respond to arm-twisting, at least for as long as it is maintained. But apparent gains are easily lost.

Since the fall of the Soviet Union, which had been one of its patrons, Vietnam's economic transformation has greatly exceeded its political advance, but earlier levels of repression fell before Vietnam's accession to the World Trade Organization (WTO) in 2006 and its securing of Permanent Normal Trade Relations (PNTR) with the United States. The 2004 Ordinance Regarding Religious Beliefs ordered the relevant authorities to '[r]aise public awareness about the need to create favourable conditions' for Protestant congregations to carry out their religious practices 'in conformity with the law'. And in 2011, British human rights monitors were told that evangelism was tolerated with knowledge of the authorities at local levels in many areas. In the same year, an interviewee from Lai Chau province reported being allowed to evangelise in surrounding villages, and to do so among those from different ethnic groups. He told a visiting Christian Solidarity Worldwide team that church services in the district were open to visitors without restriction. Another contact, from Tuyen Quang province, said that he was free to evangelise with the knowledge of local authorities. A pastor from the Nop ethnic group in Lam Dong province disclosed that he, and members of his church, were free to evangelise in neighbouring villages and districts. On occasion, village police had seen him engaging in evangelism, though the reaction was mixed. He was told by one policeman, 'It's OK to share your beliefs with others, but please don't force anyone to convert to Protestantism.'

The situation remains extremely patchy overall. The Communist Party is defined by Article 4 of Vietnam's constitution as 'the force leading the state and society'. The provision apparently granting freedom of religious belief to Vietnamese citizens

(Article 70) also contains the question-begging caveat that no one may 'misuse beliefs and religions to contravene the law and state policies'. This ambiguity is also reflected in documents such as the 2005 Decree on Religion, as well as the 2004 Ordinance. In 2006, after the thaw already outlined, Vietnam was removed from the American State Department's Countries of Particular Concern list. Three years later, Hanoi rejected forty-five recommendations to improve its human rights record made at the UN Periodic Review, including a request that it cease its longstanding use of arbitrary detention. And in 2010, the Obama administration faced public calls to recognise Vietnam's human rights abuses.[9]

To Communist ideologues, of course, Christianity represents a highly subversive threat. Part of the abiding animus can also be ascribed to the Churches' success, especially in tribal areas. About 2,000 young people were baptised at the Easter vigil in Ho Chi Minh City (formerly Saigon) in 2009;[10] another noteworthy statistic is that Vietnam now has more than 1,500 Catholic seminarians. The torment faced by Christians is shown by the problems endured at Tam Toa Church in Vinh diocese, south of Hanoi:

During the Vietnam War, the historic church was bombed by US planes, leaving only the façade and the tower standing. Parishioners were too poor to rebuild the structure, but continued to hold religious services there. In 1996, the People's Committee of Quang Binh Province confiscated the property to turn it into a 'memorial site'. In July 2009, rumours began circulating that it was due for demolition so a tourist resort could be built. During a protest against the plans, plainclothes police and party activists attacked Catholic worshippers, beating men, women and children. Seven Catholics were arrested. Two priests, Fathers Paul Nguyen Dinh Phu and Peter Nguyen The Binh, ended up in

Dong Hoi Hospital, the first with broken ribs and head wounds, the second in a coma. General Hoang Cong Tu, from the Public Security Ministry, denied that any violence had been used against the priests. The diocese responded by posting online pictures showing the priests and the wounds. General Tu announced that the seven Catholics accused of 'disorderly conduct' would be put on trial. A few weeks later bulldozers demolished what was left of the church, leaving only the tower standing.[11]

Many further abuses have taken place besides. Vietnam's Prime Minister, Nguyen Tan Dung, announced in early 2009 that none of the 2,250 properties seized from the Catholic Church before 1991 would be returned. Anyone protesting against this would be deemed guilty of 'social disorder', he added.[12]

At about the same time, in the north-western Son La province, the local authorities launched a bid to eradicate Christianity, promoting ancient indigenous cults as an alternative. Welfare benefits were withdrawn from Christian families resisting this move. Two notable acts of desecration took place in the summer of 2009: bulldozers destroyed the Convent of the Brothers of the Sacred Family of Banam in Long Xuyen, capital of An Gang province; and in Thu Thiem, a suburb of Ho Chi Minh City, a community of nuns were ordered to vacate the premises that their order had occupied for 170 years. The 3.5 hectare site included not just a church, but also a school, care facility, clinic, farm, and kindergarten for 400 children.[13] Finally, at Easter in 2010, a layman, Sung Cua Po, became the latest of many Vietnamese to pay an extremely heavy price for converting to Catholicism. He and his family fled into the forest after Mr Po had received seventy blows to his head and back from local officials and policemen. His 'offence' was to argue with his father over the validity of making religious offerings to ancestors: on this pretext, the Dien Bien Dong authorities demolished his house and confiscated forty sacks of rice – the family's annual supply.[14]

*

What of other Christians? The only recognised Protestant bodies are the state-sponsored Evangelical Church of North Vietnam (ECVN-N) and the Evangelical Church of South Vietnam (ECVN-S). Even though hundreds of ethnic-minority congregations are recognised by ECVN-N, the government still often views them as illegitimate. Persecution for 'illegitimate' worship and religious instruction includes imprisonment, fines, physical assaults, threats of violence, and other forms of intimidation. Among the most vulnerable minorities are the Hmong, Giay, and Yao, who live in Vietnam's Central Highlands and north-western fringes.

These days the registration system, even for congregations affiliated to recognised Churches, has slowed significantly. Some pastors are now asked to provide the names of members of their congregations, which is not a requirement of the relevant legislation. The three-tier system for registration under which denominations, congregations, and meeting places are required to be registered separately is also widely described as confusing and undefined. For a denomination to become legally recognised, it must prove twenty years of 'stable operation', leaving groups that have operated for less than twenty years in a legal grey area. This trickles down to congregations that are part of such unregistered denominations, who may have their registration rejected on the basis that they are part of a group not recognised by the government.

We can learn a good deal about the shape of an undernoticed cluster of problems – including the unpredictability of the authorities – by looking in more detail at the trials faced by unregistered Protestants who told their stories to Christian Solidarity Worldwide monitors. Interviewee A – naming names appears too dangerous in this context – is of Flower Hmong ethnicity and belongs to one of the fastest-growing expressions of free-range Evangelical Christianity in the world: he is pastor of eight unrecognised house churches in the northern Ha Giang province.[15] There is a Christian majority in his village, where only three families are non-Christians out of a total of twenty-six. The village church has 143 members. Most of them converted as a result of hearing Christian Far East Broadcasting Corporation (FEBC) radio broadcasts in the Hmong language during the early 1990s. In March 2011, Interviewee A was told by the village policeman that he was not allowed to evangelise non-Christians. The policeman said, 'We will allow you to worship God in your church building and give sermons there. But you are not allowed to travel to give sermons in other churches, nor are you allowed to travel to other villages to evangelise.' If the village police find out that he or a member of his flock has been preaching, Interviewee A says, then they are fined or threatened with imprisonment. He adds that if any Christians visit the church from another village, the church will be fined between 60,000 to 300,000 dong (£2–10) per person. Interviewee A said that this policy is endorsed by district-level officials.

In November 2010, Christians in the village applied for their family registration documents and ID cards. According to Interviewee A, the district-level officials did not allow him to write 'Protestant' in the religion category on the form; instead, the official took the form off him and wrote 'None' on his behalf. The local police then said, 'We do not allow Protestants in Ha Giang province.' A few weeks later, Interviewee A travelled to a Nung ethnicity village six hours away from home. He spoke to the residents about Christianity and afterwards two Nung families decided to convert to Christianity. As a first step, they destroyed their traditional altars in their homes. After one month, the village policeman found out what had happened and forced the two families to rebuild their altars. One family succumbed to the pressure and did the policeman's bidding. The other decided to leave the village: its members are now living among a group of Hmong Christians in a neighbouring district. In February 2011, Interviewee A wanted to invite the sixteen leaders from the eight churches he oversees to his house for a meeting. Those who came to the village from other locations were prevented from entering it by the local policeman, so the gathering could not take place. The following month, Interviewee A left his village to travel to Hanoi. On setting off, he was summoned by district-level police who wanted to know details of his journey, and whom he was planning to meet. He was told he needed official permission to proceed.

Interviewee C is from the same province as Interviewee A, and shares his ethnicity. He leads an unregistered congregation of sixty-three members. He is also in charge of nine churches in his area with a combined membership of over 700 people. They are fairly free to worship at home with family or in larger groups. Officially, however, they are not allowed to engage in evangelistic activity or travel to other villages, though the rule is often flouted. Interviewee C reports that: 'We are not allowed to have "Protestant" listed as the religion on our ID cards and family registration documents. When I complained to the district-level policeman, he said, "In this province we do not allow anyone to be Protestant. When the government allows you to be Protestant, then we will allow you to write Protestant on your ID cards."'

Interviewee D ministers at four churches that are also in Ha Giang province, all of which belong to an unregistered denomination. In his home village, there are two local churches with a total of 267 Christians from 43 families, out of a total of 300 families. The authorities do not allow the two churches to meet together to worship, even though they are in the same village. The police are reported to have told Interviewee D, 'In the past there were not any Hmong Christians. Then you became Christians and we have already allowed you to worship in your homes, and then in a big group. Now we do not want you to join the two churches together because there are already enough of you. If you do not obey, we will fine you 150,000 to 500,000 dong (£5–18) for every person who attends worship in the wrong [sic] place.'

Interviewee D has told human rights monitors of his distress at the inability of Christians in the village to worship together. He also says that the non-Christian villagers are hostile towards the Christians, and that churchgoers suffer some mild harassment from their neighbours as a result. This is encouraged by the village policeman. Interviewee E is of Flower Hmong ethnicity, from Tuyen Quang province, which abuts Ha Giang. He leads an unregistered congregation. He also oversees eight local churches with a total of 861 members. He reports that the general situation for the church is good, and that members of his flock are allowed to engage in evangelism, including travelling to different villages. Yet none of the 861 Christians has been allowed to have 'Protestant' listed on their ID cards or family registration documents, which say 'none' in the religion category.

In the north-western Lai Chau province, Interviewee F, of White Hmong ethnicity, oversees nine churches in his area, all of which belong to an unregistered denomination. Interviewee

F reports that '[t]he village and district level police do not allow us to gather together church leaders from different villages. This is problematic, as I need to have regular meetings with eighteen leaders serving under me to discuss our plans. I have been told by the village police that if I do not obey this order I will be fined, but they did not say how much.' He has also been told not to engage in evangelism or visit other villages to meet Christians there. He does preach to the unconverted, but only from time to time, so as not to attract suspicion. He is too scared to do more. In February 2010, he sent an application to register his main worship space, but had not received a reply a year later. The village authorities have told him that he is free to worship in one church with his members, but other people are not allowed to join in. In 2010, he submitted an application form for his family registration documents and ID cards, and wrote 'Protestant' in the religion category. On submission he was told, 'We do not recognise Protestantism in our province.'

Interviewee G, of Black Hmong ethnicity and from the far north-western Dien Bien province, leads a church belonging to the officially recognised Evangelical Church of Vietnam-North. He also oversees five churches in the surrounding area, all of which belong to ECVN-N. They have not tried to register the meeting places, even though they are part of a registered denomination, as they feel it would be too difficult. The church congregation meets for worship in the pastor's home. They would like to build a chapel, but feel that this would be too difficult at present, owing to a lack of support from the village People's Committee.

Interviewee M is part of a small unregistered congregation belonging to the unregistered Mennonite church on the outskirts of Ho Chi Minh City. A member of the congregation, Pastor Dung Kim Khai, is serving a prison sentence for his involvement in the Vietnamese Democracy organisation, Viet Tan. Because of this, the church has been under scrutiny by local officials who are wary that prayer sessions and other worship could be used to attract recruits to the democracy movement. M is particularly susceptible to accusations of this nature because of his outspoken support for democracy. On Sunday 27 February 2010, he left his home as usual to travel to the church service. He was stopped by three policemen waiting at the checkpoint outside his house who prevented him from leaving. He remained at home for the morning instead. The following Sunday, he again left home to travel to the service. Once more the police asked him not to go, but they did not stop him physically. He duly got on his motorbike and went to church as usual. En route, a police car hit him from behind, before driving in front of the bike and preventing him from continuing his journey. He was then taken to the police station against his will. On arrival, a senior officer told him, 'You need to stop your posts on the internet. You have written many disrespectful and offensive essays about Uncle Ho [Ho Chi Minh] and the Vietnamese Communist Party. As a result, many high-level people are angry with you. If you don't stop, then when you leave your house thugs will beat you up and we will not be able to help you. I cannot guarantee your safety – they may beat you to death.'

M challenged the policeman, explaining that he needed to take responsibility for what he was saying, because the policeman was implicating himself in any future ill-treatment or beating M might suffer. He then shared his faith with his interrogator before explaining, 'I have been writing many things on the internet for ten years. I have now written everything I need to say – it's enough. I promise that I won't write anything else about the Communist Party.' The policeman replied, 'You need to stop going to the church as well. The church you go to is the Vietnam headquarters for the Viet Tan party. You should not involve yourself in politics.'

At the beginning of March, M's landline, Internet and mobile phone were disconnected without his prior knowledge. Communications were only restored after a week. This had not happened before. On Sunday 13 March, he attended the church service without restrictions. Although he was followed there, he was not prevented from preaching.

All these testimonies bear witness to the continuing struggle for freedom of religious belief for a variety of ethnic groups spanning several geographical areas. One source of hope for the future is economic. Hanoi is not averse to diplomatic pressure – especially as economics tends to supplant ideology in its hierarchy of concerns. Another lies with the scale of Christian philanthropy. In general, the authorities have refused to cede control of areas such as healthcare to non-government agencies, even though standards of provision can be poor. This has been especially true for the sharply rising numbers of people with HIV and AIDS over the past twenty years. In Ho Chi Minh City, Fr John Toai opened the Mai Tam House of Hope several years ago, a centre for HIV-positive women and orphans. It now treats 2,000 people a week,[16] and received official government recognition in 2007 – one of the very few church-run initiatives to have done so. The implications of this were recently spelt out by Mgr Peter Nguyen Van Kham, an auxiliary bishop in Ho Chi Minh City. Opening the door to faith-based initiatives would make Vietnam 'more human, more equal, and – what matters a lot to the Party – more stable', he said.[17]

*

And so to North Korea – or as close as we can get. Since the country is usually called the most isolated and repressive in the world, evidence about devotional or many other sorts of activity there is extremely hard to come by. Public religious observance was banned in the North after the Korean War, and was probably stamped out more comprehensively than anywhere else. In 1950, there were about 300,000 North Korean Protestants and 57,000 Catholics.[18] In 2002, according to official statistics, there were a mere 12,000 Protestants and 800 Catholics.[19] The ideologues were especially active at the beginning. Christians were hung on crosses and burnt to death over fires,[20] thrown off bridges, and crushed under steamrollers.[21] Fears about the transmission of faith across the generations meant that believers' children were sent to prison camps for ideological re-education. Since some offspring of Christian couples were tricked into informing on their parents, never to see them again, a good number of believers decided with great reluctance not to share their beliefs with their children.[22] Buddhism, Christianity, and other belief systems such as Cheondokyo (a modern, monotheistic movement) were replaced by a febrile idolisation of the country's founding leader, Kim Il-Sung. Once again, North Korea's constitution contains a commitment to 'freedom of religious belief', but the undertaking is plainly not observed. A significant proportion of expatriate dissidents have reported that they knew no religious vocabulary, and even had no word for God, at the time of their defection. On learning about Christianity, they maintain that attributes usually ascribed to the Almighty are instead projected onto their founding leader. The veneration is enforced through the use of song, incantations, and Stalinist holy writ.

Like other believers, Christians are obliged to join government-controlled organisations. While there are one Catholic and two Protestant churches in the capital, Pyonyang, very little can be said about congregations elsewhere – though it is estimated that 500,000 people (2 per cent of the population) are underground

Christians.[23] It has been reported that Catholics form the only faith group without a single minister.[24] The Vatican has declared the country's three dioceses to be vacant sees, but still lists Francis Hong Yong-ho as Bishop of Pyonyang, even though he vanished from view in 1962 and would now be more than a hundred years old if he were still alive. Underground believers whose activities come to light may still be killed on the spot. This was the fate of three members of a congregation in the southern city of Pyongsong who were arrested in August 2010. Twenty of their fellow worshippers were sent to the Yoduk prison camp.[25]

The story of Lee Sung Ae, an astonishingly brave exiled Christian, tells us much about the unsurpassed ruthlessness and inhumanity to which North Korea has been subjected since Kim Il-Sung came to power in 1948. Her problems flared up dramatically during the mid-1990s. She was widowed at this time and left with four malnourished young sons. They managed to escape across the tightly patrolled border with China in search of help from a cousin. Too poor to assist, Mrs Lee's relative introduced her to a Christian pastor who took her and her children under his roof for a month. After this she converted to Christianity, deciding to return to North Korea with Bibles and supplies of food and clothes. She testified about the aftermath of her conversion during a visit to London in 2009:

> I told ten friends about my faith, and between us we formed a small Bible study group. However, my neighbours became suspicious and reported me to the police, who then deported me to an interrogation centre. I went through six months of extreme torture and interrogation. I was repeatedly beaten and nearly suffocated; my teeth were knocked out, my nails extracted and raw chilli put in my wounds. I used to be 170 cm tall, but after my time there, I was only 150 cm. I refused to give the names

of my friends, because I knew that they and their families would just experience the same brutality as I had.

After that I was sentenced to four years in Kyo-Haw-So prison. Our cells had no roofs, so we were forced to dig holes with leaves for shelter. Around 30 or 40 people were dying there every day. We were so hungry that we would take food from the mouths of dead people, or fight for the undigested corn husks found in animal faeces. Once I was so weak that I was given up for dead, and put on the pile of corpses awaiting burial.[26]

On her release in 2003, Mrs Lee and her sons went back to China. They eventually reached Mongolia, from where they applied for political asylum in South Korea. She is now involved with trying to get Bibles, clothes and other aid from China into North Korea.

The system Mrs Lee is campaigning against is many-tentacled. A principal foundation of North Korea's social ordering dates from 1957, when the so-called *songhun* model was introduced. The entire population was classified into three main groups – the 'core' class, the 'basic' (or wavering) class, and the 'complex' (or hostile) class. A further fifty-one sub-divisions were introduced reflecting shades of loyalty to the regime. These classifications governed access to healthcare, education, and employment. They resembled a caste system in being hereditary.[27] The 'complex' class consists of former landowners and businessmen, religiously active people, and those whose parents collaborated with South Korea during the war between the two countries. Encompassing more than a quarter of the population, this group remains especially at risk of food shortages or arbitrary detention.

The aim of eliminating Christianity from North Korea was voiced by Kim Il-Sung at intervals during the 1960s and 70s. The following quotations from his speeches do not need glossing:

Through court trials, we have executed all Protestant and Catholic church cadre members and sentenced all other vicious religious elements to heavy punishment. The repentants [*sic*] have been given work, but non-repentants have been sent to concentration camps . . .[28]

We cannot carry such religiously active people along our march toward a Communist society. Therefore, we tried and executed all religious leaders higher than deacon in the Protestant and Catholic churches. Among other religiously active people, those deemed malignant were all put to trial. Among ordinary religious believers, those who recanted were given jobs while those who did not were held at concentration camps . . . Therefore in 1958 we completely and thoroughly apprehended that group of people and had them executed. That is how we found out that the only way to fix the bad habit of these religious believers is for them to be killed . . .[29]

The guidelines for dealing with religious believers are clearly set out in our Party's public security policy. You need only to follow it. Silly old religionists need to die in order for their bad habits to be corrected. In which case, we must mercilessly eradicate them . . .[30]

Although these and other statements represent Christians as agents of 'imperialist' forces, Protestants and Catholics were still deliberately targeted as a group – a key criterion in establishing specific intent to destroy a religious community as such.[31]

Hwang Jang-Yop (1923–2010), once a leading confidant of Kim Il-Sung, who eventually became the regime's most senior defector, was well placed to shed light on official policy. Among other statements, he said: 'If anybody in North Korea publicly states that they believe in religion, they die.'[32] And Ahn Myeong-Cheol, who was a guard at a number of political prison camps, has testified that:

We do not have national or ethnic groups so the genocide definition does not apply in this regard, but the treatment of Christians precisely fits the genocide definition . . . There was a special instruction from the political leadership that all religions are [a] social evil. There was an abundance of references to Christian groups for the purposes of annihilation. There were speeches, texts, instructions, textbooks and pamphlets covering this . . . When I was on duty, I saw many Christians. One is meant to worship only the political leaders and any other worship [is] a deviation from loyalty to the regime. When North Koreans hear about God, they think they are talking about Kim ll-Sung. All North Koreans have this confusion. If anyone embraces Christianity in North Korea, they are called a crazy guy. No one could understand or imagine someone wanting to become a Christian. It is very unlikely one could find a descendant of a Christian still living . . . The purpose of the camps I was involved in was to kill the prisoners. Instead of killing them by shooting, the intention was to force them to work to the last minute. The intention was to kill, not [merely] to extract labour.[33]

Philo Kim, a leading Korean academic authority on religion in North Korea, states that:

All religiously active people have disappeared as a result of the central party's intensive guidance program . . . 900 pastors and some 300,000 followers have either been killed or forced to recant their faith . . . 260 Catholic fathers [priests], nuns, [and] monks, and 50,000 Catholic followers were killed because they refused to recant their faith. In addition, some 800 or 1,600 Buddhist monks and nuns and their 35,000 Buddhist followers have been wiped out. And . . . 120,000 followers of Cheondokyo have disappeared or been forced to recant their faith. Because of this persecution, about 400,000 religiously active people and their families were either executed or banished to political prison camps.[34]

The conundrum posed by North Korea's possession of nuclear weapons is familiar. One commonly expressed view is that the country needs a twin-track response from the world at large, combining engagement on the one hand, and pressure (including an international commission of inquiry with a remit to investigate the regime's crimes) on the other. The current situation – rendered cloudier by the accession of Kim Jong-Un in December 2011 – is especially hard to read. Some signs are positive. For example, a Christian-run medical centre opened its doors in Pyonyang shortly before the death of Kim Jong-Il, and has been allowed to function unhindered so far. At the same time, the new leader has sought to make his mark by cracking down even further on anyone seeking to flee the country. If reform does come to North Korea, then progress is unlikely to be either swift or even.

12

THE HOLY LAND

Nadia Kinani is Principal of the Hand in Hand school in Jerusalem, a joint Jewish–Arab foundation. When she arrived for work on 7 February 2012, she found the words 'Death to Arabs' spray-painted in giant Hebrew letters on the building. The same morning, in what was probably an unrelated incident, the medieval monastery overlooking the Israeli Parliament and run by the Greek Orthodox Church was daubed with the slogan 'Death to Christians'. Two cars parked outside this property had their tyres punctured.[1] Hand in Hand is a bilingual school and symbol of coexistence in Jerusalem. Half the pupils are Arabs; half are Jews.

A police spokesman said that the words 'price tag' had also been painted on the monastery, suggesting that the culprits were Jewish settlers from the West Bank. The slogan has regularly been used in vandalism against mosques and Palestinian-owned homes in the territory; it refers to the retribution some settlers say they will seek in the event of government curbs on settlement-building.

Hate crimes against schools and church property are not condoned by the Israeli authorities, of course, and anyone seeking a silver lining to this cloud could fairly argue that the extremists must be in a corner if they are reduced to launching cowardly attacks on centres of community coexistence. Ms Kinani herself expressed this point with eloquence:

If this had happened at a Jewish-only school and someone had sprayed 'Death to the Jews', it would have caused more hatred of Arabs. If 'Death to the Arabs' had been written at an Arab-only school, it would have led to more hatred of Jews. Here at our Hand in Hand school, this kind of thing just strengthens solidarity and partnership between us. It brings our Jewish and Arab students, teachers and families closer together. Our school is the answer to this kind of racism and extremism.[2]

A spokesman for the monastery named Fr Claudio was similarly magnanimous. 'We are Christians and forgive,' he said.

Settlers are violent towards Christians and others from time to time. They occupied parts of East Jerusalem at Easter in 1990 and jostled the then Greek Orthodox patriarch; and in November 1979, as yet unidentified fanatics murdered Fr Philoumenos Hasapis, an Orthodox monk, at St Photini's Monastery beside Jacob's Well at Nablus. (This is the spot where Jesus met the Samaritan woman, according to John 4:4 ff.) The killers had already warned Fr Philoumenos to remove Christian symbols from the well, claiming that their presence made it impossible for Jews to pray there. When he refused, they gouged his eyes out and hacked off the fingers of his right hand – the one he used to make the sign of the cross – before ending his life. The current custodian, a veteran of several attacks already, has prepared his tomb for what he senses may be a sudden death.[3]

Sometimes the culprits belong to Jerusalem's ultra-Orthodox Jewish community. In December 2009, for instance, Yossi Yomtov, a Christian of Jewish ethnic origin, sought police protection after being attacked four times because of his faith. A Jerusalem resident, he said that police had been slow to investigate the assaults. In two of the instances, a youth attacked him with pepper spray and a stun-gun.[4]

On other occasions, the culprits are never identified. For example, in May 2009, around seventy graves in Palestinian Christian cemeteries in the West Bank village of Jiffna were desecrated by vandals.[5] Seventeen months later, arsonists set fire to the Alliance Church Ministry Centre in Jerusalem. The basement windows of the building were broken into, and its lower floors set on fire. Volunteer workers from the United States and Denmark sleeping at the church's overnight facilities were sent to a nearby hospital to be treated for smoke inhalation. The fire largely gutted the basement. Recently completed renovations were destroyed.[6]

Hate crime is some way from being the main concern of Christians, though. The principal source of hardship for Christians and Muslims alike lies with the 'security fence' erected around the West Bank from 2000 onwards. The government's rationale for the fence is that it has saved many lives after almost 250 Israelis were murdered by suicide bombers during the years before its construction. As an official statement puts it:

> The security fence disrupts Palestinian life. It is ugly, inconvenient, and a symbol of conflict. But responsibility for the fence lies with the Palestinian groups which compelled Israel to build it, as a last resort, in the first place. Terrorism against Jerusalem and elsewhere in Israel has 'disrupted Israeli life' too – this needs to be brought into the equation. The fence is not the inevitable result of Israeli policy, but the inevitable result of Palestinian actions which have killed 249 Jerusalem citizens, and injured and traumatised many more.[7]

This argument naturally deserves a serious hearing. Many, however, may still judge that the statement underplays the heavy cost caused by the fence, quite apart from the question of its legality. (Some also judge that the wall is very permeable, and that the true reason for the lack of suicide bombings now is that Hamas has changed its policy.) When I returned to the area in 2011 after a fifteen-year absence, I was struck by how much the situation had worsened, even compared with the near-universal gloom that followed the assassination of Yitzhak Rabin in 1995. The scarring of the handsome, lumpy landscape between Jerusalem and Bethlehem stirred another memory – of Cold War Berlin, which I'd visited as a schoolboy thirty years earlier. Travelling the six miles from my billet at the Pontifical Biblical Institute, on the edge of the Old City, to Bethlehem took an hour. Had I been making the same journey in reverse at 7 a.m., like the Institute's Palestinian cooks, it could have taken a good deal longer.

A diplomatically worded protest against the wall and its effects was voiced by Pope Benedict on his visit to the Holy Land in May of 2009:

> In a world where more and more borders are being opened up –
> to trade, to travel, to movement of peoples, to cultural exchanges
> – it is tragic to see walls still being erected. How we long to see
> the fruits of the much more difficult task of building peace! How
> earnestly we pray for an end to the hostilities that have caused
> this wall to be built! On both sides of the wall, great courage
> is needed if fear and mistrust is to be overcome, if the urge to
> retaliate for loss or injury is to be resisted.[8]

A more forthright statement of Roman Catholic – and broader Christian – opinion came shortly afterwards from the Latin Patriarch of Jerusalem, Archbishop Fouad Twal. 'Discrimination, always present in Israel, threatens both Christians and Muslims,' he said.[9] Turning directly to the effects of the security barrier, the patriarch added: 'We have a new generation of Christians that cannot visit the holy places of their faith, which are just a few kilometres from where they live.'[10]

In October 2010, the Synod of Middle East Bishops in Rome broadened the argument by emphasising concerns over the rising emigration of Christians from the region – in Israel/Palestine alone, the Christian presence has fallen from 20 per cent of the population in the 1940s to a mere 2 per cent (under 150,000 souls) today. The difficulties faced by other faith groups were not neglected. While noting the 'suffering and insecurity' of Israelis, the final communiqué also stated: 'We have taken account of the Israeli–Palestinian conflict on the whole region, especially on the Palestinians who are suffering the consequences of Israeli occupation: the lack of freedom of movement, the wall of separation, and the military check-points, the political prisoners, the demolition of homes, the disturbance of socio-economic life, and the thousands of refugees.'[11]

Admittedly, some Christian numbers have risen. Israeli officials regularly point out that Christian numbers in Israel are rising – a statistic linked to the arrival of Christian Zionists. But this is not a positive sign in itself. The Christian population of Saudi Arabia is also rising, thanks to immigrant labour, but that does not legitimise Saudi policy towards minorities. More revealing is the Israeli government's policy of making it harder for foreign clerics and members of religious orders to enter the country. Visas are now valid for only one year rather than two. 'We do not know whether [this] reflects ministerial policy, or whether certain officials have dragged their feet. Perhaps the ambiguity is intentional,' says Fr Pierbattista Pizzaballa,[12] Custodian of the Holy Land, an official Catholic post. Visas are hard to obtain for seminarians training under the wing of the Latin Patriarchate, which covers Israel, the Palestinian territories, Jordan, and Cyprus. Restrictions are growing tighter, especially for Jordanians, who form two-thirds of the student body. Their visas are very often valid for only one entry per year. Before the clampdown of the past decade, they were able to return to their families much more freely.[13]

During the Holy Week and Easter ceremonies of 2010, the Israeli authorities limited the number of permits for Christians from the West Bank and Gaza who wanted to travel to Jerusalem. Fr Raed Abousahlia, the Catholic parish priest at Taybeh, in the West Bank, said he could only get 200 permits for the members of his congregation, a third of the allocation for previous years.[14] In Ramallah, Archbishop Atallah Hanna of the Greek Orthodox Church said that Israel's attitude showed a desire 'to violate religious freedom', and called for Jerusalem 'to remain an open city for all Christians'. Yusef Daher, a spokesman for the World Council of Churches, argued that the Israelis were undermining a tradition of religious freedom that had lasted for 900 years.[15]

So it is fair to say that official Israeli attitudes have grown more unyielding. But Israel can point with justice to the colossal intransigence displayed by Hamas and other hardline Islamist groups; to their call for Israel to be replaced by a unitary Palestinian state with no special privileges for Jews; and to the separate but telling fact that levels of Holocaust-denial among Muslims across the Middle East are alarmingly high.[16] The essential consideration for our purposes is that Christians are caught in the middle: mistrusted and disliked by the hard men among Israeli and Palestinian ranks alike.

A mere 5,000 Christians live among 1.5 million Muslims in the Gaza Strip. Until the end of the 1980s, nationalism played a larger role than religion in shaping Palestinian identity. Some infer from the change that faith is now far more influential, but this entails a misconception. It would be more accurate to suggest that the nationalist campaign and its rejection by Israel have been 'religionised'. Hamas remains deeply nationalist; and it has been supported in the parliamentary elections by many Christians, because they were seen as more honest and ethical than their Fatah counterparts.

It is nevertheless a source of regret and anger to many that Christian women have been expected to observe Islamic dress codes during the ascendancy of Hamas, and Christians have been stopped from selling alcohol. Tailors have been told to remove mannequins displaying lingerie; bare-chested men at Gaza's beaches are now ordered to cover up. Attacks on Christian-owned homes, shops, and churches have become regular events.[17] The alleged link between Christianity and the West was repeated with less deference to reality than ever after Israel's invasion of Lebanon in 2006 and its subsequent bombardment of Gaza in 2009. In August of that year, schools in Gaza City imposed a new dress code on girls, requiring them to wear traditional Islamic sleeved robes and to cover their hair. Boys and girls were separated and put into different buildings. The rules were also enforced on the Christian minority in state schools. (Thus far, though, private Christian schools have been exempted.)

There is a notable irony here, because Christians such as Fr Ibrahim Ayad (d.2005) helped give birth to Palestinian nationalism – some early PLO meetings were held in his sacristy – and other prominent Palestinian Christians such as Hanan Ashrawi, Asmi Bishara, and the late Emile Habibi have tended to stress nation before religion. But the perceived failure of secular nationalism has given Islamists the chance to provide an alternative focus for the hopes and frustrations of Muslims. On a visit to Tantur, the Catholic-run university on the edge of Jerusalem, I met Yazeed Said, who straddles several worlds as Israeli citizen, Palestinian Arab, and Anglican priest. He gives a bracing overview of his country's current predicament:

Looking at the Holy Land today, one sees a very dim picture of religious [coexistence]. Judaism does not come across as the religion of faith and promise and witness, but that of a settler land-grab. The Christian stress on nationalism has not been terribly successful, and all the nation states that arose as a result of Arab-wide national aspirations ended up with regimes that seem to be more accountable to the State Department in Washington than to their own people. As a result, Islamic religious fanaticism came in to fill the gap. Hamas [got] voted into power, while suicide bombers [have] destroyed the lives of many.[18]

*

This view is rendered more sobering still by background events, including the decline of the Middle East's Christian population over a much longer time frame.[19] The curve had been pointing downwards for decades before the Second World War – Christian numbers fell by 13 per cent between 1922 and 1931, for example – but this was small beer compared with the effects of the Nakba, or catastrophe, which followed David Ben-Gurion's declaration of a Jewish state and the ensuing 1948 Arab–Israeli War. Urban middle-class Christians escaped in advance to avoid arrest or death. Between 50,000 and 60,000 were condemned to refugee status.[20] The gaps left in Jerusalem neighbourhoods such as Qatamon, Talbiyeh, and Baka have caused a distinguished sociologist such as Salim Tamari to describe the former Arab areas of East Jerusalem as a 'phantom city'.[21]

Only about a third of the Arab Christian population (32,000 people) remained within Israel's borders.[22] East Jerusalem was cut off from the rest of Israel under Jordanian rule between 1948 and the Six Day War of 1967, after which Israel took control of the Gaza Strip, the Sinai Peninsula from Egypt, the

West Bank and East Jerusalem from Jordan, and the Golan Heights from Syria. Christians in Israel were no longer able to visit their holy sites, except with special permits issued before certain major feast days. These people were 'a defeated and demoralized minority, without leadership and without much hope',[23] in the words of Merav Mack, a scholar of the period based at the Van Leer Institute in Jerusalem. Among them were residents of Christian villages such as Iqrit and Fafr Bir'im, near the Lebanese border. Their evacuation was presented as a short-term measure that would be reversed at the end of hostilities. In the event, the villagers were never allowed to return to their homes. Iqrit and Fafr Bir'im were bulldozed in 1951. The land was then granted to a new Jewish population.

As Israel expanded after 1967, it defined as 'absentee property' the homes, smallholdings, and other land that Palestinians were forced to vacate. Though obliged under the law to respect the integrity of religious sites, the Israeli government found it hard to reconcile this understanding with its desires for security and expansion. Muslim-owned religious property was treated with even less deference than that of Christians. And Muslim *waqf* (religious endowments) were often confiscated before a change in the law in 1965.[24]

Gentler forms of official pressure have been in evidence as well. For two decades after 1948, even though the Greek Orthodox Patriarchate stood in what was then the Jordanian side of Jerusalem, the Israeli government paid rental fees on church-owned land in its territory. Israel thus acquired title or long-term leases to hundreds of acres of church land in West Jerusalem. Had it not cooperated, the Patriarchate would have risked losing all of its property in Israel. The details of land negotiations are extremely complex, and individual Churches have not escaped criticism for acting out of self-interest, as well as in ways that have risked causing harm to other Christians. But the broad picture has seen successive Israeli governments incrementally strengthening the hand of the state. In March 2011, the Greek Orthodox Patriarch, Theophilos III, drew fire from fellow Christians and others when he renewed a lease on property and land in Jerusalem for an additional ninety-nine years, even though it was not due to expire till 2051. The inducement for the Church is said to have been 80 million shekels.[25]

To some extent, it is fair to suggest that Christians have been victims of a divide-and-rule policy. But with the conspicuous exception of Christian Zionists, most of the Churches have also formed a common front against the Israeli authorities' perceived intransigence. As the first and second Intifadas (uprisings) beginning in 1987 and 2000 respectively served to galvanise the forces of Palestinian nationalism, including among Arab citizens of Israel, they also promoted what has been termed the 'Palestinianisation' of the Churches in Jerusalem. The city's three patriarchs (Latin, Greek, and Armenian) and other senior pastors have voiced loud support for the Palestinians in recent years, producing regular joint statements for the first time on political and humanitarian subjects. Twice in 1988, for instance, soon after the start of the first Intifada, senior clerics publicly deplored 'the grievous suffering of our people on the West Bank and in the Gaza Strip'.[26] They also came to a much-needed accord on planning repairs to the Church of the Holy Sepulchre before the turn of the millennium,[27] thus easing a series of small-minded squabbles between the site's various Christian custodians dating back many years.

Perhaps the most significant document compiled under church auspices has been *A Moment of Truth (Kairos Palestine)*, put out in December 2009.[28] Published by the World Council of

Churches and endorsed by the leaders of the historic Churches in Jerusalem, it stresses the need for freedom of religion for everyone:

> Trying to make the state a religious state, Jewish or Islamic, suffocates the state, confines it within narrow limits, and transforms it into a state that practises discrimination and exclusion, preferring one citizen over another. We appeal to both religious Jews and Muslims: let the state be a state for all its citizens, with a vision constructed on respect for religion but also on equality, justice, liberty and respect for pluralism, and not on domination by a religion or a numerical majority.[29]

*

Detailed political analysis of the Israeli–Palestinian conflict lies beyond my remit. It seems to me adequate here to note that we are confronted with a historical tragedy brought about because two ancient peoples were led to believe that they had a right to nationhood: the Jews through the Balfour Declaration, and the Arabs through the support for their Revolt of 1916–18 given by figures such as T.E. Lawrence. Britain's own divide-and-rule tactics, and British diplomats' fondness at this time for saying different things to different parties, had lethal consequences.

The background most appropriate to our discussion is theological, given both the persecution of Jews by Christians on a monumental scale in the past and the allied problem arising from core Christian self-understanding – including the Church's claim to be the new Israel, both supplementing and fulfilling the revelation held by Jews and Christians alike to be set out in the Hebrew Bible or Old Testament.

There is a second important basis for a theological perspective. We must grant that the political deadlock is fuelled by Christians to a marked extent – in this case Protestant fundamentalists, largely from the United States, whose brand of Zionism translates into uncritical support for settlers in the West Bank as part of a warped reading of both the Old and New Testaments. A small number of Christians are Zionists in exactly the same sense as Jewish Zionists; but far more Christian Zionists support Zionism simply as a staging post before the projected conversion of the Jews as a prelude to the Second Coming of Christ. Resting on a literalistic approach to the picture language of the Book of Revelation, this world view can only be dismantled on its own terms.

A more responsible and theologically informed Christian argument might deploy the following points. The doctrinal dispute between Christians and Jews centres on whether God's purported revelation in Christ as the climax of Israel's calling is essential to the story of God's people or not – and the allied Christian belief that this calling is to be extended beyond the ethnic limits of Israel to the worldwide community that is the Church. Hideous consequences have sometimes followed from an affirmative answer to this question. Many Christians have seen it as a licence for anti-Semitism, and many Jews, unsurprisingly, have concluded that Christianity is by definition antithetical to them. But to believe that Jesus is the Messiah need not in any way entail a brushing aside of Israel's significance. On the contrary, for the Christian, a careful reading of the most authoritative text on this subject – chapters 9–11 of St Paul's Letter to the Romans – buttresses the conviction that Jews retain their special calling by God's grace.

I have already argued – both at the outset of this book and in my biography of him – that Rowan Williams is one of the most judicious contemporary guides to the interface between Christianity and geopolitics, a status enhanced by his having led the world's second-most international Church between 2002 and 2012. His instincts on the Middle East are especially astute, as can be seen from the Sabeel Conference lecture, 'Holy Land and Holy People', which he gave in Jerusalem in 2004.[30] This text has stood the test of time – despite unforeseeable events such as the Fatah–Hamas split, the Arab Spring, and the arm-wrestling of Binyamin Netanyahu and Barak Obama. It provides a grid for recognising the integrity of the state of Israel without giving unconditional support to its every move. Both extremes of the argument rest on highly questionable interpretations of Scripture. One reading has it that there is nothing to be said about the Jewish people and the state of Israel from a Christian standpoint. The second, 'Zionist' reading, is based, as I have argued, on an apocalyptic myth. There is plainly a political as well as a theological imperative to resist these twin errors.

Williams's discussion begins with the question of the Covenant and its meaning. The answer supplied by Leviticus and much of the prophetic tradition in the Hebrew Bible (the Old Testament to Christians) is that Israel is called to be what Williams terms the 'paradigm nation', namely

> the example held up to all nations of how a people lives in obedience to God and justice with one another. This is how a nation is meant to be: living by law, united by a worship that enjoins justice and reverence for all, exercising hospitality, with a special concern for those who have fallen outside the safety of the family unit (the widow and orphan) and those who fall outside the tribal identities of the people (the resident alien, the 'stranger within the gates'). What is more, as Deuteronomy insists (4:5–6, 32–34; 7:7–8), this is a people, a community, that exists solely because of God's loving choice; they have been called out of another nation specifically to live as a community whose task is to show God's wisdom in the world.[31]

But a high calling entails heavy responsibilities. This is one reason why the prophets of the Old Testament are so scathing about injustice in ancient Israel and Judah. The corollary to all this is spelt out by the Evangelical writer Gary Burge in his book *Whose Land? Whose Promise?: What Christians are not being told about Israel and the Palestinians*.[32] One of Burge's main arguments is that if a biblical warrant is sought to justify the state of Israel, then biblical expectations – including the thrust of the prophetic critique – must be brought into play as well. In fact, the Bible abounds in stories of Gentiles such as Job and Ruth who highlight Israel's real calling.

Furthermore, the land is to be seen as lent or leased from God, who is its ultimate owner. The prohibition against selling off the land in Leviticus 25 should be understood in this light: it should not be a means of building up private wealth, but rather a conduit for maximising equitable provision for all. 'Take away this vocation,' Williams adds, 'and the history makes no sense. A "chosen people" that has become not only powerful but oppressive in its practice has made nonsense of God's calling to them . . . [and] if the land has to be defended by ceaseless struggle which distorts the very fabric of the common life, it ceases to be a . . . mark of God's calling . . . but becomes a prison, not a gift.'[33]

The thrust of this argument will be apparent to all who deplore anti-Semitism (and its theological bedfellow, anti-Judaism), but who yet feel that in Israel former victims have themselves become aggressors. Security for both sides should be the priority in the Holy Land: good news for one being good news for the other. 'There can be no more important matter to insist upon at present,' Williams urges, which is why . . . every suicide bomb in Israel is an appalling injury to the Palestinian people, and every demolition of a house, every collateral death of a bystander or child in the Palestinian territories, is a wound to Israel in the long run. There is no good news for Palestinians in the proclamation of a programme to humiliate and destroy Israel; there is no good news for Israelis in a 'security' that sets in stone the impotent anger and resentment of Palestinians . . . it would be the bitterest irony if the State of Israel were simply encouraged to subvert its own moral essence in order to survive, encouraged and enabled to become not a paradigm for the nations, but a nation deeply caught in the same traps of violence and self-interest that affect us all.[34]

Given the horrors to which Jews have been subjected in other eras, especially in the West, their right to call Christians to account should be taken for granted. The Church's claim to embody the new Israel is challenged by a legacy of deep prejudice. It is also incontestable that Islam is perverted in the attitudes of suicide bombers. The challenge arises when Christians and Muslims nonetheless feel a need in their turn to hold Jews to account, too. Yet this is simply a matter of treating them as responsible equals, not as permanent victims.

My brief encompasses reportage and analysis, not sermonising, but it seems right all the same to end this chapter on a confessional note. Christianity is the only major monotheistic faith to originate in an explicit repudiation of religious violence. For this reason, and despite all the countless betrayals of Jesus's message by his followers, the tradition he inaugurated retains potent resources for nourishing contemporary peace-making across the globe. In 1996, during my first trip to the Holy Land, I visited St George's Anglican Cathedral, a little corner of Jerusalem that is forever Barchester – at least visually. The Dean,

John Tidy, poured me a drink as we sat on a terrace looking across the city, and reflected that he had 'started to understand why God had incarnated himself here, in the midst of all this'.

Here was a comment drawn from Christian piety, certainly, but no less solidly rooted for that in a grasp of problems affecting the Holy Land, and many other strife-torn places besides.

13

SIX COUNTRIES AT A GLANCE

This chapter differs from the previous dozen in giving brief outlines of the problems facing Christians in six countries. Our survey begins in **Cuba** and **Venezuela**. This may be surprising to some who do not see these societies as obvious zones of religious persecution, whatever their other problems, and who recall that church news in Latin America has often mainly concerned either internal divisions (including Vatican clampdowns on liberation theologians during the 1980s and 1990s) or accusations of poaching voiced by established Christians against Pentecostals. Yet reasons for a focus on Latin America are not hard to find. The Catholic Church has long been heavily politicised in the region – whether through the witness of an anti-poverty campaigner such as Archbishop Hélder Câmara of Recife in Brazil; or Archbishop Oscar Romero of San Salvador, martyred by a right-wing death squad in 1980; or, by contrast, through the ill-famed alliances between bishops and military dictators in countries including Chile and Argentina before their transition to civilian rule. Mercifully, the continent has moved on in crucial respects over the past two decades, despite abidingly high levels of poverty – and growing violence – in some places. My focus on the regimes of the Castro brothers and of Hugo Chávez is simply a reflection of where current difficulties chiefly lie, given the eclipse of the far right and the advance of democracy.

It may also seem surprising to start by drawing a parallel between the Cuban regime and hardline Muslim governments on the other side of the world. But one crucial resemblance between Communism and Islamism is the denial of alternative sources of authority. This helps explain the Castros' antipathy for the Church through much of their reign, even though Fidel and his brother, Raúl, were educated by Jesuits, and were later saved from execution by a local bishop and family friend, Enrique Pérez Serantes, who intervened with the Batista regime after the Castros had been convicted of attacking the Moncada Barracks in 1953.

As the profile of Cuba in *Religious Freedom in the World* makes clear,[1] many Catholics felt initial sympathy for the revolutionaries, or at least for the sentiment underlying their rejection of entrenched privilege and inequality. A number of priests even ministered as chaplains to Fidel's forces. But Church–state relations deteriorated at a gallop after the new leader's declaration in December 1960 that 'to be anti-Communist is tantamount to being anti-revolutionary', and after the failed Bay of Pigs invasion four months later. Many clergy and laypeople, and all the bishops, were arrested; then all church-run schools were taken over by the state. Public devotions were banned, foreign missionaries expelled, and the number of priests on the island fell to 200. Cuba was declared an atheist country in 1976. Both before and after this time, official permission was rarely given to extend or even repair church property.

But from the late 1980s onwards, and partly motivated by the end of Soviet economic subsidies, Castro began to make life a little easier for the Catholic Church. (He had always been more indulgent towards *santería*, the fusion of Catholic, African, and Caribbean spiritualities popular in Central America, because devotees of this tradition lack a clear institutional voice.) Christmas was reinstated as a public holiday in 1997, shortly before Pope John Paul II visited the island. To the amazement of many Cuban Catholics, the Archbishop of Havana, Cardinal Jaime Lucas Ortega y Alamino, was even asked to broadcast a series of homilies on television.

Progress on religious liberty since then has been halting: after Raúl Castro succeeded Fidel in 2008, a nationwide appeal was launched to raise funds for Our Lady of Charity of Cobre, Cuba's national shrine, where devotions had been banned as recently as the late 1990s. Cardinal Ortega protested vigorously when the police broke up a demonstration of the 'Ladies in White', relatives of political detainees, in 2010. The government duly gave way, allowing similar events to go ahead. Two other significant events occurred at around this time. Cardinal Ortega acted as intermediary in talks leading to the release of fifty political prisoners; and on Easter Day 2010, up to 3,000 Christians took to the streets in the town of Santa Clara in a spontaneous display of faith. Even though they marched for two kilometres, the police did not try to arrest them. Observers are nevertheless clear that church action in crucial fields including health, education, and charitable outreach remains severely hampered. Practising Christians continue to face discrimination in the workplace. Scarcely any progress has been made in negotiations to return church-owned buildings seized during the 1960s. Individual priests who take a more robust stance in favour of human rights can expect trouble.

A notable victim of persecution is Fr José Conrado, parish priest of Santa Teresita del Niño Jesús, a renowned church in Santiago de Cuba. He is known as 'the Cardinal of the people' for his outspoken opposition to the regime and his human rights campaigns. For his pains he has suffered frequent break-ins at his home for years. He is also scarcely ever allowed to receive foreign visitors. Catholic lay leaders who have spoken out in favour of religious freedom also report various forms of provocation, including having loud music played outside their homes day and night, and vandalism to their property.[2]

Two further details deserve emphasis: the treatment of non-Catholic Christians, especially house-church members; and the worsening situation faced by Christians in the very recent past. Church leaders who have openly called on the government to respect religious freedom, or criticised political interference in internal church affairs, those who have refused to work on behalf of the government (for example, by acting as informers, or by publicly endorsing government policy), and church groups who fail to register with the authorities: all these have been targeted for harsh treatment. The six-year sentence handed down in July 2009 to one pastor (the most lengthy penalty inflicted on a religious leader in decades), and the ongoing persecution of another senior leader who resisted pressure on the organisation he led, are sources of regular concern to human rights campaigners. They see this and other evidence as proof that Cuba is not moving towards a more open society under Raúl Castro. Rather the reverse.

The bigger picture is reflected in the case of Adalberto Ramírez, a Methodist pastor in Pilón, Granma province. He reported in July 2008 that the authorities were threatening to confiscate his church. The unregistered premises had been the base for a ministry to about 150 people for seven years. Shortly afterwards, Mr Ramírez was ordered to disband his congregation. If he did not comply, the building would be confiscated. Another pastor, Yogli González Pérez, was evicted from his house in Santiago de Cuba at about this time; the building was then confiscated by the government. Mr González Pérez was ministering at the

Pentecostal Congregational Church. Items belonging to him, his wife, and their four-year-old son were taken away.

Another body, the Western Baptist Convention, has faced sustained collective pressure. The government targets both congregations and specific pastors, encouraging them to report any dissident activity. When this ploy failed, an attempt was made to strong-arm the convention into changing its constitution. That, too, proved unsuccessful, after which the authorities retaliated by confiscating several pieces of church property.

Among Christians targeted for their activism is Pastor Omar Gude Pérez, leader of a new Christian body, the Apostolic Movement, who was jailed for six-and-a-half years in 2008 on trumped-up charges. Though he was released in early 2011, his activities have been strictly curtailed. His application to move to the United States, which had offered him asylum, has been refused. It is fair to infer that Raúl Castro's government fears the tide of poor publicity that would probably follow Pastor Gude Pérez's move overseas.

Christians face regular beatings from security officials and their thugs; no one has been held accountable for these attacks to date. Requests for investigations are ignored. The assaults have several features in common. 'Victims have all been church leaders in smaller denominations or independent churches, meaning they do not have an organised network to call on for support,' CSW reports.[3] Furthermore, the targets of violence have tended to be those based in more out-of-the-way areas, away from the main tourist trails. In each instance, the victim has challenged the authorities in some way before being attacked. The case of Reutilio Columbie, leader of a Pentecostal congregation in the eastern Moa area, is especially harrowing. When he protested against the illegal confiscation of a church-owned vehicle by Communist Party staff, he was beaten up and left for dead. Discovered by passers-by, Mr Columbie received emergency medical treatment, but has suffered long-term brain damage marked by symptoms such as memory loss, constant dizziness, and nausea.

The worsening situation is all the more surprising given the regime's evident wish to project a good image of itself during the visit of Pope Benedict in March 2012. The truth is that the event prompted a behind-the-scenes clampdown. Hundreds of activists, most of them Catholics, were rounded up in advance and placed under house arrest or in prison to stop them from taking part in any of the events on the papal itinerary. Part of the reason for this is procedural. Policy towards religious bodies is controlled by the Office of Religious Affairs of the Cuban Communist Party, not by a government institution. This leaves faith groups at the mercy of party officials, who are often hostile in principle during negotiations on matters ranging from construction and upkeep of church buildings to permits for foreign travel and the importing of catechetical materials.

It was certainly notable that restrictions were not eased after Pope Benedict's departure: some of those detained have since been forbidden to attend Sunday worship. One victim of this policy is Caridad Caballero, a member of the Ladies in White group. She and several of her relatives have been manhandled by the authorities, and subjected to verbal abuse, on numerous occasions. At the time of writing they are still placed in solitary confinement on Sundays.

A snapshot of Venezuela shows it to be a parallel case in core respects. The regime is widely accused of flouting the rule of law, including carrying out extra-judicial killings and heavy media censorship. In 2009, a decade into President Hugo Chávez's rule, a source close to the country's Catholic bishops told religious-freedom monitors that the government was 'intent on eliminating the work of the Church'. Education is naturally a critical battleground: the Archbishop of Caracas, Cardinal Jorge Urosa Savino, alleged in 2009 that recently introduced legislation 'takes out religion from schools', even though religious education is 'a right which is in the constitution'.[4] 'Going beyond the national constitution,' the cardinal wrote a year later, '[Chávez] and his government want to lead the country on the path to Marxist socialism, which monopolizes all spaces, is totalitarian and leads to a dictatorship, not of the proletariat, but of the leadership that governs.'[5]

The government in turn has harried the Church via various channels, including La Piedrita, the self-styled 'people's revolutionary collective', which serves as an urban guerrilla force for Chávez. For example, members of this group launched six tear-gas attacks on the home of the Apostolic Nuncio between 2007 and 2009; and in September 2009, a Caracas daily carried an article headlined 'The cardinal's administrative error', which alleged that Cardinal Urosa had circulated an email endorsing class divisions in schools. Urosa strenuously denied doing so.

Chávez has described his country's Catholic bishops as 'a bunch of cavemen';[6] they in turn welcomed National Assembly elections in 2010 that reduced Chávez's majority. The result, they announced, would make the chamber more democratic and less 'fearful'.[7] The stand-off between Church and state betokened by these remarks has a long way to run.

*

The denial of alternative sources of authority was manifestly one of countless vices displayed by the Soviet Union and its satellites, with large consequences for religious freedom. Yet many older churchmen and women in Central and Eastern Europe feel that younger generations are guilty of amnesia over the horrors endured by Christians in their own backyards within living memory. The complaint is fair. Travel through a country such as Hungary today and you will see signs at places such as Kistarcsa and Recsk, with no indication at all that they were sites of concentration camps at which clergy and other believers were murdered in their thousands as recently as the 1950s. The once huge levels of violence seen in this part of the world have fallen dramatically, of course. But the oppression continues in pockets of the former Soviet bloc barely touched by reform.

Belarus stands out as the only European country discussed in this book, and also as a place where Christians are taunted by some of their fellow believers, as well as by the secret police and other operatives of the state. Alexander Lukashenko, who began a fourth term as President after disputed elections in 2010, has long shown the style of a Communist-era dictator. A panoply of human rights reforms in the early 1990s appeared to herald a better future. But in 1995, Lukashenko banned Catholic priests from holding public Masses without permission. Four years later, a decree laid down that foreign clergy could minister only under the aegis of bodies officially recognised by the State Committee for Religion and Ethnic Affairs.

Predictably, government enmity towards Christians increases in proportion to their involvement in social and political activism. The year 2002 saw the passing of the Law on Freedom of Conscience and Religious Organisation, which claimed to guarantee religious freedom – just as the 1929 Law on Religious Associations had done in the Soviet Union. Like its Soviet precursor, the Belarusian law employs the principle of registration as a means of exercising control, while also making registration difficult in the first place.

Once more, it is newer Christian groups who tend to fare the worst of all. Pentecostals in the Brest region sought permission to conduct public baptisms in a lake in 2006. When no official response was forthcoming they went ahead with the ceremony, but it was quickly broken up. Two of the participants were sent to prison for a fortnight. At around the same time, Georgi Vyazovsky, a Baptist minister in Minsk, was jailed for conducting worship at his home without permission. The experience of registered congregations that had previously operated quite legally is also revealing. The 1,000-member Pentecostal New Life Church (NLC) in Minsk offers a disturbing example. It was refused re-registration in 2004. Undeterred, the congregation moved to a disused cowshed which they had bought two years previously. This new venue was raided by the police, the pastor was given a heavy fine, and officials threatened to demolish an extension that had been built by the worshippers themselves. Giles Udy, a close observer of religion in Belarus, reports that demolition was only prevented by the support of foreign ambassadors. The confrontation is now approaching its ninth year: recently, NLC was accused of 'polluting' its grounds, fined $100,000, and had its bank account frozen. Worshippers are appealing for foreign help to save their building.[8]

Similar clampdowns have taken place more recently. Alexander Yermalitsky, a Baptist leader, was fined in January 2009 for hosting 'a religious event at which the Bible was read' in his home.[9] Two Danish visitors were deported a year later for voicing 'ideas of a religious nature'. They had been filmed worshipping at the Living Faith Church in Gomel, Belarus's second city.[10] Another Protestant, Viktor Novik, was fined in July 2010 for preaching out of doors.

These cases point to the country's position as a throwback to a world many thought had been extinguished. Today's

Thought Police in Belarus are known as ideology officers. Describing these figures, Mr Udy writes that they promote official state ideology at all levels of government and in all state enterprises and institutions. 'They also recruit informers to report on illegal religious activity. It is not untypical for groups comprising officials, police, and sometimes KGB officers to raid religious meetings and initiate prosecutions against believers.'[11] Udy cites an example from October 2009, when an ideology officer and four policemen raided a house in the eastern town of Chavusy, where a Full Gospel Protestant group was holding a service. Every member of the fellowship was interrogated; reading material was confiscated. Elsewhere, Udy adds, 'a state ideology officer shut down a seminar on family relationships held by a Protestant pastor in the town's Palace of Culture. Fifteen Palace of Culture employees were then sacked as a warning [that they should not] associate with or accommodate believers.'[12]

The chauvinism displayed by some in the Belarusian Orthodox Church (BOC), an exarchate or offshoot of the Russian Orthodox Church, should be placed on the record. From their headquarters at the Moscow Patriarchate, several senior church leaders worked for the KGB during Soviet times; among their recruits was Metropolitan Filaret of Minsk. The Religion Law of 2002 reflected strong ties between Orthodoxy and nationalism: the BOC was accorded a privileged position, and shortly before the law's enactment, the then Patriarch of Moscow, Alexei II (also a former KGB agent), awarded President Lukashenko the prize of 'the Unity of Slavic Peoples' as a mark of his service to Orthodox identity. The relationship was sealed with a concordat the following year that endowed the BOC with the sole right to call itself 'Orthodox' (thereby sidelining other Orthodox communities), along with a role in resisting 'pseudo-religious structures that present a danger to individuals and society' – a barely coded reference to Protestants.

Orthodox prejudice and paranoia partly spring from the terrible persecutions of the Communist era (an irony not lost on bemused observers of today's bedfellows in Church and state), and a deeper resentment against the West over historical injuries, some real, others greatly overstated, extending back at least as far as the sacking of Constantinople during the Fourth Crusade in 1204. But Russian Orthodoxy's poor record on toleration, and on speaking truth to power, should serve as a reproach to Christians convinced that 'ethno-religion' and its associated ills are only a problem for those of other faiths.

*

Sri Lanka fits a template common in this book. First, the country's general human rights record is poor. Opposing forces were both guilty of multiple war crimes during the long civil conflict that ended in 2009. Although the government has signed treaties such as the International Covenant on Civil and Political Rights and the Convention against Torture, neither measure has been properly implemented.[13] Criticism from the international community has prompted the Sri Lankan authorities to boost economic links with China.

A second factor is that there is a close fit between religious and ethnic differences. Three-quarters of the 20 million-strong population are Sinhalese; most of this group are Buddhist. About 8.5 per cent of the population are Tamils, mostly Hindu. The Muslim community is of roughly comparable size, and regarded as a separate ethnic body. Christians, forming just over 6 per cent of the population, are of both Sinhalese and Tamil ethnicity. Four-fifths of Christians are Catholics.

Only they and other 'traditional' Christian groups such as Anglicans, Methodists, and Baptists are officially recognised by the government. The National Christian Evangelical Alliance of Sri Lanka (NCEASL), representing new Protestant congregations for the most part, is 'routinely denied permission' for any request it makes, according to CSW.[14] Official sources consistently tend to represent Sri Lankan identity as an interlacing of Sinhalese ethnicity and Theravada Buddhist culture.[15] Buddhist nationalism thus menaces Sri Lanka in a way that stands comparison with that of Burma.

The roots of this tendency lie to a large degree in a reaction against colonialism, and thus against Christianity, during the nineteenth century. By then the island had seen successive waves of rule by Christians – Catholics, Dutch Reformed, and eventually, Anglicans – over a 300-year span. A Buddhist revival began across the territory (then Ceylon) shortly before the turn of the twentieth century; this received a nationalist twist under the influence of Anagarika Dharmapala (1864–1933). He glorified the achievements of Sinhalese culture as 'a way of infusing [his people] with a new nationalist identity and self-respect in the face of humiliation and restrictions suffered under British rule and Christian missionary influence', in the words of the Sri Lankan scholar Stanley Tambiah.[16]

The tradition grew in weight during the twentieth century. Just after the Second World War, Walpola Rahula, a monk and historian, set out a mythologised account of the alleged role played by monks in championing the Sinhala Buddhist nation in his book *Bhiksuvage Urumaya (The Heritage of the Bhikkhu)*.[17] Composed with an eye on the contemporary situation, this work offered an intellectual underpinning for militancy among Buddhists during the following decades. The shift was reflected in changes to the country's constitution. Its initial (1947) version held Ceylon to be religiously neutral, but the revised wording of 1978 defined Buddhism as having 'the foremost place' in society.

The practical consequences of this were far-reaching. CSW reveals that in 1991, a presidential commission investigating NGOs soon came to focus on the activities of the Churches, introducing the language of 'unethical conversions' to classify a wide range of social projects carried out by Christians.[18] The individuals and groups examined by the commission were not given the opportunity to defend themselves. The inquiry prompted the media to cast local congregations in a negative light, which in turn provoked violent anti-Christian attacks.

Stephen C. Berkwitz, an anthropologist with long experience of Sri Lanka, has traced a contemporary echo of Dharmapala in the writings of Gangodawila Soma Thero (d.2003), a hot-headed but popular monk given to scattergun condemnations of 'foreign' forces ranging from Christian missionaries to the World Bank, from Norwegian peace monitors to the Tamil and Muslim populations. Jathika Hela Urumaya (JHU), the party of Buddhist monks founded in 2003, has displayed a particular animus against Christians. Its spokesmen favour the complete outlawing of conversion. The party is still relatively small (it won three seats in the 2010 elections); anti-conversion laws have not been introduced so far. But it wields influence with the Sri Lankan government all the same. Even denominations that have been legally incorporated by an act of Parliament, such as the Assemblies of God and the Church of the Foursquare Gospel, are often faced with threats of closure on the basis that they are not 'legitimate' Churches; refusal of permission to construct places of worship; refusal of burial rights; or denial of admission to schools for their members' children.

The problem extends far beyond the domain of legal wrangles. A Pentecostal pastor's house (also used as a church) was burnt down in Matugama, 45 miles south of Colombo, on 16 January 2010. When he went to the police station to report the matter, the pastor found a crowd of Buddhist monks and villagers protesting against Christian worship in the area. A few weeks later, the pastor of Creator Almighty God Believers' Church at Getalawa, in the north-central Anuradhapura district, was assaulted, warned that he should abandon his ministry, and threatened with being thrown into Kokawewa Lake. The police issued those responsible with a warning. But several days later, two Buddhist monks threatened the pastor again after his church service. On 19 February, the Living God Prayer Centre was attacked by a mob late at night in Thiruperunthurai, a village on Sri Lanka's east coast. And shortly after this (in the town of Kalutara), the dedication service for an Evangelical pastor's residence was invaded by a mob of over a hundred, led by several Buddhist monks. The rioters declared that Sri Lanka was a Buddhist country; Christians could only conduct services with official permission. Police advised the monks against violence, but demanded that the pastor show evidence of authorisation for religious activities, which is not a legal requirement.

The hardline monks of Kalutara have kept up their campaign. On 10 October 2010, six of them led a crowd into the Foursquare Gospel Church during Sunday morning worship, where they assaulted the pastor, and destroyed furniture and musical instruments. Police filed a complaint. On 18 January 2011, at Norachcholai, in the north-western Puttalam district, a mob came to the rebuilding site of an Assemblies of God church that had been burnt down three times. The builders were told to stop work. An official, the 'divisional secretary', instructed the pastor to halt building work as well, but he refused, on the grounds that the church had received all necessary permissions. The divisional secretary later issued a letter repeating his demand.

Finally, in Galkulama, Anuradhapura, on 20 February 2011, a mob led by six Buddhist monks forcibly entered the home of a Christian man who was hosting a birthday celebration for his daughter. They had been joined by the family's pastor and several of the pastor's relatives. The mob assaulted the pastor and his son; then they stole items that were being used at the celebration. The Christians went to file a complaint with police, who began an investigation five days later, and told the victim that 'religions which are not recognized' were unwelcome. And so the melancholy saga continues.

*

Laos well exemplifies the Communist iron fist with Far-Eastern characteristics. A group of people in the village of Katin, part of the Ta-Oyl district in Salavan, a southern province, gathered for worship one Sunday in mid-January 2010. Suddenly, their service was halted when about a hundred police and local officials hurried into the building. Forty-eight members of the congregation were marched at gunpoint to a spot four miles away. The belongings of eleven Christian families were confiscated; six Christian-owned homes were completely destroyed. The families made homeless were given pieces of plastic sheeting for protection. Then strenuous attempts were made to force them to renounce their faith. A month later, a senior local official returned to visit the dispossessed Christians, telling them that they must take down the makeshift shelters they had put up. The adults refused, pointing out that the youngest of twenty children in their care was just two years old.

This was not the first ordeal that the Christians – most of whom were recent converts – had faced. Six months beforehand (on 5 July 2009), officials broke into the new believers' pig pens and confiscated one pig from the holdings of each of nine families, each one worth six weeks' salary. The Christians were told that this was their punishment for disobeying an order forbidding them to convert. At a meeting the following day, a local official made an announcement:

> Those who follow the Christian faith are practising a foreign religion, not a religion of Laos. We have banned the Christian faith in our village. Thus, the residents of Katin village should follow only the belief in the spirits, which is considered the Lao religion. If any villager . . . is found following the Christian faith without renouncing that religion, he or she will no longer be under the official provision and protection of the village.[19]

The pendulum on religious freedom has swung violently in Laos, where half of the population of almost 7 million is Buddhist, and most other people profess traditional religions. There are 150,000 Protestants and 40,000 Catholics. Pathet Lao guerrillas seized power in 1975, setting up a one-party Communist state governed by the Lao People's Revolutionary Party (LPRP). The economy was in tatters within fifteen years. There followed a measure of economic liberalisation accompanied by a qualified easing of political and cultural fetters, then another move backwards. Christians faced particular trouble after 1998, for example. Many believers were sent to prison if they failed to renounce their faith. Some were obliged to demonstrate the reality of their change of heart by taking part in animist rituals, smoking (a practice which is anathema to Christians in Laos), and drinking blood. Then such pressure was eased after a tide of international pressure around the turn of the millennium.

Fewer Christians were arrested; some churches were allowed to reopen.

In common with that in many other authoritarian societies, the legal position in Laos is ambiguous. Articles 30 and 31 of the country's constitution provide for freedom of belief and freedom of speech respectively. But a prime ministerial edict on religious liberty (Decree 92) allows officials to ban activities considered to encourage 'social division' or 'chaos'. Religious proselytising is only permitted with the approval of the Lao Front for National Construction (LFNC), the public face of the LPRP. In practice, such permission is rarely forthcoming.

Non-registered Christian fellowships thus operate at considerable risk. Arrests and detentions of members of unauthorised churches occurred during 2009–2010 in Luang Namtha, Phongsali, and Savannakhet provinces. During April of 2010, one of the Christians expelled from Katin village the previous January died after an outbreak of diarrhoea and dehydration in the displaced community.[20] And in January of the following year, police arrested eleven Christians at gunpoint in the Hinboun district of Khammouan Province. Three of the church leaders remain in prison at the time of writing for 'holding a secret meeting'.[21]

Typically, though, acrid conditions can generate heroism as well as misery. The widow of a murdered pastor, a woman identified simply as Abigail, has testified that 'Christianity is spreading in Laos – despite persecution – and Christians are growing strong in the faith.' She added that if she were confronted with her husband's murderer, she would tell him 'about God's love . . . even when I do something wrong He always forgives me, so I will tell [the killers] that I love him, because God loves him too – and God will forgive him.'[22]

*

Magnanimity of this kind is also a source of healing in **Sudan**, the scene of suffering as abhorrent as anywhere on any continent. Until the long-delayed vote for partition that led to the founding of South Sudan in 2011, this immense country was split between the Arab- and Muslim-dominated north and the black south, where most people are either Christians or adherents of traditional spiritualities.

Turf wars over land and resources have long been as common in Sudan as in many other places. But a profound change arose in the early 1980s, when the authorities in Khartoum sought to introduce sharia law in the southern city of Bor. Tensions proliferated from 1989 onwards, the moment when a more hardline body, the National Islamic Front, took power and launched a jihad against its opponents. We have already noted that around 2 million people died in the ensuing civil war, which officially ended with a peace agreement in 2005. Vast numbers of others were deeply marked by the conflict: tens of thousands were enslaved; 4 million displaced. The legacy for ravaged communities of malnutrition, disease, and lost educational chances will naturally be felt for generations.

Obviously, the war had many political causes. But the religious dimension was rarely far from the surface. Asked to renounce their faith in return for receiving government aid, many Christians chose to risk starvation. In their book *The Very Stones Cry Out*,[23] Caroline Cox and Benedict Rogers cite the case of a blind and almost naked mother in Bahr el Ghazal (now part of western South Sudan) who declared in 1994 that she 'could go to another area where the government of Sudan is in charge and receive food, medicine, clothes. But I know that if I do, I will have to convert to Islam – and that I will not do. We are Christians – and I would prefer to live and die as Christians.'[24] The authors' reflection on this comment is apposite: 'While this would be a challenging decision to make for oneself, it must be infinitely . . . harder to make the decision to sacrifice one's child. Such is the price paid by countless people in Sudan who refused survival for themselves and their children in order not to betray their faith.'[25]

This example needs to be seen in the context of a wider campaign to impose Islam on southern Sudan by any means. The epicentre of violence spread to the western province of Darfur after 2005. The Catholic Bishop of Khartoum, Daniel Adwok Kur, spoke for many two years later in suggesting that the government was exploiting the Darfur situation as 'a smoke screen to spread Islam into the mainly Christian south'. Addressing an international conference, he said that his government was operating hand-in-glove with Islamist groups in the Middle East to fund schools, hospitals, and mosques to promote religious conversions.[26]

Separate tragedies have unfolded in the Nuba Mountains (or southern Kordofan, as the area has been renamed, against local wishes) and in the north of the country, where Christians have long been an embattled minority. With the secession of South Sudan, Sudan is now more manifestly an Islamist state. Sharia law applies to all, converts from Islam are at grave risk, church life is very tightly controlled. As I read the literature, various stories of Sudanese Christian converts stood out for me, among them that of Halima Bubkier, a woman from Sinarr, near Khartoum, now in her late thirties. She became a Christian after seeing a film about the life and message of Jesus. At first, her husband acquiesced in her decision. But local hardliners were horrified, banning Mr Bubkier from attending communal meals during Ramadan. He then turned on his wife, according to later testimony, threw a chair at her, and injured her back. He later removed his belongings from their home and set fire to the building. Mrs Bubkier tried to take refuge with her elder brother, who beat her and threatened to stab her. Yet it was she who ended up in prison, on a charge of 'disrespecting Islam', in April 2009. Fortunately, she was released within a few days, thanks to the intervention of a Coptic priest, though her husband has retained custody of two of their three children.[27]

A little earlier (in March of the same year), two Protestant churches were destroyed in the Chat area of the Nuba Mountains, probably because the International Criminal Court in the Hague had indicted Sudan's President, Omar al-Bashir, for war crimes. Similar acts occurred in the centre of the country: the Anglican church at Shatt Mazarik was bombed on 7 March; a similar attack took place on the Catholic church at Shatt Damman a fortnight later. Christians reported that the local authorities made no effort to investigate.

Another recent hate crime that stands out is the attempted murder of the Archbishop of Khartoum, Cardinal Gabriel Zubeir Wako, in October 2010. A man later named as Hamdan Mohamed Abdurrahman drew a dagger and ran towards the cardinal as he celebrated Mass, but was intercepted by a member of the clergy and handed into police custody. Another Catholic bishop, Eduardo Hiiboro Kussala, said that his colleague had been targeted for assassination on various occasions, but had shown very strong faith under pressure.

Grace under fire provides a fitting focus on which to end. My text is a passage from a sermon preached by Macram Gassis, exiled Catholic Bishop of El Obeid, who risked his life by visiting his flock in the company of Baroness Cox in 1995. Standing under a tamarind tree, the bishop spoke thus:

Here we are, in this beautiful cathedral, not made by human hands, but by nature and by God – and it is filled with the people of God, and especially with children. You people here in Sudan still smile, in spite of suffering, persecution and slavery. Your smiles put us to shame. Many of you have been captured and taken into slavery. If that happens to you or to those whom you love, remember that that is not real slavery. The real slave is a person who does injustice to brothers and sisters and who kills them. But you are children of God . . . no longer slaves, but free: children of liberty and truth.

Many of you are naked and embarrassed by your nakedness. Don't be embarrassed. Yours is not true nakedness. True nakedness is to be without love. Therefore, be clothed in love – that is true Christianity – and show your love to those who do not know our Lord of love. Do not think that we will forget you. You will be remembered as those who are closest to God, because every day you are obeying Christ's command to take up His cross and to follow Him.[28]

The point of quoting words as tender and life-enhancing as these is not just to balance bad news with something more cheering. The deeper lesson – that evil can pave the way for the victory of good – takes us to the root of the Christian story.

CONCLUSION

I trust that this book has helped establish that Christians are afflicted on a great scale and in many places. I also hope that one of my main secondary arguments has been demonstrated: that the injustice remains under-reported, despite the admirable work of a small number of individuals and NGOs. Part of the reason for this lies with what I earlier called a bien-pensant blind spot. This consists of a generalised belief that religion is a greater cause of conflict than other factors such as access to resources or status, or questions of honour, or ethnic or political solidarity, or the use of superior power to exploit or eliminate rivals. The truth is that these elements are permanent features of intergroup relationships. They have continued to provoke strife under secular regimes into the present. The idea that religion is especially to blame derives from an Enlightenment narrative whereby the state, itself a major source of conflict, offloads blame onto Churches and other faith communities in particular.

Despite its pretensions to objectivity, this world view (which is often accompanied by the belief that a secularised providence has led to a liberal, God-free present) rests on a pile of lazy assumptions. Since all religions are seen as irrational sources of violent behaviour, this means that when a particular body of believers is targeted, sympathy gets withheld on the basis that the victims would inflict comparable aggression against others were they able to do so. In the case of the Churches, this is compounded by the association over the past two centuries of Christianity with Western imperialism, as though the link between institutions and wielders of power were not a much more general and tangled phenomenon. Exponents of this view tend to forget that all imperialisms, secular or religious, are linked to ideologies of domination. A further ingredient in this mix is drawn from the tension that developed in the early twentieth century between Christian missionaries on the one hand and, on the other, anthropologists promoting the ideology of 'authenticity' – often in alliance with the interests of postcolonial elites. This meant that Christians in countries such as Pakistan could be written off as part of the detritus of empire. As it happens, academic anthropology widened its horizons years ago – a shift encapsulated by a recent book such as *Missions and Empire*[1] in the Oxford History of the British Empire. But many hardline secularists, especially in politics and the media, remain stuck in old grooves.

Being clear that religion is over-blamed for conflict is hardly to suggest that it should not be blamed at all, though. Pascal's famous warning – that men never do evil so completely and cheerfully as when they do it from religious conviction – retains a blistering relevance. But different traditions cannot be lumped together in an undifferentiated mass. The repertoires of the major faiths are in some respects very different.

Statistics speak more powerfully than opinions in this regard. The chart in Appendix A shows the results of the survey of religious liberty carried out by the Freedom House think-tank published in 2008. Of the forty-one countries that were judged free in religious terms – that is, scoring 1, 2, or 3 on a scale of 1 to 7 – thirty-five are traditionally Christian. Only two traditionally Christian countries out of forty-five, Belarus and Cuba, were deemed to be 'not free' – that is, scoring a 6 or a 7. The other countries rated highly included three traditionally Buddhist domains: Japan, Mongolia, and Thailand. Buddhist societies scoring poorly were those with Communist governments: China, Tibet, Laos, North Korea, and Vietnam. Among the small number of Hindu-majority countries, Nepal scored poorly on both political and religious freedom, while India, unusually, was rated highly in the former category, and badly in the latter. This apparent anomaly is usually ascribed to the growth of Hindutva over recent decades.

The survey makes clear that the greatest curbs on religious freedoms take place in Muslim-majority countries. 'This pattern parallels problems with democracy, civil liberties and economic freedom, but the negative trend with respect to religious freedom is even stronger,' the scholar and campaigner Paul Marshall writes.[2] It is worth emphasising that religiously free Muslim countries do exist – Senegal, for example. But Muslim-majority societies formed twelve of the twenty 'unfree' ones surveyed, and of the seven territories receiving the lowest possible score, four were Muslim. This phenomenon extends outside the Middle East. Islamic democracies such as Indonesia and Bangladesh also score poorly: not, in their cases, because of government repression, but through the spread of Islamist terrorism. These findings are corroborated by an even more recent survey published in Brian J. Grim and Roger Finke's major study *The Price of Freedom Denied: Religious Persecution and Conflict in the Twenty-First Century*.[3]

So we must also confront directly a question which has haunted a large portion of this book. Is there a problem with Islam as such, or is the trouble more a matter of contingencies? (After all, large parts of the Christian world were saturated with unsurpassed levels of violence seventy or a hundred years ago.) Part of the answer to this question is theological. There is a theory that the idea of jihad is more deeply embedded in Islam than related notions in the other world religions – and therefore that Islam is more susceptible to violent extremism – because of the martial context in which Islam took root. It does not help that for the first half of the Muslim era, Muslims thought of themselves as being on top, both culturally and in terms of military power, for understandable reasons. The *ummah* extended from Córdoba in the west, to Baghdad, and in due course to the Far East: a vast belt of land greatly surpassing the reach of Christendom – and at times threatening to overwhelm it.

Defence advocates tend to reply that the Prophet Muhammad's ministry took place in a very hostile context, and that Islam's matrix was connected with the need to defend the community against dangerous opponents from the start. Supporters of this argument can sometimes turn the tables on Christianity by suggesting that although the New Testament is brimming with the language of peace, Christ's followers would in time become extremely violent towards non-Christians and perceived heretics. Thousands of 'witches' were murdered in early modern Europe and America; Thomas Aitkenhead was executed in Scotland for blasphemy as recently as 1697. This is to say nothing of earlier inquisitions, or of the anti-Jewish pogroms that took place later in Christian societies. Nor is Christian-backed violence a thing of the past. In the 1970s and 1980s, Lebanese Phalangist militias were dominated by Maronites in communion with the see of Rome. During the 1990s, Orthodox Christians (and ex-Communists who used their religious heritage as a flag of convenience) were guilty of extreme aggression against Muslims and Catholics in the Balkans.

As is the case with the Bible, selective quotations from the Qur'an are unlikely to advance the discussion: it contains both the aggressive-seeming 'sword' verse (9:5 – 'When the sacred months are over, slay the idolaters wherever you find them. Arrest them, besiege them, and lie in ambush everywhere for them. If they repent and take to prayer and render the alms levy, allow them to go their way. Allah is forgiving and merciful'), and the tolerant-seeming 'Let there be no compulsion in religion' (2:256), traditionally seen as underlining the right of non-Muslims to convert freely. A more solid account of the Muslim position would focus on its concentric understanding of faith, with Islam at the centre; Jews and Christians, so-called People of the Book, in an intermediate position; and the representatives of *shirk* (polytheism) and *kufr* (those who reject religion out of ingratitude) at the edge.

We have noted that in Muslim polities, Jews and Christians were traditionally given the status of *dhimmis*. They paid a special tax and enjoyed qualified rights. Notwithstanding the inequality of this relationship – and, of course, its monotheistic bias – it is reasonable to hold that the *dhimma* arrangement was a precursor of the public international law that did not evolve in Europe until the early seventeenth century. Another important consideration is that some Muslim jurists were prepared to extend the definition of 'People of the Book' to cover Hindus, because of the scriptural status of the *Bhagavad Gita*. The Mughal Empire had an enormous non-Muslim population of Hindus and others.

Christianity's trajectory has been very different. It did not develop a formal understanding of interfaith toleration, despite the ethic of radical self-giving love towards all set out in the Gospels. Landmarks in the history of Europe such as the Treaty of Westphalia (1648) are reminders of how long it took for the principle of toleration to be accepted even *between* the Christian denominations. Nevertheless, as the anthropologist Jonathan Benthall has suggested in an important essay on the history of religious toleration, Christianity eventually became more self-critical – and subversive of its own apparent strictness – than Islam. One fruit of Jesus's special emphasis on the poor and marginalised has been a tradition of positive discrimination in the modern era. In Islam, the right to criticise the dominant faith rarely extends to the forces of *shirk* and *kufr,* who are condemned so comprehensively in the Qur'an. It is also significant that Islam never evolved into movements analogous, say, to Liberal, Reform, and Orthodox Judaism. Muhammad Abduh (1849–1905), a Grand Mufti of Egypt, and Muhammad Iqbal (1877–1938), who ministered in what is now Pakistan, were two major reform-minded thinkers whose ideas failed to take wing. Today, Christians and others are surely right in calling on liberal Muslim intellectuals to show greater robustness in confronting awkward questions, including the crisis of institutional authority in Islam.

Yet as Benthall emphasises, the situation should not be considered static. The lesson of the past is clear, he writes.

Islam has proved to be just as flexible as Christianity in accommodating popular forms of belief and practice. Second, its scholars were able to recognize Hindus as People of the Book, though on most objective criteria they would have fallen more naturally into the category of *shirk*. If this leap of toleration could be made for the Hindus, albeit for reasons of state, why not today for other belief systems such as the indigenous cosmologies of Africa, Indonesia and Malaysia?[4]

Just as Christianity has evolved, then, there are reasonable grounds for thinking that Islam will do so, too. It seems right to finish on an irenic note by emphasising that the points of contact between the two traditions are at least as significant as the differences. When they are true to their guiding principles, both faiths insist on the sanctity of the person as a seeker of God, and from this should duly follow a recognition of religious freedom as the first of human rights.[5] Whether this awareness will spread is not for me to predict. For the Christian, it is hope – not more malleable impulses towards either optimism or pessimism – that really counts. Hope, in St Augustine's resonant words, 'has two beautiful daughters: their names are anger and courage. Anger that things are the way they are. Courage to make them the way they ought to be.'

Appendix A:
RELIGIOUS FREEDOM BY RELIGIOUS BACKGROUND

Religious Freedom Rating	Catholic	Protestant	Orthodox	Mixed Christian
1	Hungary Ireland	Estonia United States		
2	Austria Brazil Chile Ecuador Guatemala Italy Lithuania Portugal Spain	Botswana Denmark Norway South Africa Sweden	Ukraine	Australia Canada Latvia Namibia
3	Argentina Belgium France Nicaragua Peru Philippines Venezuela	Kenya	Bulgaria Greece Romania	Germany
4	Mexico Slovakia	Tanzania	Armenia Georgia Macedonia Moldova Russia Serbia	
5	Columbia	Zimbabwe		
6	Cuba		Belarus	
7				

☐ 'Free' ▨ 'Partly Free' ▧ 'Not Free'

270

Hindu	Buddhism and Related Religions	Islam	Other	Mixed Muslim / Christian
	Japan	Mali Senegal		
	Mongolia Thailand		Israel	
		Jordan Kosovo Kyrgyzstan Malaysia Morocco Oman		Cameroon Lebanon
India Nepal	Laos Sri Lanka	Algeria Azerbaijan Bahrain Comoros Egypt Indonesia Kazakhstan Kuwait Libya Syria Tajikistan Tunisia Turkey Yemen		Chad Ethiopia Nigeria
	China Vietnam	Afghanistan Bangladesh Mauritania Pakistan Palestinian Areas		
	Burma China-Tibet North Korea	Iran Iraq Maldives Saudi Arabia Sudan Turkmenistan Uzbekistan		Eritrea

NOTES

Introduction

[1] The 200-million figure includes Christians who face discrimination and other forms of hardship falling short of active persecution. See, for example, the findings published by the World Evangelical Alliance (www.worldevangelicals. org).

[2] *Washington Times*, 16 March 2012 (www.washingtontimes.com/news/2012/mar/16/destroy-all-churches).

[3] Timothy Samuel Shah and Monica Duffy Toft, 'Why God is Winning', *Foreign Policy*, 9 June 2006 (www.foreignpolicy.com).

[4] ibid.

[5] Jonathan Sacks, *The Dignity of Difference: How to Avoid the Clash of Civilizations* (Continuum, 2002), Introduction.

[6] Tony Judt, *Postwar: A History of Europe Since 1945* (Vintage, 2010).

[7] David Martin, *The Times Literary Supplement (TLS)*, 17 December 2010.

[8] John Micklethwait and Adrian Wooldridge, *God is Back: How the Global Rise of Faith is Changing the World* (Allen Lane, 2009).

[9] Andrew Chandler (ed.), *The Terrible Alternative: Christian Martyrdom in the Twentieth Century* (Cassell, 1998).

[10] ibid., p.4.

[11] Jon Sobrino, *The True Church and the Poor* (Maryknoll, 1981), p.173.

[12] Jonathan Sacks, 'The Pope is right about the threat to freedom', *The Times*, 3 February 2010 (www.thetimes.co.uk).

1. Egypt

[1] Alaa al-Aswany, *On the State of Egypt: What Caused the Revolution* (Canongate, 2011), p.129.

[2] See for example, Yaroslav Trofimov, 'As Islamists flex muscle, Egypt's Christians despair', *Wall Street Journal*, 11 June 2011 (www.wsj.com).

[3] BBC News, 1 November 2011 (www.bbc.co.uk/news).

[4] Nina Shea, 'Egypt's Copts: Will the region's largest non-Muslim religious community simply disappear?' *New Republic*, 10 June 2011 (www.tnr.com).

[5] ibid.

[6] Febe Armanios, *Coptic Christianity in Ottoman Egypt* (Oxford University Press, 2010).

[7] I am most grateful to Dr Sebastian Brock of the Oriental Institute at Oxford University for his guidance on this subject.

[8] Abd al-Rahman al-Jabarti, *History of Egypt*, Text vol., 3, 69 (Marcus Wiener Publishers, 2009).

[9] Alastair Hamilton, *The Copts and the West, 1439–1822: The European Discovery of the Egyptian Church* (Oxford University Press, 2006).

[10] ibid., p.279.

[11] Habib C. Malik, 'Christians of the Middle East: A story of accelerating erosion', in Paul A. Marshall (ed.), *Religious Freedom in the World*, pp.23–8.

[12] ibid., p.27.

[13] Christian Solidarity Worldwide, 'Egypt: Religious Freedom Profile', September 2009. Available online (www.csw.org.uk).

[14] ibid., p.19.

[15] ibid.

[16] Reuters, 'Lover rumour sparks Muslim–Christian clash in Egypt', 13 February 2007 (www.alertnet.org/thenews).

[17] Paul A. Marshall (ed.), *Religious Freedom in the World* (Rowman and Littlefield, 2008), p.159.

[18] ibid.

[19] CSW, 'Egypt: Religious Freedom Profile', pp.4–5.

[20] ibid., p.7.

[21] Court of Cassation, Case No. 475, 478, 481, Judicial Year 65, 1172.

[22] 'Egypt: Religious Freedom Profile', p.8.

[23] ibid., p.9.

[24] Paul Marshall, 'Apostates from Islam: The case of the Afghan converts is not unique', *Weekly Standard*, 2 April 2006 (www.weeklystandard.com).

[25] Congressional Hearing on 'The International Religious Freedom Report', 15 November 2005, p.80 (www.foreignaffairs.house.gov/archives).

[26] 'Sectarian Violence in Gabal-el Teir', *Watani*, 11 November 2009 (www.wataninet.com).

[27] 'An unprecedented move', *Watani*, 30 December 2007.

[28] 'Egypt: Religious Freedom Profile', p.11.

[29] *Tablet*, 14 May 2011 (www.thetablet.co.uk).

[30] *Church Times*, 9 December 2011 (www.churchtimes.co.uk).

[31] ibid.

[32] ibid.

[33] *Guardian*, 23 January 2012 (www.guardian.co.uk).

2. Iraq

[1] See, for example, the statement put out by the Irish Catholic Bishops' Conference (www.catholicbishops.ie) on 16 March 2011, during the visit of Archbishop Bashar Warda to Armagh.

[2] ibid.

[3] Anthony O'Mahony, 'Chaldeans' Last Stand', *Tablet*, 30 June 2007.

[4] I reproduce Archbishop Warda's statistics used in his address cited above.

[5] ibid.

[6] ibid.

[7] www.globalissues.org/article/105/effects-of-sanctions.

[8] Hala Jaber and Christine Toomey, 'Why Have You Forsaken Us?', *Sunday Times* magazine, 24 April 2011.

[9] Zenit News, 6 December 2010 (www.zenit.org).

[10] ibid.

[11] Aid to the Church in Need, *Persecuted and Forgotten?: A report on Christians oppressed for their faith*, 2011, p.67 (www.acnuk.org).

[12] House of Lords Hansard text for 9 December 2011 (www.parliament.uk).

[13] ibid.

[14] Anthony O'Mahony, 'Eastern Christianity in Modern Iraq', in Anthony O'Mahony (ed.), *Eastern Christianity: Studies in Modern History, Religion and Politics* (Melisande, 2004), pp.11–43.

[15] The lot of the Oriental Orthodox was to be known by the equally unfortunate term 'Monophysite', a definition that persisted for many centuries. Nestorianism (named after Nestorius, sometime Patriarch of Constantinople during the early fifth century, but actually deriving from a school of thought associated with the city of Antioch) is the view that there were two separate persons in the incarnate Christ, one human and the other divine – in contrast to the orthodox conviction that Christ was a single person, at once God and man. Monophysitism holds that Christ incarnate had only one nature, not two, and this teaching has thus tended to be seen from outside as the mirror image of Nestorianism – a kind of equal and opposite heresy.

[16] Aidan Nichols, *The Latin Clerk: The Life, Work, and Travels of Adrian Fortescue* (Lutterworth Press, 2011), p.105.

[17] ibid., p.109.

[18] ibid., p.110.

[19] Philip Jenkins, *The Lost History of Christianity: The Thousand-Year Golden Age of the Church in the Middle East, Africa, and Asia – and How it Died* (HarperCollins, 2008).

[20] ibid., p.6.

[21] Anthony O'Mahony, 'Christianity in Modern Iraq', *International Journal for the Study of the Christian Church*, Vol.4, No.2, July 2004, p.129.

[22] ibid., n.55, p.133.

[23] Marshall, *Religious Freedom in the World*, p.213.

[24] O'Mahony, 'Chaldeans' Last Stand', *Tablet*, 30 June 2007.

[25] ibid.

[26] O'Mahony, 'Christianity in Modern Iraq', p.127.

[27] ACN News (www.acnuk.org), 3 June 2011.

[28] ibid.

[29] ACN News, 3 August 2011.

[30] See note 1 above.

3. Iran

[1] *The Times*, 29 September 2011.

[2] Ben Macintyre, 'Oil and history fuel Iran's extreme paranoia', *The Times*, 21 February 2012.

[3] 'Iran 1994: The year of assassinations', report by Middle East Concern, 1995, p.10.

[4] Christian Solidarity Worldwide (CSW), 'Iran: Summary of Concerns and Recommendations', August 2011 (www.csw.org.uk).

[5] ibid.

[6] Paul Marshall, *Their Blood Cries Out: The Worldwide Tragedy of Christians Who Are Dying for Their Faith* (Word Publishing, 1997), p.25.

[7] ibid., p.35.

[8] Catholic News Service (CNS), 26 August 2011 (www.cnsnews.com).

[9] ibid.

[10] Obituary of Bishop Hassan Dehqani-Tafti, *Daily Telegraph*, 1 May 2008, (www.telegraph.co.uk).

[11] Marshall, *Their Blood Cries Out*, p.24.

[12] Marshall, *Religious Freedom in the World*, p.208.

[13] ibid., p.209.

[14] *The Times*, 29 September 2011.

[15] www.foreignpolicy.com/articles/2010/11/02/the_end_of_christianity_in_the_middle_east? page=0.1).

[16] Michael Nazir-Ali, 'Christianity in Iran: A brief survey', *International Journal for the Study of the Christian Church*, Vol.9, No.1, February 2009, pp.32–41.

[17] ibid., p.34.

[18] ibid., p.37.

[19] BBC Persian Service, 23 June 2009 (www.bbc.co.uk/persian/iran/2009/06/090623_rs_stoning_ban.shtml).

[20] Christian Solidarity Worldwide, 'Iran: Religious Freedom Profile', September 2009, p.5.

[21] ibid.

[22] ibid.

[23] Compass Direct News (CDN), 25 June 2008 (www.compassdirect.org).

[24] Mr Nadarkhani's story has been covered extensively on the CSW website.

[25] 'Iran: Religious Freedom Profile', p.5 ff.

[26] ibid.

[27] CDN, 20 May 2009.

[28] Associated Press (AP), 11 January 2011 (www.ap.org).

[29] CSW press release, 5 January 2011.

[30] Ali Rahnema, *Superstition as Ideology in Iranian Politics: From Majlesi to Ahmadinejad* (Cambridge University Press, 2011).

[31] *The Times*, 15 February 2012.

[32] Amir Taheri, *The Persian Night: Iran Under the Khomeinist Revolution* (TradeSelect, 2009).

[33] Amir Taheri, 'Why bombing Iran would suit Khamenei', *The Times*, 17 February 2012.

4. Pakistan

[1] See www.archbishopofcanterbury.org.

[2] ibid.

[3] Christian Solidarity Worldwide news report, 'No justice one year after the assassination of Shahbaz Bhatti', 2 March 2012.

[4] CSW Pakistan report, 'Religious Freedom in the Shadow of Extremism', June 2011, p.34. (www.csw.org.uk).

[5] Farzana Shaikh, *Making Sense of Pakistan* (Hurst, 2009).

[6] Anatol Lieven, *Pakistan: A Hard Country* (Allen Lane, 2011).

[7] ibid., p.151

[8] 'Religious Freedom in the Shadow of Extremism', p.34.

[9] *Third Way*, November 2011 (www.thirdwaymagazine.co.uk).

[10] Marshall, *Religious Freedom in the World*, p.323.

[11] 'Religious Freedom in the Shadow of Extremism', p.13.

[12] ibid., p.16.

[13] *Tablet*, 30 May 1998.

[14] 'Religious Freedom in the Shadow of Extremism', pp.22–3.

[15] This section of Faisalabad has witnessed a higher than average number of attacks on Christians in recent years, partly owing to a greater concentration of Christians in the neighbourhood, and partly because of more concerted anti-Christian campaigns led by a minority seeking to create a Muslim-only zone.

[16] Ziya Meral, 'No Place to Call Home: Experiences of apostates from Islam: Failures of the international community' (CSW, 2008).

[17] ibid., p.4.

[18] The examples cited are taken from the CSW's Pakistan report, where individuals are identified by letters of the alphabet. I have given them fictional names.

[19] ibid., p.27.

[20] ibid., p.31.

[21] Lieven, *Pakistan: A Hard Country*, p.160.

[22] ACN News, 8 August 2011.

[23] 'Religious Freedom in the Shadow of Extremism', p.37.

5. Turkey

[1] John Eibner, 'Turkey's Christians under siege', *Middle East Quarterly*, Spring 2011, pp.41–52 (www.meforum.org).

[2] ibid.

[3] ibid.

[4] *Persecuted and Forgotten?* p.126.

[5] ibid.

[6] *Instrumentum Laboris* 2010 (www.vatican.va).

[7] Christian Solidarity Worldwide, 'Turkey: Religious Freedom Profile', September 2009, p.10.

[8] The Pew Forum is an especially reliable source of demographic statistics and other information (www.pewforum.org).

[9] See note 15 for chapter 2 above.

[10] The comment was cited by Türker Alkan in his column in the *Radikal* newspaper, 17 May 2002 (www.radikal.com.tr).

[11] 'Turkey: Religious Freedom Profile', p.8.

[12] 'Missionaries the new Crusaders', *Turkish Daily News*, 24 February 2005.

[13] 'Turkey: Religious Freedom Profile', p.9.

[14] ibid., p.10.

[15] ibid., p.9

[16] William Dalrymple, *From the Holy Mountain: A Journey in the Shadow of Byzantium* (HarperCollins, 1997).

[17] ibid., p.32.

[18] ibid., p.33.

[19] ibid., p.43.

[20] ibid., p.63.

[21] See David Gaunt, *Massacres, Resistance, Protectors: Muslim–Christian Relations in Eastern Anatolia During World War I* (Gorgias Press, 2006).

[22] Dalrymple, *From the Holy Mountain*, p.83 ff.

[23] Compass Direct News, 30 August 2011.

[24] Asia News, 10 June 2010 (www.asianews.net).

[25] Eibner, 'Turkey's Christians under siege', p.24.

[26] 'Lawyer involved in journalist murder case found dead', www.bianet.org, 7 June 2010.

[27] Eibner, 'Turkey's Christians under siege', p.51.

6. Nigeria

[1] *Church Times*, 30 December 2011 (www.churchtimes.co.uk).

[2] ibid.

[3] I am very grateful to Fr Ralph Madu and his colleagues at the John Paul II Centre in Abuja, my base during a visit to Nigeria in 2012.

[4] Marshall, *Religious Freedom in the World*, p.310.

[5] ibid., p.311.

[6] ibid., p.312.

[7] Eliza Griswold, *The Tenth Parallel: Dispatches from the Faultline Between Christianity and Islam* (Farrar, Straus and Giroux, 2010).

[8] ibid., p.46.

[9] ibid., p.47.

[10] ibid., p.50.

[11] ibid., p.52.

[12] ibid.

[13] Rupert Shortt, *Rowan's Rule: The Biography of the Archbishop* (Hodder & Stoughton, 2008), p.313.

[14] Griswold, *The Tenth Parallel*, p.56.

[15] ibid., p.67.

[16] Compass Direct News, 11 November 2011.

[17] CDN, 27 September 2011.

[18] Christian Solidarity Worldwide, 'Nigeria: December 2009 Visit Report', pp.4–5.

[19] ibid., p.6.

[20] ibid.

[21] Names have been changed.

[22] 'Nigeria: December 2009 Visit Report', p.11.

[23] ibid., pp.11–12.

[24] ibid., p.12.

[25] ibid., p.13.

[26] ibid., p.14.

[27] See, for example, the Human Rights Watch report on these events: www.hrw.org/news/2-11/05/16/nigeria-post-election-violence-killed-800.

[28] ibid.

[29] CSW, 'Nigeria: overview of recent violence' (January 2012), concluding section.

[30] Statement by the UK Christian–Muslim Forum, 9 January 2012 (www.christianmuslimforum.org).

[31] See, for example, Rafiq A. Tschannen, 'Muslim groups protect churches in Nigeria', *Muslim Times*, 29 April 2012 (www.themuslimtimes.org).

7. Indonesia

[1] Marshall, *Their Blood Cries Out*, p.59.

[2] Marshall, *Religious Freedom in the World*, p.203.

[3] Griswold, *The Tenth Parallel*, p.180.

[4] Marshall, *Their Blood Cries Out*, p.59.

[5] Marshall, *Religious Freedom in the World*, p.202.

[6] Musdah Mulia, 'The Problem of Implementation of the Rights of Religious Freedom in Indonesia', EU–Indonesia conference: 'Human Rights and Faith in Focus', Jakarta, 24–25 October 2011.

[7] Gomar Gultom, 'CCI's Vision and Mission in the Context of Rising Fundamentalism and Capitalist Challenge', keynote speech to the Eukumindo General Assembly, 21–23 October 2010, Ede, the Netherlands.

[8] Franz Magnis-Suseno SJ, 'Protecting the Rights of Minorities in Law and Practice', 'Human Rights and Faith in Focus' conference.

[9] See, for example, www.globalvoicesonline.org2011/04/09/indonesia-ministry-orders-removal-of-buddha-statue/

[10] 'Indonesia: "Christianisation" and Intolerance', Asia Briefing No.24, November 2010 (www.crisisgroup.org).

[11] Christian Solidarity Worldwide, 'Indonesia Briefing' covering visit in May/June 2011, p.10.

[12] ibid., p.11

[13] ibid., p.12.

[14] ibid.

[15] ibid.

[16] ibid., pp.12–13.

[17] ibid., p.13.

[18] ibid., p.14.

[19] ibid.

[20] ibid., p.15

[21] ibid.

[22] UCAN, 2 November 2010 (www.ucanews.com).

[23] CDN, 25 March 2010.

[24] UCAN, 7 May 2010.

[25] Magnis-Suseno, 'Protecting the Rights of Minorities in Law and Practice'.

[26] CSW, 'Indonesia Briefing' covering visit in October 2011, p.8.

[27] ibid., pp.9–10.

[28] 'Cikeusik Ahmadi leader gets six months in prison', *Jakarta Post*, 15 August 2011 (www.thejakartapost.com).

[29] CDN, 4 October 2011.

[30] 'GKI Yasmin members in Bogor harassed again', *Jakarta Post*, 1 November 2011.

[31] CSW October briefing, pp.9–10.

[32] CSW May/June briefing, p.27.

[33] ibid.

[34] Marshall, *Their Blood Cries Out*, p.61.

[35] See, for example, *Economist*, 18 February 1995.

[36] Marshall, *Their Blood Cries Out*, p.61.

8. India

[1] *The Christian Century*, 24 February 1999.

[2] David Griffiths, 'Conversion, Re-Conversion and Violence in Central Orissa' (an M.A. thesis researched at the University of London's School of Oriental and African Studies), p.43.

[3] Robert Eric Frykenberg, *Christianity in India* (Oxford University Press, 2010).

[4] See, for example, William Dalrymple, *White Mughals: Love and Betrayal in Eighteenth-Century India* (Harper Perennial, 2004).

[5] Christian Solidarity Worldwide India report, 'Communalism, Anti-Conversion and Religious Freedom', June 2011 (available online www.csw.org.uk).

[6] ibid., p.9.

[7] ibid., pp.12–13.

[8] Sita Ram Goel, *Vindicated by Time: The Niyogi Committee Report on Christian Missionary Activities* (Voice of India, 1998), Vol.1, Part IV, chapter 1, par. 3.

[9] For an example of accusations based on what many fair-minded observers consider to be conspiracy theories, see www.harekrsna.com/sun/features/04-07/conversions.pdf.

[10] Report of the Special Rapporteur on freedom of religion or belief, Asma Jahangir: Addendum: Mission to India, 26 January 2009, par. 70 (www.2ohchr.org/english/bodies/hrcouncil/10session/reports.htm).

[11] ibid., par. 50.

[12] Asia News, 1 July 2004 (www.asianews.net).

[13] Report of the Special Rapporteur, par. 30.

[14] See note 2 above.

[15] Angana P. Chatterji, *Violent Gods: Hindu Nationalism in India's Present: Narratives from Orissa* (Three Essays Collective, 2009), p.109.

[16] 'Communalism, Anti-Conversion and Religious Freedom', p.26.

[17] Griffiths, 'Conversion, Re-Conversion and Violence in Central Orissa', p.38.

[18] 'Communalism, Anti-Conversion and Religious Freedom', p.29.

[19] ibid.

[20] ibid., p.30.

[21] ibid.

[22] ibid., p.31.

[23] ibid.

[24] ibid., p.35.

[25] ibid.

[26] ibid., p.37.

[27] Asia News, 4 April 2010.

[28] 'Communalism, Anti-Conversion and Religious Freedom', p.39.

[29] ibid., p.40.

[30] ibid., p.39.

[31] www.persecution.in.

[32] Compass Direct News, 22 April 2011.

[33] CDN, 17 August 2011.

[34] CDN, 15 April and 20 May 2011.

[35] ACN UK News, 7 September 2011.

[36] ibid.

[37] ibid.

[38] Asia News, 8 April 2011.

[39] ACN UK News, 23 August 2011.

[40] Griffiths, 'Conversion, Re-Conversion and Violence in Central Orissa', p.47. See also pp.12–12, in which the author discusses the clash between Hindutva and Christian paradigms of conversion.

9. Burma

[1] See, for example, the Chin Human Rights Organisation's report 'Religious Persecution: A campaign of ethnocide against Chin Christians in Burma' (2004), and Anne Schreiber, 'Human Rights in Myanmar/Burma: The Church under military dictatorship (Pontifical Mission Society Human Rights Office, 2004).

[2] Benedict Rogers, 'Carrying the Cross: The military regime's campaign of restriction, discrimination and persecution against Christians in Burma' (a Christian Solidarity Worldwide report available on the organisation's website).

[3] Rogers also draws on the researches of bodies such as the Karen Human Rights Group, the Chin Human Rights Organisation, the Free Burma Rangers, Christian Freedom International, the US State Department, and the US Commission on International Religious Freedom.

[4] Women's League of Chinland, 'Hidden Crimes against Chin Women', 2006.

[5] Rogers, 'Carrying the Cross', p.10.

[6] Michael Jerryson and Mark Juergensmeyer (eds), Buddhist Warfare (Oxford University Press, 2010).

[7] Katherine Wharton, review of Buddhist Warfare in the TLS, 1 October 2010.

[8] Rogers, 'Carrying the Cross', p.12.

[9] 'Religious Persecution: A campaign of ethnocide against Chin Christians in Burma', p.31.

[10] Rogers, 'Carrying the Cross', p.15.

[11] Christian Solidarity Worldwide, 'Burma Visit Report', November 2010, p.3.

[12] Rogers, 'Carrying the Cross', p.32.

[13] ibid., p.33.

[14] ibid.

[15] ibid., p.35.

[16] 'Witness: Christians persecuted in Burma; starvation, abuse rampant', *Christian Post*, 8 December 2005 (www.christianpost.com).

[17] Rogers, 'Carrying the Cross', p.36.

[18] ibid., p.37.

[19] 'Burma Visit Report', p.11.

[20] CSW news report, 21 October 2011.

[21] CSW news report, 8 November 2011.

[22] CSW news report, 26 March 2012.

[23] Rogers, 'Carrying the Cross', p.42.

[24] ibid.

[25] ibid., p.43.

10. China

[1] Gerolamo Fazzini, Joseph Zen and Michael Miller (eds), *The Red Book of Chinese Martyrs: Testimonies and Autobiographical Accounts* (Ignatius Press, 2008), pp.114–15.

[2] ibid.

[3] See, for example, David Aikman, *Jesus in Beijing: How Christianity is Changing the Global Balance of Power* (Monarch; revised edition, 2006).

[4] For a reliable and absorbing recent account of the terrain, see Robert Bickers, *The Scramble for China: Foreign Devils in the Qing Empire, 1832–1914* (Allen Lane, 2011).

[5] Victor Goossaert and David A. Palmer, *The Religious Question in Modern China* (University of Chicago Press, 2011).

[6] ibid., p.69.

[7] See, for example, R.C. Bush, *Religion in Communist China* (Abingdon Press, 1970).

[8] Goossaert and Palmer, *The Religious Question in Modern China*, p.67. Other observers argue that even during the toughest of times, underground congregations were growing explosively.

[9] Marshall, *Religious Freedom in the World*, p.128.

[10] See www.vatican.va

[11] Audrey Donnithorne, *Tablet*, 18 September 1999.

[12] Goossaert and Palmer, *The Religious Question in Modern China*, p.400.

[13] Simon Scott Plummer, *TLS*, 6 April 2012.

[14] For a lucid overview of problems faced by Protestants, and of other kinds of restriction on religious freedom in China, see the joint CSW–ChinaAid report, 'China: Persecution of Protestant Christians in the Approach to the Beijing 2008 Olympic Games', June 2008.

[15] Marshall, *Religious Freedom in the World*, p.129.

[16] ChinaAid briefings, November 2011 (www.chinaaid.org).

[17] Marshall, *Religious Freedom in the World*, p.129.

[18] *Persecuted and Forgotten?* pp.27–8.

[19] ChinaAid briefing, 23 August 2009.

[20] Reuters, 11 December 2009 (www.uk.reuters.com).

[21] *Persecuted and Forgotten?* pp.29–30.

[22] ChinaAid briefings, April 2011; Reuters, 3 April 2011.

[23] UCAN, 4 July 2011 (www.ucanews.com).

[24] Interview with Lawrence Braschi, December 2011.

[25] Katherina Wenzel-Teuber, 'Sino-Vatican Relations Reach a New Low', *Religions and Christianity in Today's China*, no. 2 (2011), (www. china-zentrum.de).

[26] ChinaAid briefings, July 2011.

[27] CDN, 29 July 2011.

[28] Scott Plummer, *TLS*, 6 April 2012.

11. Vietnam and North Korea

[1] Interviews conducted in 2011 in conditions of strict anonymity.

[2] See, for example, Robert Royal, *The Catholic Martyrs of the Twentieth Century: A Comprehensive World History* (Crossroad, 2000), Chapter 17.

[3] Thomas A. Dooley, *Deliver Us from Evil: The Story of Vietnam's Flight to Freedom* (Farrar, Straus and Cudahy, 1956).

[4] ibid., pp.174–5.

[5] Royal, *The Catholic Martyrs of the Twentieth Century*; see n.2 above.

[6] Dooley, *Deliver Us from Evil*, pp.182–3.

[7] François-Xavier Nguyen Van Thuan, *The Road to Hope: A Gospel from Prison* (Pauline Books, 2002), p.15.

[8] François-Xavier Nguyen Van Thuan, *Thoughts of Light from a Prison Cell* (New City, 1997), p.45.

[9] *Christian Post*, 18 August 2010.

[10] *Persecuted and Forgotten?* p.130.

[11] ibid., p.131.

[12] For a discussion of this subject, including the reluctance felt by some Catholics to seek the restitution of church property, owing to more pressing pastoral concerns, see Alessandro Speciale, 'Sin Cities', *Tablet*, 3 March 2012.

[13] *Persecuted and Forgotten?* p.132.

[14] Compass Direct News, 1 April 2010.

[15] All the following examples are taken from the CSW 'Visit Report' on Vietnam, May 2011.

[16] Speciale, 'Sin Cities', *Tablet*, 3 March 2012.

[17] ibid.

[18] 'North Korea: A case to answer, a call to act' (a CSW report available on the organisation's website), n.284, p.65.

[19] ibid., p.65.

[20] ibid., n.205, p.53.

[21] ibid., n.206, p.53.

[22] ibid., n.207, p.53.

[23] *Persecuted and Forgotten?* p.94.

[24] ibid.

[25] US State Department, 'International Religious Freedom Report, 2010', North Korea section (www.state.gov).

[26] Christian Solidarity Worldwide news report, 'Cry Freedom: Mrs Lee's long escape from North Korea', 1 March 2012.

[27] 'North Korea: A case to answer, a call to act', n.49, p.19.

[28] ibid., n.266, p.63.

[29] ibid., n.267, p.63.

[30] ibid., p.63.

[31] ibid.

[32] ibid., p.64.

[33] ibid.

[34] ibid., p.65.

12. The Holy Land

[1] www.Haaretz.com, 7 February 2012.

[2] www.handinhand12.org/News/Vandalism.

[3] I am most grateful to Fr Jamal Bulos Daibes of Bethlehem University for discussing this and related cases during a wide-ranging interview in November 2011.

[4] Compass Direct News, 30 December 2009.

[5] International Christian Concern (ICC), 26 May 2009 (www.persecution.org).

[6] CDN, 4 November 2010.

[7] For a statement of the Israeli government's point of view, see www.beyondimages.info/b160.html

[8] *Persecuted and Forgotten?* p.75.

[9] ibid.

[10] ACN News, 11 August 2009.

[11] Holy See Press Office, 23 October 2010 (www.vatican.va/news).

[12] *Persecuted and Forgotten?* p.76.

[13] ibid., p.76.

[14] ibid., p.79.

[15] ibid., p.79.

[16] For a brief discussion of this, see, for example, Mehdi Hasan, 'Thunderer', *The Times*, 12 January 2012.

[17] Assist News Service (ANS) 1 August 2009 (www.assistnews.net).

[18] These views are expressed in an unpublished essay by Dr Said, a Research

Fellow at McGill University, and formerly Acting Dean of St George's Cathedral, Jerusalem.

[19] Merav Mack, 'Christian Palestinian Communities in Israel', in Marshall J. Breger, Yitzhak Reiter and Leonard Hammer (eds), *Sacred Space in Israel and Palestine: Religion and Politics* (Routledge, 2012); n.10, p.305.

[20] R.B. Betts, *Christians in the Arab East: A Political Study* (John Knox Press, 1978), pp.67–8.

[21] S. Tamari (ed.), *Jerusalem 1948: The Arab Neighbourhoods and Their Fate in the War* (Institute of Jerusalem Studies, 1999).

[22] Mack, 'Christian Palestinian Communities in Israel', n.10, p.305.

[23] ibid., p.286.

[24] ibid., p.292.

[25] See R. Nahum-Halevy, 'The Greek Orthodox Church Sells Jerusalem Land to Jewish Investors: NIS 80 Million Deal Solves Capital's Leasing Problems Through 2051' (*sic*), *Marker*, 18 March 2011.

[26] M.A. May, Jerusalem Testament: Palestinian Christians speak, 1988–2008 (Eerdmans, 2010), n.28, p.20.

[27] R. Cohen, *Saving the Holy Sepulchre: How Rival Christians Came Together to Rescue Their Holiest Shrine* (Oxford University Press, 2008), pp.230–5.

[28] *A Moment of Truth (Kairos Palestine)* (2009) (www.kairospalestine.ps).

[29] ibid.

[30] Rowan Williams, 'Holy Land and Holy People', 14 April 2004 (www.archbishopofcanterbury.org).

[31] ibid.

[32] Gary Burge, *Whose Land? Whose Promise? What Christians are not being told about Israel and the Palestinians* (Pilgrim Press, 2004).

[33] Williams, 'Holy Land and Holy People'.

[34] ibid.

13. Six Countries at a Glance

[1] Marshall, *Religious Freedom in the World*, p.144ff.

[2] Christian Solidarity Worldwide, 'Cuba: Religious Freedom Report' May 2012 (available online). My evidence in this chapter also derives from three Cuban interviewees who asked to remain anonymous. I am indebted to them, and to Rosa María Valverde, Marta Villanueva, and José Peré for their guidance.

[3] 'Cuba: Religious Freedom Report'.

[4] Catholic News Service (CNS), quoted on the *Catholic Review* website (www.catholicreview.org), 18 August 2009.

[5] Zenit, 9 July 2010.

[6] CNS (www.catholicnews.com), 16 July 2010.

[7] *Tablet*, 5 October 2010.

[8] *Keston Newsletter* No.15, 2012, published by the Keston Institute (www. keston.org).

[9] Forum 18, 11 June 2009 (www.forum18.org).

[10] ibid., 11 February 2009.

[11] *Keston Newsletter*, p.5.

[12] ibid.

[13] CSW, 'Sri Lanka: Prospects for Religious Inclusiveness', May 2011 (available online), p.6.

[14] ibid., p.7.

[15] ibid., p.10.

[16] ibid.

[17] Walpola Rahula, *The Heritage of the Bhikkhu* (Grove, 1974).

[18] 'Sri Lanka: Prospects for Religious Inclusiveness', May 2011, p.6.

[19] Caroline Cox and Benedict Rogers, *The Very Stones Cry Out: The Persecuted Church: Pain, Passion and Praise* (Continuum, 2011), pp.75–6.

[20] Compass Direct News, 14 May 2010.

[21] ibid., 6 January 2011.

[22] Cox and Rogers, *The Very Stones Cry Out*, p.79.

[23] See note 19 above.

[24] ibid., p.124.

[25] ibid.

[26] *Persecuted and Forgotten?*, 2008 edition, p.91.

[27] CDN, 13 April 2009.

[28] Cox and Rogers, *The Very Stones Cry Out*, pp.122–3.

Conclusion

[1] Norman Etherington (ed.), *Missions and Empire* (OUP, 2008).

[2] Marshall, *Religious Freedom in the World*, p.4.

[3] Brian J. Grim and Roger Finke, *The Price of Freedom Denied: Religious Persecution and Conflict in the Twenty-First Century* (Cambridge University Press, 2011); see especially p.169.

[4] Jonathan Benthall, 'Confessional Cousins and the Rest: The structure of Islamic toleration', *Anthropology Today*, vol.21, No.1, February 2005, p.20.

[5] For a significant recent example of deepening dialogue between Muslims and Christians, see Miroslav Volf, Ghazi bin Muhammad, and Melissa Yarrington (eds), *A Common Word: Muslims and Christians on Loving God and Neighbor* (Eerdmans, 2010).

ACKNOWLEDGEMENTS

I am most grateful to my publishers at Rider/Random House. The kindness and efficiency shown by Judith Kendra, Sue Lascelles, Sally Wray, Martin Bryant, Alex Cooper, and their colleagues means a great deal. I am also deeply indebted to the staff of two charities in particular – Christian Solidarity Worldwide and Aid to the Church in Need – whose commitment to religious minorities (not just to their fellow believers) is reflected in an exemplary mixture of intellectual rigour and big-hearted outreach. I offer no apology for purveying the findings of these and other bodies, including Amnesty International, to as wide an audience as possible. Such material, always assembled with great care, forms one of the foundations of my narrative, even though I am naturally responsible for any errors of interpretation.

For agreeing to be interviewed, or for offering advice or practical help, I thank Fr Isaac Achi, Adesina Adesanya, Maureen Allen, David Alton, Bishop Angaelos of the Coptic Church in Britain, Fr Michael Barnes SJ, Annabelle Bentham, Fr Secondo Bongiovanni SJ, Fr Frans Bouwen, Lawrence Braschi, Ollie Brock, Sebastian Brock, Clare Carlisle, Archbishop Mor Filuksinos Yousf Cetin, Andrew Chandler, Yolande Clarke, Sébastien de Courtois, Caroline Cox, Chris Cox, William Crawley, Fr Michael Czerny SJ, Lucy Dallas, William Dalrymple, John Dayal, Xenia Dennen, Cédric Duroux, Jo Evans, Julia Evans, Archbishop Michael Fitzgerald, Khataza Gondwe, Katharine

Gorka, the Revd David Gosling, Ingrid Gregg, the Revd Stephen Griffith, David Griffiths, Eliza Griswold, Eileen Gunn, Ibrahim Habib, Harry Hagopian, Bishop David Hameed, Alastair Hamilton, the Revd Chris Hancock, Diana Healey, Fr Raymond Hickey OSA, David Horspool, Robert Irwin, Barbara James, the Revd John Kennedy, Nicholas Kerton-Johnson, Fr Jamal Khades, Paula Johnson, David Jowitt, Neville Kyrke-Smith, Jane Leek, Thea Lenarduzzi, Anatol Lieven, Ian Linden, Stefano Lodigiani, Fr Timothy Lowe, Regina Lynch, Fr Ralph Madu, Fr Matthias Nasr Mancrious, Gabriel Malan, Paul Marshall, Robert Mickens, Abs Moosuddee, Catharine Morris, Abdal Hakim Murad, Erasmus Ndukuba, Fr David Neuhaus SJ, Aziz Nour, Louismary Ocha, Ignatius Okoli, Anthony O'Mahony, Giulio Paletta, Fr Jean Jacques Pérennès OP, John Pontifex, Robert Potts, José Prado, Fr Vito del Prete, Isobel Reid, Max Rodenbeck, Ben Rogers, Bishop Geoffrey Rowell, David Ryall, Fr Saliba Sabri, Yazid Said, Hany Samir, Simon Scott Plummer, Timothy S. Shah, Seamus Shortt, Nader Shoukri, Samia Sidom, the Revd Patrick Sookhdeo, Ben Spotts, Rory Stewart, Peter Stothard, Edward Stourton, Fr Rod Strange, Adrian Tahourdin, Mervyn Thomas, Monica Duffy Toft, Fr Philippe Verdin OP, Brendan Walsh, George Weigel, Kate Wharton, Canon Guy Wilkinson, Archbishop Rowan Williams, Jenny Willis, Stuart Windsor, Fr Timothy Wright OSB, and Engin and Mine Yildirim.

I received generous grants from several people and organisations – Graham Hutton, Michael Berry, Oliver Pawle, Tim Syder, John Booth, Silvia and Piers Le Marchant, Brian Griffiths, the Porticus Trust, the Earhart Foundation, the Society of Authors, Civitas, and the Royal Literary Fund. This backing enabled me to visit seven countries in Africa, the Middle East, South Asia, and Europe, and to interview dozens of Christians and others on the ground. It was all the more valuable at a time of heavy financial constraints. Blackfriars, Oxford, offered me a visiting fellowship while the research unfolded. I look back with delight on my time spent with the friars and other scholars in this highly stimulating and hospitable environment.

Finally, I am very thankful indeed for the sustenance provided by my agent, Sam Copeland; and by four exceptionally acute observers of the interface between religion and society – Glyn Paflin, Bernice Martin, David Martin, and Jonathan Benthall.

With thanks to the following organisations for use of their copyright material: Christian Solidarity Worldwide; Aid to the Church in Need for *Persecuted and Forgotten?*; Lutterworth Press for *The Latin Clerk* by Aidan Nichols; Rowan & Littlefield for *Religious Freedom in the World* by Paul Marshall (ed.); Ignatius Press for *The Red Book of Chinese Martyrs* by Gerolamo Fazzini (ed.); HarperCollins for *From the Holy Mountain* by William Dalrymple; Penguin for *Pakistan: A Hard Country* by Anatol Lieven; Canongate for *On the State of Egypt* by Alaa al-Aswany; and Farrar, Straus and Giroux for *The Tenth Parallel* by Eliza Griswold.

INDEX